D0969789

# Island

## BOOK ONE

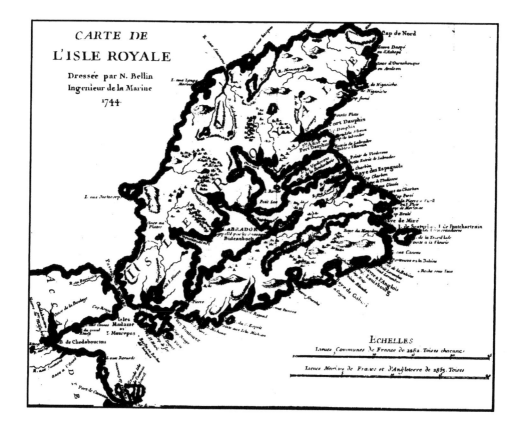

CARTE DE
L'ISLE ROYALE

Dressée par N. Bellin
Ingenieur de la Marine
1744

ECHELLES
Lieues Communes de France de 2282 Toises chacune

Lieues Marines de France et d'Angleterre de 2853 Toises

# Cape Breton Island

# Rise Again!

## The Story of Cape Breton Island

BOOK ONE

Robert J. Morgan

Breton Books

© 2008 Robert J. Morgan

Editor: Ronald Caplan; Production Assistant: Bonnie Thompson; Graphic Coordinator: James Fader

**Author's Note:** For their help in preparation of this book, I want to thank Ronald Caplan and Bonnie Thompson of Breton Books and *Cape Breton's Magazine*; Anne MacLean and Anne Connell and Catherine Arsenault, Manager, and Greg Bates, student assistant—all of the Beaton Institute, Cape Breton University; and Don Ward of the Cape Breton Regional Library, Sydney. Thanks as well to Diane Chisholm, Mi'kmaw Resource Centre, Cape Breton University.

**Our thanks to** the Beaton Institute, Cape Breton University for the generous contribution of the following images in their collection and their time to prepare them for this book: Miniature portrait on ivory of Ranna Cossit (1744-1815), first Anglican Minister in Sydney, founder of St. George's Church, ca. 1795, artist unknown, 79-1167-4147. Engraving entitled: "A Plan of the City and Fortifications of Louisburg," 1758, *The London Magazine*, Map #719. The Jerseyman's Church at Point Cross, 1978, Owen Fitzgerald, 79-1056-4036. St. Peter's Canal–the locks with the "Marion" going through, 1880, Harold Medjuck Photo Collection #1, 78-724-247. Drying cod fish on Ingonish Beach. (copy) ca. 1917, Cabot Archives, North of Smokey Collection, 79-688-3668. Carte de L'Isle Royale, 1744, Jacques Nicolas Bellin (1703-1772), Map #71. Our thanks, as well, to Owen Fitzgerald for permission to include his photograph of the Jerseyman Church.

The images of Nicolas Denys and of Charles Robin are taken from paintings by Lewis Parker in the collection of the Cape Breton University Art Gallery. Reproduced courtesy of Lewis Parker, Copyright 1982.

Our thanks to Scott Robson, Curator, for recommending the H. N. Binney watercolour of "Mi'kmaq Encampment," c. 1790, History Collection, Nova Scotia Museum. "Sydney from Hardwood Hill" by Major E. Sutherland, 1853, is courtesy McConnell Memorial Library.

We acknowledge the support of the Canada Council for the Arts for our publishing program.  Canada Council for the Arts / Conseil des Arts du Canada

We also acknowledge support from Cultural Affairs, Nova Scotia Department of Tourism, Culture and Heritage. NOVA SCOTIA Tourism, Culture and Heritage

We acknowledge the financial support of the Government of Canada through the Book Publishing Industry Development Program (BPIDP) for our publishing activities. Canada

**Library and Archives Canada Cataloguing in Publication**

Morgan, Robert J, 1938-
    Rise again! : the story of Cape Breton Island / Robert J. Morgan.
Includes bibliographical references and index.
Contents: Book 1.
ISBN 978-1-895415-81-0 (bk. 1)
    1. Cape Breton Island (N.S.)—History. I. Title.
FC2343.5.M673 2008        971.6'9        C2008-902633-0

Printed in Canada

# Contents

Illustrations between pages *58* and *59*

INTRODUCTION

# The Geology
# of Opportunity

WHEN I BEGAN MY CAREER at Xavier Junior College in 1962, we were happy to have the resources to teach Canadian history. We had no hope of presenting courses in Cape Breton history; indeed, we did not begin teaching history of the Maritimes until the 1970s; there just were not enough published studies. I remember when I proposed giving a course in early Cape Breton history, discussion centred on whether there was enough material for a half course!

The development of research in the history of Cape Breton Island has made great strides over the past half century.

After World War Two, Cape Breton began producing its first professional historians. Historians at the Fortress of Louisbourg National Historic Park contributed new knowledge about the island's history in the 18th century. The 20th century labour history was researched and published as well as Cape Breton's colonial period (1784-1820). More recently, works on the military history and 19th century political and economic history have been published. And in the last 30 years, considerable work has been done on the folklore—the oral history that gives the man-on-the-street portrait (actually on the trawl line and in the field)—the rich daily life of Cape Breton's citizens. When we add to this the numerous local histories that have been stimulated by the heritage movement on

1

the island, and the songs, poetry and fiction that tell our story, a considerable amount of new material has become available.

It seems time to take the plunge and write a history of the island. Such a project has not been tackled since Richard Brown's *A History of the Island of Cape Breton* in 1869. Like Brown, I feel it is time our young people as well as the "more seasoned" read their history and draw together the lines of our island's heritage. Like Brown's, I expect this book will invite more focused and detailed stories. I hope it will encourage work from our local town historians. We have not one current county history. I look forward to books devoted to our sports history, women's issues as they emerged on Cape Breton, biographies of so many deserving Cape Bretoners we should all know more about. And family histories. And more. For now, I offer this book as a tribute to the historians who came before me—from well-trained academics to passionate amateurs.

THIS IS THE STORY OF AN ISLAND. It is located in the North Atlantic Ocean, close enough to the mainland to be influenced by what goes on there, but far enough away to have developed its own ways. People have fought over it, bargained for it, exchanged it, bought and sold it. It has been a crossroads of history and a backwater; a centre of wealth and of poverty; people have made fortunes from its resources, others have been ruined. Cape Breton Island is one of the most beautiful places on the planet, and one of the most desecrated. Its sons and daughters are often quick to leave, but then they hanker to return. It has been called "Nature's Masterpiece" and "little isle of trouble." Its peoples have been called "unpleasant and disagreeable," "an indolent rabble who don't have the sense to emigrate," "deceitful and unprincipled characters," its early settlers the "refuse of the three Kingdoms," while one governor of Nova Scotia went so far as to call its people "lawless rabble."

The Reverend John MacGregor remarked on the "honesty

and hospitality" of the people; others wrote of their "unbounded kindness" and "the good cheer and a wholesome zest for living" displayed there. How have circumstances created such diverse views? Why do Cape Bretoners feel they are a people apart, and how has such a small piece of the earth influenced so much of history?

To say Cape Bretoners are a separate people does not mean that they all think alike. Indeed, the diversity of the island's terrain—the western side of the island facing the mainland and the east the open Atlantic—its ethnic make up, and its size have contributed to a diversity of outlook that has played an abiding role in the island's history. There's a fierce attachment to individual identity—ethnic, religious, political, even county!—and yet Cape Bretoners feel a sense of island identity. Still, outside influences have prevented their home from becoming "an island, entire of itself." Cape Breton's shores have been the home of wars, economic disasters, international greed, ideological movements. Today it is more her beauty and her culture that involve her in the outside world, and the vagaries of economic change or simple adventure that lure her people away.

I DISCOVERED CAPE BRETON on a September day in 1962 on my way to my first teaching position at Xavier Junior College. I was with my future bride Barbara MacKinnon, herself an Invernesser, when we stopped at the St. Ann's lookoff on Kelly's Mountain. The combination of water and cloud shadows scudding over the hills awed me with a sense that this island would be my home forever. The people were just as enticing, and it was not long before I was surprised to learn of the diverse history and geology of Cape Breton. A trip around the island was a trip through the history of the earth.

One interest led to another, and I learned that this beautiful rock in the sea—actually, this island composed of islands—was born about 1.2 billion years ago. It appears that some of Cape

Breton Island was part of an archipelago located off the coast of what would become South America, which geologists call Avalonia. Eventually Cape Breton was assembled from this and three other parts. The Blair River Complex in the northwest portion of the island was part of Laurentia, part of Canada's precambrian shield, the ancient core of North America. The other two components formed at or near the edges of some continent, possibly Africa or even part of Europe (called Baltica), because these continents were joined together at that time. This region—Avalonia—split off about 700 million years ago. Avalonia drifted northward from its location south of the equator, near South America, and collided with Laurentia and with the other components—Aspy and Bras d'Or Terranes—driving up mountains that included the whole of present-day Cape Breton Island.[1]

Cape Breton's voyage was not over.

About 750 million years ago, all of the continents came together in one great land mass or supercontinent, which we call Pangea. As Pangea gradually crept northward, Cape Breton was approaching the equator and the climate was warming.[2] Seawater flooded into the low-lying areas of what would become Atlantic Canada from the east along a trough, forming an inland sea, the Windsor Sea. Interchange between this inland sea and the distant ocean became restricted and marine incursions became intermittent, resulting in repeated flooding and drying of the inland sea. The salts within this evaporating body of water became increasingly concentrated and precipitated to form the gypsum deposits along the seacoasts and the Bras d'Or Lakes, the source of later gypsum mines near Chéticamp, River Denys, Dingwall, and Port Hawkesbury (Plaster of Paris Cove), and inland wherever the interior valley extended, such as Margaree and Lake Ainslie.

Continental movement broke up Pangea. North America was still attached to Asia, until they too rifted apart. Sea levels rose and fell, and river basins drained the highlands and deposited fertile silt. Cape Breton was transported from the hot, arid interior of the continent. The climate became more temperate and very wet, giving rise to newly-evolving tree ferns and other lush jungle-like vegetation. This was compressed, covered by more silt, and again covered by vegetation. Plant remains that accumulated in these basins—floodplains, swamps, bogs, shallow lakes, estuaries, and seacoasts—were covered by stagnant water which prevented decomposition, and they became compacted into peat. The basins were covered by rocks eroding from the surrounding hills, by sediments deposited by meandering rivers, and by marine sediments. The peat was buried. Millions of years of pressure resulted in coal, vast beds of which extended not only through what is today coastal Cape Breton, but through the then-adjoining regions such as today's Britain and eastern United States.

As Pangea continued to break up, about 230 million years ago, the Atlantic Ocean began to form. North America, with Cape Breton in its arms, drifted northwestward. The resulting geological pressures and tensions caused ruptures or faults to occur and sedimentary layers of coal and other minerals to tilt, bend, and even get flipped over.

Twenty million years ago, another period of crustal uplift began, which in turn led to erosion as streams cut their way to the sea, exposing granite and gypsum that had formed in earlier times. The stress of the earth's movement caused cracks to form, as seen in the Aspy Fault along which the North Aspy River flows today.[3] Formed at the same time was the long, straight range of hills known as the Aspy Escarpment, which we climb as we drive over North Mountain.[4]

After the latest cycle of uplift, sea levels rose and inundated the lower land we know as the Bras d'Or Lakes.[5] As North America drifted further northward, the climate became cooler and drier. Eventually ice began to form in North America, culminating in the Great Ice Ages. Ice sheets spread over the present Maritime

Provinces 500,000 years ago and have advanced and retreated several times since. As glaciers melted, huge amounts of water gouged out the Laurentian Channel in the Gulf of St. Lawrence and the Cabot Strait between Cape Breton and Newfoundland. When the ice sheets re-advanced they scraped the best topsoil from the island and deposited it in banks now far under the sea—grounds that produced the magnificent cod fishery which attracted Europeans from the 15th century on, while condemning Cape Breton to be much less of an agricultural island than it might have been.

The ice caused extensive erosion in the highlands but did not much alter the lay of the land; valleys simply deepened and widened to become U-shaped, such as Grande Anse and the Clyburn Valley.[6] In the lowlands, however, ice tore boulders and earth, carving the landscape. Lake Ainslie was formed as the ice left huge amounts of earth behind, damming up the melt water which eventually found a channel to the Gulf of St. Lawrence via the Margaree River. Rocks from the Coxheath Hills are found in the yards of Sydney homes.

Ocean levels rose and fell as the ice advanced and retreated. As the last ice melted about 11,000 years ago, the rising sea levels broke the connection to the mainland and formed today's Strait of Canso—despite the Canso Causeway, a lasting symbol of Cape Breton's separate identity. The glaciers were slower to melt in the highlands than elsewhere, but by 9,000 years ago they were gone. Forests of spruce and birch made their appearance, followed by pine. Increased warmth saw the arrival of hemlock, maple, oak, and beech.

Animals followed. No insular race of mammals evolved on Cape Breton Island. However, in comparison to other islands in the Gulf of St. Lawrence, Cape Breton received a rich mammal population with only five mainland Nova Scotia species missing: the porcupine, the skunk, the arctic and smoky shrews, and the white-footed mouse. These species arrived in mainland Nova Scotia too late to take advantage of the ancient land link. Three species of ungulates or hoofed mammals were endemic here: the caribou, the moose, and the white-tailed deer. The surrounding waters offered a rich variety of sea life. Mammals such as seals arrived with their pups in the spring and dwelled on the shores in summer. Fish like the northern cod, mackerel, shrimp, and squid teemed on the nearby fishing banks; salmon, eels, and inshore species inhabited the island's rivers and the Bras d'Or Lakes. Along the coasts of both the ocean and the lakes, particularly in river estuaries, clams, mussels, and oysters abounded. Their populations rose and fell in response to climate change.

Beautiful Cape Breton Island consists of a high plateau to the north of the Bras d'Or Lakes, and an uneven topography with hills and valleys to the south. Its climate is what we might call modified continental: the surrounding ocean, though cold due to the Labrador current, moderates the winter cold and the summer heat. The growing season, due to the late, wet, cold spring, is short—especially in the highlands which, according to the growth rings on the spruce, can have years without a single frost-free month—but it is generally sufficient to allow the ripening of grains and other temperate climate crops. And pockets of good soil, particularly the eastern and intervale lands of Inverness County and Boularderie Island, have supported agriculture and cattle production for generations.

This was the land of the Mi'kmaq that Europeans found. The physical evolution and natural geography of Cape Breton Island put it in the path of history, and have presented its inhabitants not only with a magnificent setting, but with challenges, opportunities and inspiration.

# 1

# In the Land of the Mi'kmaq

## Early European Settlement on Cape Breton Island

"For the Micmac [the historic period] apparently began with the discovery of Cape Breton by the French Bretons in 1504. Thus, the Micmacs were exposed to European influence and trade for almost one hundred years before a successful attempt was made to colonize their territory, and before the written records become at all adequate."[1]
— Bernard G. Hoffman

THE EARLIEST HUMAN INHABITANTS of Cape Breton probably arrived within a few thousand years of the last melting of the glaciers. Archaeological evidence suggests that an early group inhabiting Cape Breton was replaced by the Mi'kmaq people who came here from the Canadian Shield.[2] Their social organization, certain tools, hunting techniques, and spiritual beliefs reveal their Algonquian links. However, between five and seven thousand years ago, the island environment soon changed their way of life. Fishing proved a more reliable source of food than hunting, and any agriculture they may have previously pursued was replaced by food gathering. Why toil over crops where the season was short, the soil was thin, and a rich harvest of berries, sea

9

life, and mammals was available? They called their sea-girt land—so different from their earlier home in the continental interior—"Unama'ki," the foggy land, and they likened the island to a head, with the mainland of today's Nova Scotia its torso.

To take advantage of the wealth of sea life, the Mi'kmaq moved in small groups between the ocean and the Bras d'Or Lakes. During the summer, extended families lived together in villages on the Bras d'Or. As winter approached, they divided into fishing and hunting units composed of three to five households of perhaps twelve to fifteen people. In the spring they came together again in large groups at the mouths of streams and harbours along the ocean where they trapped and speared trout and cod before returning to the Bras d'Or Lakes for the summer.[3] Favourite gathering places are remembered in place names like Malabo (today's Mabou), Naliksaak or Maliksaak (Arichat), Ubunakade (Benacadie), and Menadou (Main-à-Dieu). As winter approached, more time was spent hunting as the group broke up again to fish on the Bras d'Or and hunt in the highlands.[4]

Villages were temporary and were relocated for better hunting or fishing; shelter was portable. The conical tipi consisted of disposable poles supporting easily transported moose hide or birch bark, suitable for seasonal migration. Longer-lasting settlements consisted of wigwams, or of long-houses which were communal dwellings much larger than the single-roomed wigwam. The birch-bark canoe, toboggan, and snowshoe provided transportation. The Mi'kmaq made both local and ocean-going canoes, the latter with a distinctive hump in the gunnel. The Mi'kmaw canoe "is one of the few elements of Indian culture the whites took to immediately, making no other changes except that of increasing the size.... Normally, the entire [Mi'kmaw] family participated in construction, and building sites were often used for generations."[5]

They navigated Cape Breton, noting landmarks and describing location. With no formal maps in European terms, Mi'kmaq travellers might scratch a figure of a stream on a piece of bark indicating the number of branches they must pass before reaching a destination. Malagawatch meant "a triangular piece of land formed by a river and a larger body of water"; Baddeck is "a place with an island near"; Arichat, originally Meliksaak (variously spelled Naliksaak and Maliksaak), "worn or shivered rocks"; and Soolacadie—the Mira River—meant "mussels place."[6] Distance was reckoned by naming the significant landmarks such as capes along a river or coast, and by the length of time it took for a journey, or by the number of nights they were obliged to sleep.[7]

Social relationships in this mobile society were based on consensus and voluntary organization. The basic social unit, the family, consisted of the father, mother, married sons and daughters and their families, as well as unmarried relatives and widows. Marriage between groups was encouraged, since it provided a sense of wider identity and grounds for alliances. Social power thus came through having many relatives, and polygamy was not unknown.[8]

The larger seasonal groupings or "residential kin" were headed by a *saqmaw*, a chief or war leader, whose authority was based on persuasion and/or family connections, though obedience to him was not obligatory. To keep peoples' respect such a man would have to show superior insight or wisdom.[9] Long after European contact, these leaders continued to merit respect for their demeanour and in turn were respected by the French.

Occasionally the Mi'kmaq would meet in regional groups or bands, where wider topics were discussed—war, determination of hunting area, allocation of resources for the dispossessed, and the solidification of alliances.[10] The term "Mi'kmaq" itself means "allied people," denoting a sense of identity, a code of governance, and inter-regional trading and bartering.

Socially, the leaders or chiefs enjoyed certain limited privileges like the best meat and furs, and their word carried extra weight. Others also enjoyed respect—older men, those possessing superior abilities in war or hunting, and those with wide social connections. People with no social influence were "slaves"—people captured in war. These were often released to their native bands.

In such a society which necessarily valued war and hunting prowess, women were given inferior status. They produced no staple crop but gathered food or shellfish, stitched wigwams, mended clothing, carried in fallen game, set up tents, and raised the children.[11] They were protected by males of the family; even polygamy assured them social connections and family protection.

Men, on the other hand, were called upon to undertake the hunting and fishing with expert use of bow and arrow or harpoons. When hunting, men would grease their bodies with seal oil as protection against cold and black flies, and wore breechcloths and leggings and a mantle of moose hide or tanned deerskin painted or decorated with porcupine quills. Footwear consisted of seal- or moose-skin moccasins and knee-high mukluks. In winter, robes of beaver or otter were used for added warmth. With his hair tied back and interwoven with bird feathers, shell beads, dyed moose hair, a warrior presented a formidable picture.[12]

Women, if unmarried, wore their hair long and tied back into a tail. Like the men they tattooed their faces and bodies and wore bracelets and necklaces of white or blue beadwork. And like the men they presented a fine physical appearance.[13] In 1583 Étienne Bellenger, a merchant from Rouen, France, visiting Cape Breton, described the Mi'kmaq as having

verie good disposition and stature of Bodie. They weare their hayre hanging downe long before and behynde as lowe as their browes. They go all naked saving their privities which they cover with an Apron of some Beastes skynn....[14]

Fifty years later, Father Julien Perrault was still able to write in a letter from St. Ann's Bay:

As to the people, there is nothing anomalous in their physical appearance; you see well-formed men, good-looking, of fine figures, strong and powerful.... One sees there old men, of eighty and a hundred years, who have hardly a gray hair.... You do not see in their gestures and bearing any foolishness or nonsense, but rather a certain gravity and natural modesty, which makes them agreeable.[15]

Physical dexterity was of supreme importance. Strength, endurance, and self discipline were highly prized since they could mean the difference between survival and death. While we can hardly call the Mi'kmaq a war-like people, occasional conflicts broke out between bands or neighbouring peoples over hunting territory or aggressive raids. Before any war, a band council meeting was called, and only after elaborate ceremonies, debate, and pleas for supernatural assistance was war decided upon. With the arrival of peace, chiefs met and literally buried war hatchets. Wars were sometimes carried out with the neighbouring Malecite peoples, but the most serious enemy were the "Kwedek," probably Iroquois, who sometime around 1500 tried to push their way into Mi'kmaq territory. Under the leadership of their great chief Ulgimoo, the Mi'kmaq joined with other nations to form a confederacy which lasted until the 17th century, and successfully drove the Kwedek to the north and west. Such warfare brought privileges to warriors, further encouraging the maintenance of physical prowess.

Knowledge of and insight into natural forces were raised to a high spiritual level. Europeans later noted that, as with their own ancestors, the sun played a prominent role in Mi'kmaw spirituality because of its life-giving properties, while the moon as wife of the sun was mother of mankind, protector of women in childbirth, and generally guardian of life from the dangers of the night.

The Mi'kmaw cosmology had no clear-cut division between the natural and supernatural. Since all life sprang from the ground, animals were seen as equal to humans, living in complex societies like people.[16] Because animals possessed soul-spirits, taboos regulating the use of animals were common. For example, beavers were admired for their industry and were highly respected. Their bones were not to be thrown in the fire in case misfortune might befall the people—the beaver might withdraw from an area, or the hunt could fail. It was standard procedure to apologize before killing bears.[17] Prior to the European fur trade, the Mi'kmaq believed that animal overkill would cause anger in the animal world as an act akin to genocide, leaving humans vulnerable to retaliation. Animal spirits were thus appeased and excessive hunting was taboo. Nicolas Denys, in the 17th century, remarked that before the European fur trade arose, the Mi'kmaq "did not lack animals, which they killed only in proportion as they had need of them."[18]

The practical effect was conservation in an atmosphere of respect. Prior to contact, the Mi'kmaq lived in a complex but sustainable relationship with nature which provided them with an integrated way of life. Since they raised existence above the material level, linking humans to all forms of life on the island, we have a society of people living in spiritual harmony with their surroundings. People with special insights or visions, often called *peiowin*, or shamans, were highly respected and feared.[19] The Mi'kmaq were hardly a burden to Cape Breton's wildlife, since a mobile race of hunters and food gatherers rarely results in the large populations of settled agricultural societies. Estimates put the total population of all Mi'kmaq in an area covering today's Nova Scotia, New Brunswick, Prince Edward Island, and Gaspé at around 15,000 people, with only about 2,000 in Cape Breton.[20]

BESIDES THE KWEDEK, it is possible that the Mi'kmaq in Cape Breton also came into contact with the Norse, who had begun expanding westward from Europe in the 10th century. If the Norse came to Cape Breton, they left no traces.

According to legend, around the year 1500 the Mi'kmaq began witnessing events—strange-looking floating islands were sighted off the coast, soon to be followed by men in unusual costumes, who came and went during the summer season.[21]

What should they see but a singular little island...which had drifted near to the land and became stationary there! There were trees on it, and branches on the trees, on which a number of bears...were crawling about.... What was their surprise to find that those supposed bears were men, and that some of them were lowering down into the water a canoe, into which several of them jumped and paddled ashore. Among them was a man dressed in white, a priest with his white stole on, who came toward them making signs of friendship, raising his hands towards heaven, and addressing them in an earnest manner, but in a language which they could not understand.[22]

These strange creatures from half a world away were being driven by forces the Mi'kmaq could not imagine. Europeans had entered a period of rapid economic and technical development leading to the search for new resources and ultimately their discovery of the Americas. These visitors were fishermen who, like the Vikings, had gradually extended their range westward toward Newfoundland and Cape Breton. Though they were secretive about their fishing grounds, word spread of new shores to the west. Despite skeptics and the fear of monster-laden seas, the concept of the world as a globe gradually spread. The final push to find these new lands—and India and China—came when land routes to the east Orient were cut off by the Turkish invasions and the fall of Constantinople in 1453.

In 1497, just five years after Columbus's expeditions to the Caribbean, Henry VII of England commissioned a Venetian merchant living in Bristol, Giovanni Caboto—John Cabot—to explore this new world and lay claim for Britain to any territory found there. Thirty-five days after leaving Bristol, Cabot sighted a long, rocky coastline teeming with cod. An Italian visitor in England heard tales of this voyage and told that "the sea is covered with fishes, which are caught not only with the net but with baskets, a stone being tied to them in order that the baskets may sink in the water."[23]

The earliest known map representing North America, drawn

up by a Basque mapmaker, Juan de la Cosa, indicates that Cape Breton was "Cabo Descubierto"—"the Cape that was discovered."[24] A German map dated 1544 designates the northeast corner of the mainland of North America as "prima terra vista" or first land sighted, 24 June 1497, clearly indicating Cape Breton. It also has a Spanish inscription which, besides giving the date of discovery, goes on to say:

The inhabitants wear skins of animals, use in their battles bows, arrows, lances, darts, wooden clubs, and slings. The soil is very barren, and there are many white bears and stags as large as horses, and many other beasts. Likewise great quantities of fish, pike, salmon, soles a yard long, and many other kinds, besides a great abundance of the kind called baccalaos [cod].[25]

That 1544 map was based on recollections of Sebastian Cabot who had sailed with his father but whose memory and geographical knowledge may have been fuzzy. While modern writers such as Ganong and Hoffman favour Cape Breton as the site of Cabot's landfall, Newfoundland may actually have been discovered first as its name suggests.[26]

By the time of Cabot's landfall, the Mi'kmaq were used to the sight of fishermen. Soon fishermen from all over western Europe were using the North American coast. By 1526 maps include "Cape Briton" or "Breton," indicating the prominent landmark cape at the southeast corner of the island. The name itself was likely derived from Cap Breton in the French region of Bretagne or Britanny, since its shores are on the same latitude—which was the primary method of navigation—and Cape Breton was frequented by fishermen from there, as well as by Portuguese and Basques.[27] The name has persisted on maps, making "Cape Breton" the oldest European place name transferred to America.

Between 1522 and 1524 Giovanni Verrazzano, sailing for France, explored the region. Jacques Cartier sailed along the Gulf of St. Lawrence in 1534 and saw French, probably Breton, fishing boats off the coast. While the Europeans still had only slight knowledge of the Mi'kmaq living on Unama'ki, trade and personal encounters were more frequent.

The late 16th century Europeans were increasingly interested in the region's codfish, whales and seals. An English expedition under the command of Captain Richard Strong landed in Cape Breton in 1593. Unfortunately, they clashed with Mi'kmaq, who it appeared had already experienced European aggression.[28] Strong's men came ashore for fresh water. They discovered a pond and weirs. In Strong's rendition of his crew's meeting with the Mi'kmaq, he says:

There came one Savage with blacke long hayre hanging about his shoulders, who called unto us weaving his hands downwardes...as wee drew towardes him one of our mens muskets unawares shot off.... Thereupon nine or tenne of his fellowes running right up over the bushes with great agilitie and swiftnesse came towardes us with white staves in their handes like half pikes...but we retired unto our boate without any hurt at all received.[29]

The enlightened historian Marc Lescarbot, writing thirteen years later (1606), objected to the use of the word "savages" in describing the Mi'kmaq as "abusive and unmerited, for they are anything but that." He praised their "courage, fidelity, generosity, and humanity." He added, "They are not simpletons.... They speak with much judgment and good sense."[30]

In 1525, Joao Alvarez Fagundes had led an expedition from Portugal and the Azores to form a colony in Mi'kmaw summer territory, probably at present-day Glace Bay or at St. Ann's.[31] The colony failed, but the same year another Portuguese mariner, Estevan Gomez, guided a Spanish vessel to Cape Breton in search of a northwest passage to China. That expedition was also unsuccessful, but a number of Mi'kmaq were captured and taken as slaves to Spain.

It is no wonder then that in 1597 while entering Cibou or Sydney Harbour, Englishman Charles Leigh and his crew noted that the natives fled. Leigh's men took their boat but, in an attempt to placate the natives, returned it along with gifts of knives and coats.[32]

Leigh's act of kindness was probably rooted in his need for native friendship in order to work on land. During the 16th century, methods of transporting cargoes of fish back to Europe changed. Before, most fish were caught, gutted and salted on board ship, stored in the holds, and brought back directly to Europe. This wet or green fishery was practiced particularly by the Portuguese and Spaniards, people who brought their salt with them, collected after the sun's evaporation of sea water in European tidal flats at low tide. These fishermen needed to land only for fresh water, and had slight contact with the Mi'kmaq.

By the end of the 16th and early 17th centuries, the British and French fishermen in Cape Breton's waters came from cooler climates where such evaporation for salt did not occur. They could not bring enough salt to preserve fish aboard ship, and had to come ashore for longer periods to dry their catch. On shore, fish were gutted, split and lightly salted, extracting some of the water. Then the fish were spread to dry on rocky shores before they were loaded for shipment to Europe. This was a more labour-intensive operation and needed a safe land base. It required turning the fish to protect the flesh from the sun, piling it in faggots, and covering it when it rained. These longer periods ashore opened the door for greater contact between Mi'kmaq and Europeans—and contact led to trade exchanges and other relationships.

The Europeans were especially attracted by the high quality pelts the natives offered in exchange for European goods. The Mi'kmaq quickly learned to bargain; they soon gave lesser quantities of furs for more European goods. For a brief period in the early 17th century the Mi'kmaq monopolized the fur trade, going so far as to sail out to European ships in shallops—small European sailing boats—to trade with fishermen.[33]

Native use of shallops draws our attention to the interaction of the two peoples. As they overcame their fear of Europeans, the Mi'kmaq traded for goods like clothing, utensils, boats, weapons, alcohol, and food. Consider the introduction of the simple copper stew pot to a society previously without the use of metal. The typical Mi'kmaw soup pot was a hollowed log still rooted in the ground. "The copper pot...by virtue of its portable, sturdy nature, made it easier for these people to roam the woods in search of fur bearers—easier than it would have been had they been obliged to rely on the stationary wooden cauldron."[34]

Now travel was easier and so was cooking. While growing native dependence on European goods transformed the subsistence pattern of native life, there is evidence that a powerful native spirituality remained. The copper pot was among the items ceremoniously buried with the dead as one of the tools they would need in the other world. Archeologist J. Russell Harper reported on a burial pit in which kettles were smashed—"killed"—to release their souls to travel on with the deceased.[35] Ultimately, Nicolas Denys was able to report "they have been disabused of that in the end, though with much difficulty."[36]

In any case, manufactured European goods were seen as preferable to native handwork. European food items like prunes, raisins, sea biscuits and peas entered the aboriginal diet.[37] Trade became more formalized. Each season the Mi'kmaq would bring furs to the fishing stations located on Cape Breton's east coast. The English clustered around English Harbour, today's Louisbourg; the French were based at St. Ann's Bay; the Portuguese at Ingonish and the Spanish and Basques in Spanish Bay, today's Sydney Harbour. To be ready with furs when the Europeans arrived in the spring, the Mi'kmaq spent the winter hunting. This disrupted their pattern of gathering food, and thus their subsistence base. They became more dependent on Europeans for food, without which they might face famine and social disorganization.[38]

How long could the fur resource last on a relatively small

island? The use of European firearms made short work of the local fur-bearing animals. As more Mi'kmaq ignored their symbiotic relationship with nature in the scramble for furs, they sailed to Newfoundland in the newly-adopted European shallops. By the 1730s they had even settled at Port aux Basques, trading furs with British merchants.[39] This is a rare example of native peoples extending their range after the arrival of Europeans.

On the other hand, the use of European firearms not only decimated local wildlife, but also greatly affected the Mi'kmaw lifestyle. The introduction of guns meant less need for athleticism in hunting. Moreover, regard for the spiritual relationship with animal life—so basic to Mi'kmaw spirituality—was weakened. The Europeans used alcohol as a bargaining tool with natives, to whose society it was apparently alien. Alcohol upset family ties, led to racial mixing, fractured tribal organization, and generally sapped the strength of the natives.

Nicolas Denys observed,

To buy the brandy it was then necessary that [the Mi'kmaw] sell his gun, his blanket, or other things in order to get it. This will cost them five to six skins; they will give this to the fishermen for a bottle or two of brandy. Then they commence again to drink.... They will not cease drinking so long as they possess anything. Thus the fishermen are ruining them entirely.[40]

On top of that, contact resulted in the outbreak of diseases like smallpox, measles, whooping cough, and syphilis—diseases never seen in North America and to which the Mi'kmaq had no immunity. The results were devastating.

Several waves of epidemics wracked Mi'kmaq society in the 16th and 17th centuries. It is possible that the total population of Mi'kmaq in eastern Canada declined to 2,000.[41] This would mean that, when some immunity was finally achieved, probably around 1620, there may have been only 200 Mi'kmaq living in Cape Breton. The population might have been totally decimated had not the Mi'kmaq lived in scattered settlements. This slowed the spread of epidemics and allowed the population to restore itself.[42]

We can only imagine the horror as diseases such as pleurisy, dysentery, and smallpox claimed the lives of most of the people in any family group or settlement. At La Have on the mainland, in one year alone, sixty people—most of the population there—died.[43]

These epidemics—along with alcohol and the destruction of family and tribal organizations—weakened Mi'kmaq resistance to increasing European encroachment. And as the value of dried codfish grew as an essential European commodity, the French and English recognized the need for permanent settlements from which fish could be processed easily for shipment to Spain, Portugal, and the West Indies. Ignoring the natives, royal governments were ready to grant exclusive rights to the fishery and fur trade to those willing to pay for them, and willing to transport settlers to North America.

IN 1603 THE KING OF FRANCE, LOUIS XIII, granted the Sieur de Monts all the territory in coastal America lying between 40 and 46 degrees latitude—essentially today's New England and the southern half of the Maritimes. Known as La Cadie—meaning "a place" in Mi'kmaw and corrupted to "Acadie"—the territory included most of Cape Breton Island.

De Monts left France in 1604 with settlers and priests. One of his ships landed at present-day Louisbourg before joining the rest of his expedition on the Nova Scotia mainland at Port Mouton.

Though De Monts established no settlement on Cape Breton, the handwriting was on the wall. In 1606 the King of England, James I—totally ignoring any French, Mi'kmaq, or other claims—granted the whole of eastern North America lying between 38 and 45 degrees latitude to a group from Plymouth, England. The overlapping claims of the French and English to Acadie would prove to be the root cause of European conflict in North America until the Treaty of Utrecht in 1713.

Before long, King James I handed out even more land. This

time it went to a Scot, Sir William Alexander—a courtier, poet, and dreamer—who convinced the King, himself a Scot, that just as there was a New France, a New Spain, and a New England, there should be a New Scotland. He was given a fur and fishing monopoly which ignored French claims and embraced Acadie and the Gaspé. The grant charter, in Latin, described the territory as Nova Scotia.

In 1622 Alexander planned a fishing settlement on Cape Breton Island, but the expedition was blown off course. Many of the settlers died, joined fishing crews, or simply returned home.

Undeterred, Alexander came up with the idea of establishing an order of "Baronets of New Scotland." Anyone who promised to provide for male colonists during the first two years in New Scotland was offered land and a baronetcy. No one took the bait until the grants were given directly by King James. Then, eight candidates signed on.

Alexander's son led an expedition together with new baronet James Stewart—Lord Ochiltree—and 60 settlers in two vessels which arrived at Baleine, on the southeast corner of Cape Breton Island, 1 July 1629. They quickly cleared some land and built a stockade—Fort Rosemar—which stood on a point with water on two sides. Ochiltree rashly began enforcing his fishing monopoly, demanding a tribute of one-tenth of their catch from foreign, mainly French, fishermen.

This was a foolhardy move since the French saw Cape Breton as *their* territory. They had identified land around St. Ann's Harbour—long France's chief fishing and fur post—as a possible permanent settlement. The Company of New France, which had been organized with the purpose of settling the St. Lawrence Region, had sought the aid of André and Charles Daniel, two swashbuckling master seamen, to help establish their planned settlements.

The Daniel brothers from Dieppe had been engaged in fishing off Cape Breton while battling with Basque and English over access to the fishery. In 1629 they were put in charge of the Company's flotilla. On its way to Canada, it was blown off course. Charles Daniel sailed on to Cape Breton where he listened to the complaints of French fishermen about the tribute they had been forced to pay Ochiltree. In September, Daniel attacked Fort Rosemar. His description of the attack gives a clear insight into the daredevil braggadocio of these seadogs:

At about two o'clock in the afternoon I had my men advance toward the fort according to the instructions I had given them; which were to attack at different points and make plentiful use of grenades, fire-pots, and other fire-works, notwithstanding the resistance and musket-fire of the enemy. The latter, seeing themselves hard pressed, were seized with fright, and quickly appeared on their rampart, waving a white flag, begging for life and quarter from my lieutenant. Meantime, I was approaching the gates of the fort, which I immediately burst open, and I entered the said fort, followed at once by my men and captured the said lord, whom I found armed with a pistol and a sword which he was holding in his hand, and all his men...having disarmed them all, I ordered down the standards of the King of England, and put up instead those of the King, my master.[44]

Charles Daniel had Fort Rosemar demolished and took his Scottish prisoners to St. Ann's Harbour. There, he put these captives to work building a new French fort, Fort Sainte-Anne, even using some of the materials found at Baleine. According to Ochiltree, his settlers were then shipped to England:

Fifty men women and children being enclosed in the hold of the schipe in so little bound that they were forced to ly upon [each] other as thy hayd beein so many fisshes lying in thair owin filthe and fed upon bread and water. That by famine and the pestiferous smell of their owin filth many of them wer throwin in the sea throu famin the mothers lossing their milk the poor souking childrin lost their lyffe and were throwin in the sea.[45]

Those that survived and had any wealth were held for ransom. The rest were left in England. All in all, this was a tragic ending for the first attempt of Scottish people to settle Cape Breton Island, but it gives an indication of how high were the stakes for what was considered the right to lay claim to an increasingly valuable piece of real estate.

Fort Sainte-Anne—near where the Englishtown ferry crosses today—contained a storehouse, a chapel, and quarters for a forty-man garrison and two Jesuit priests. However, when he set sail with the prisoners in November, the impulsive Charles Daniel failed to leave sufficient trade goods for the Mi'kmaq, who in turn brought neither furs, greens, nor meat. As a result scurvy broke out, killing over one-third of the garrison. As the winter wore on, tempers flared, and the garrison captain, Gaude, murdered Daniel's lieutenant, Martell. Gaude was put in confinement, but he escaped—never to be seen again.[46]

In the spring, Charles Daniel returned with supplies and his brother Antoine, a Jesuit priest. Antoine was just as energetic and single-minded as his brother, only his intended conquest was that of souls. He began the christianization of the island's Mi'kmaq. He stayed in Cape Breton for less than a year, leaving to work among the natives in the St. Lawrence River-Great Lakes region. It was there he was killed, a martyr. He was canonized in 1930.

In 1632 two more Jesuits, Vimont and Vieuxpont, arrived. They set to work converting the Mi'kmaq to Christianity. The Mi'kmaq were now long accustomed to hard bargaining with the Europeans, as Daniel's settlers had found out; but France was interested in working with the Mi'kmaq to keep English settlement at bay, and what better tool than religion? The Mi'kmaq had witnessed the French surviving plagues that had devastated their own people. Their shamans had been powerless against European disease.[47] Their own religious beliefs strained, they grew curious about French spiritual practices, especially the external symbols like Holy Water and ritual gestures. The Jesuits were quick to notice this and set up a chapel, thus keeping a promise made to their patroness, Anne of Austria, the mother of the King of France. They dedicated this first chapel to St. Anne, the grandmother of Christ.[48]

24

Since they had high regard for grandmothers, the Mi'kmaq themselves were probably touched by the Jesuit's selection of this name.

It was also in 1632, with the Treaty of Saint-Germain-en-Laye, that France and England decided on a peace settlement which stabilized French control of Acadie and the Québec region up the St. Lawrence River. The promise of the fur trade—and of new souls to convert in the vast territory to the west—lured people like Charles Daniel and Father Antoine Daniel away from smaller fur-producing areas like Cape Breton. And as they departed, the value of the Mi'kmaq fur trade declined, leading the Jesuits to close their mission in Cape Breton and move westward. The last Jesuits left in 1641.

This meant that the Mi'kmaq, now converted to Catholicism but bereft of many of their own spiritual practices, were left without clergy. They had to travel for baptism all the way to Miscou, an island off the northeast coast of present-day New Brunswick.[49]

The St. Ann's post continued to exist, but on a smaller scale. In 1634 another trading and colonizing enterprise, the Compagnie du Cap-Breton, purchased monopoly rights to the fur trade and fishery of the whole island, and along with it control of Fort Sainte-Anne. Pierre Desportes de Lignières, the driving force behind this venture, opened a second post in 1636 on Cape Breton's southwest coast, known as Saint-Pierre (St. Peter's). This site was strategically located near a narrow stretch of land that separates the Bras d'Or Lakes from the Atlantic Ocean, not far from what the French called Détroit de Fronsac, today's Strait of Canso. It lay along a traditional Mi'kmaq trade route between the Bras d'Or Lakes and the adjoining mainland, barely 48 kilometres away.[50]

Both outposts prospered, but they were soon confronted with problems caused by France's colonial policy. While that country was ready to confront foreigners trying to assume control of her coastal colonies, she allowed almost free rein to her own people who were given trade monopolies. The result was frequent fights over territory and general confusion as to ownership. So in 1647 the little outposts in Cape Breton were suddenly attacked by forces of the governor of Acadie, Charles Menou d'Aulnay. To ensure his authority—and ignoring the rights of the Company of Cape Breton—D'Aulnay took over the post at St. Peter's.[51]

Both posts—St. Ann's and St. Peter's—continued to operate. In 1650 they came under the control of merchants Nicolas Denys and his brother Simon. Nicolas Denys would leave a deep mark on the history of Cape Breton, emerging as the first European we can identify with a clear-cut character that featured endurance, energy, intelligence, and physical strength. Called "La Grande Barbe" because of his long beard, he had to use all of these abilities in the rapacious struggles for territory.

Nicolas was born in Tours, France, in 1598. Despite little formal education, he had soon become involved in fishing and lumbering businesses, so that in 1632 he became agent for the Company of New France, recruiting settlers to be sent to Acadie under the auspices of Isaac de Razilly. The settlers arrived near La Have, Nova Scotia, that September, and Denys began a fishing operation. He branched out into cutting timber for export to France but at Razilly's death in 1635 his lieutenant, Charles Menou d'Aulnay, assumed control and rescinded Denys' right to export his timber. Denys had no choice but to return to France.

Denys was not to be thwarted. He continued fishing and trading trips to Newfoundland, so that by 1645 he obtained a concession from the Company of New France to erect a commercial settlement at Miscou Harbour in today's New Brunswick. His implacable enemy D'Aulnay refused to recognize the grant in what he felt was his own territory, and in 1647 D'Aulnay seized the post and expelled Denys. Denys was powerless to act until D'Aulnay's death three years later, when he and his brother Simon went to Cape Breton where they quickly fortified the post at St. Peter's. The settlement contained dwellings, storehouses for furs and food items, and even a little chapel to which Nicolas managed to attract three Capuchin friars who served both his settlers and the Mi'kmaq that brought furs to the site.

The Mi'kmaq and the Denys brothers continued the inter-dependency that had developed between the native peoples and the French. In order to cement that relationship, one of Denys' sons married an aboriginal woman, perhaps introducing the Denys surname now common among the Mi'kmaq people. Meanwhile, Simon concentrated his energies on St. Ann's where he continued the fishery and established one of the first farms on Cape Breton Island. He planted apple trees which were to persist there for many years.

Once again their hopes were dashed. Jeanne Motin, the widow of Charles d'Aulnay, continued her husband's feud with the Denys brothers. In 1651 she sent soldiers who took both posts and captured Simon and Nicolas, sending them as prisoners to Québec. They complained to the authorities there that Madame d'Aulnay's actions were illegal, and were allowed to return to St. Peter's. Simon, however, left for France, leaving Nicolas to continue the struggle in Cape Breton.

And struggle it was. He had just returned to St. Peter's when another enemy appeared in the person of Emmanuel Le Borgne, a merchant to whom d'Aulnay had died heavily in debt. Since he assumed the debts, Le Borgne also assumed D'Aulnay's rights in Acadie, which he took to include control of Cape Breton. With a troop of soldiers he ambushed and captured Denys in 1653 and sent him prisoner to Port Royal on the Nova Scotia mainland. Denys fought for his release and returned to France where once again his rights were upheld by the Company of New France.

This time, to ensure his safety, Denys purchased from the Company rights to the coasts and islands of the Gulf of St. Law-rence, including Cape Breton, and was given the title of Governor and Lieutenant-General of the region.

He could now turn his attention to St. Peter's. Realizing the importance of the fur trade there he once again welcomed Mi'kmaq travelling between the mainland and the Bras d'Or Lakes, encouraging them to bring their furs to the narrow isthmus at Fort Saint-Pierre. To facilitate European use of the isthmus, Denys had a haulover road of wooden skids built for the transportation of heavier boats between the lakes and the Atlantic.[52]

Denys cultivated 80 acres of land at St. Peter's, and explored Cape Breton Island in search of new business opportunities. He spotted coal and sent samples to France, obtaining the right to collect royalties on any coal shipped there. He explored the use of birch in shipbuilding: "It is lighter [than beech], and does not split nor crack in the sun, or very little. I have had several vessels built of it...."[53] He recognized elm trees as excellent for the manufacture of gun carriages for the mother country.[54] He mentioned maple syrup which he praised since "it does not inconvenience the stomach" and was as good as water from mineral springs in France. "This is the drink of the Indians, and even of the French, who are fond of it."[55]

Denys quickly turned St. Peter's into a busy centre of the fur and fish trade. Taking advantage of the ice-free harbour and its proximity to the fishing banks, he dried the fish and had them ready for spring export even before the annual crop of European fishermen arrived.

He imported cattle and more settlers to begin the growing of wheat. He experimented with a flour mill, and began making beer, which he hoped would replace the wine imported from France.[56]

With St. Peter's as his headquarters, in 1659 he set up another fishing station at Chedabuctou (Guysborough) on the nearby mainland. This led to trouble; it was not long before yet another rival attacked the post. As the attacks persisted Denys went once again to France to reaffirm his rights. The following year, 1668, tragedy again struck when the settlement at St. Peter's went up in flames. The conflagration destroyed his holdings there and led to financial ruin. By now he was 70 years old and could not face the rebuilding of St. Peter's. Instead he moved with his family to a post he had built at Nipisiguit, now Bathurst, New Brunswick.[57]

In the midst of this busy life, Denys found time to observe and write about the Acadian region. This was perhaps his greatest gift not only to Cape Breton but to the Maritime Provinces. His 1672 publication, *The Description and Natural History of the Coasts of North America (Acadia)*, included the most extensive, clearest and most reliable study of the island, its native population, and its agricultural, timber, fishing, hunting, and mineral resources. Denys drew attention to the settlement potential of Cape Breton: "One can live there with as much satisfaction as in France itself," if only "the envy of the French, one against another, does not ruin the best-intentioned plans."[58] It would take a war and another 40 years before France realized the truth and wisdom of these words.

DENYS' ABANDONMENT OF HIS POSTS in Cape Breton marks the end of the early period of contact between European and Mi'kmaq. Sexual relations and intermarriage between the two peoples had left, in some instances, a mixed race highly influenced by French. Denys noted that most earlier Mi'kmaq customs persisted. The great change was in hunting methods, where the gun replaced the arrow, and fishing spears were tipped with iron instead of bone. As well,

The axes, the kettles, the knives, and everything that is supplied them, is much more convenient and portable than those which they had in former times, when they were obliged to go to camp near their grotesque kettles, in place of which to-day they are free to go camp where they wish. One can say that in those times the immovable kettles [hollowed-out logs filled with water and heated with hot stones] were the chief regulators of their lives, since they were able to live only in places where these were.[59]

The Mi'kmaq had left the stone age culture. Their population had suffered the ravages of strange diseases, their spiritual and

29

social worlds had been deeply shaken and reorganized, and now they had a growing dependency on an outside race of people.

Europeans had sought to exploit the economic potential of Cape Breton Island. Though they had realized some limited success, imperial rivalries and opposing land claims thwarted sustained economic development.

# 2

# Isle Royale, The First Boom

## 1713-1758

"Il sera l'entrepost et le refuge des vaisseaux qui
reviennent des grandes Indes, des Indes Espagnoles,
des Isles de l'Amérique et de tous ceux qui
fréquentent les mers de Canada."[1]
—Anonymous, 1692

"[Cape Breton] will become a centre of trade and
safety for ships returning from the greater Antilles, the
Spanish Indies and the islands near America—indeed
for all those regularly sailing the seas off Canada."

FOR ALMOST FORTY-FIVE YEARS after Denys' withdrawal, Europeans were scarce on the island of Cape Breton.
France's interests lay in the fishery off Placentia, on the south coast
of Newfoundland; in the fur trade in Canada, as their colony along
the upper St. Lawrence River was called; and to a lesser extent in
Port Royal, their mainland headquarters. While French officials
recognized the potential value of Cape Breton as a fishing base
and a focus for intercolonial trade, as long as they controlled
Placentia and Port Royal, Cape Breton was of secondary interest.[2]
The Island's Mi'kmaq continued to trade with whatever fishermen came along, and carried trade goods along the Bras d'Or

31

Lakes-St. Peter's corridor to the adjoining mainland, as they had done in the days of Nicolas Denys.

The situation changed abruptly when England and France went to war over the succession to the Spanish Throne (1701-1714). Battles were fought in Europe and America. In Acadie, New England troops captured Port Royal and Placentia, putting eastern Newfoundland under British control.

At the ensuing peace negotiations in the Dutch city of Utrecht, Cape Breton Island—which had been at the sidelines during these battles—suddenly leapt to prominence when France refused to give up her islands in the Gulf of St. Lawrence, especially Isle St. Jean (Prince Edward Island) and Cape Breton. Cape Breton's location made it the most valuable since it lay near the great fishing banks and at the entrance to the Gulf of St. Lawrence, from where it could control the mouth of the St. Lawrence River. France realized that without Cape Breton she had no hope of a significant fishery, upon which thousands of families in Western France depended for their livelihood. She also needed an ice-free location to compensate for the winter isolation of Canada (Québec). Even more important, Cape Breton's location on the same latitude as Brittany in France placed it on the triangular route for ships bringing French-made goods to North America, transporting fish to the West Indies and France, and hauling produce from the West Indies to North America and France.[3]

Since Britain, too, saw the significance of Cape Breton, treaty talks almost collapsed over its possession. When the Treaty of Utrecht was finally signed in 1713, France had given up claims to Acadie, the Hudson Bay territory, and Newfoundland—so long as she got ownership of, and the right to fortify, Cape Breton Island.

France moved quickly to ensure her possession of the island. Placentia was vacated in the late summer of 1713; 149 settlers and 100 soldiers sailed from Newfoundland to Havre à l'Anglais—English Harbour in Cape Breton—the future Louisbourg. There they encountered Mi'kmaq who, though they had not been consulted about France's plans for the island, were willing to deal with their long-standing trading partners and co-religionists.

The royal government in France needed the friendship of the Mi'kmaq to carry out its new colonial policy in North America. Gone were the earlier trading monopolies which had resulted in conflict and had failed to produce lasting settlement. Instead, the government assumed control of Cape Breton and was willing to pay for the operations and fortifications of the colony out of its own coffers.

A sign of the new policy was the change of place names. Cape Breton Island became "Isle Royale," putting it firmly under royal control. Old place names were replaced by ones that sounded more official: Havre à l'Anglais became Louisbourg, named for King Louis XIV and for the patron saint of France, the Crusader King, St. Louis. Today's St. Peter's was now Port Toulouse after one of the sons of the King. St. Ann's became Port Dauphin, the title of the heir-apparent to the throne.

In an effort to increase settlement, attempts were made to attract Acadians from the Nova Scotia mainland, now under British rule. Only a small number of Acadians were lured from their homes in the fertile Annapolis Valley to the sparer soil and cold-water fishery off Isle Royale. Those Acadians who did come favoured Port Toulouse, where they would be nearer their mainland relatives.[4] Port Toulouse and the whole southwestern end of Cape Breton retained for both French and Mi'kmaq their importance as centres for trade and for smuggling with the adjoining British mainland. Port Dauphin was even more important since it was closer to the fishing banks. Both sites eventually became centres of local administration, protected by forts and garrisons.

But when it came to choosing a capital, Louisbourg—actually, the fishery—won out.

Louisbourg had a deep harbour nearer to traditional fishing

ports such as Baleine and Gabarus. Administrators had favoured Port Dauphin; they felt it would be easier to defend. Defense of Louisbourg, which was situated in a low-lying area backed by hills, would require expensive fortifications. Fishermen, however, chose Louisbourg as their chief port since it was near the fishing banks and—unlike Port Dauphin—was ice-free throughout the year.

In 1717, after four years of dithering, the administrators led by Governor Joseph St. Ovide de Brouillon and Jean-François de Verville, Chief Engineer, settled in at Louisbourg and began plans for the Fortress. One historian has pointed out that the fortification could have been located either on the north side of the harbour, where the lighthouse was eventually erected, or on the south side. The north side was higher, with no surrounding hills, making it far less pregnable. But the south side won because, although it was backed by hills, it had a beach for the drying of cod. The needs of the fishery prevailed.[5]

Having been forced to build the Fortress in an exposed situation, the French compounded the problem with the type of fortification they selected. Despite France's difficult financial straits Vauban, the master of fortifications, advocated a complicated fortress. Given that determination, the simplest way to combine economy with complexity would have been to erect earthwork walls covered, or revetted, with masonry. A large fortification could have been erected capable of sustaining the pounding of cannon, yet relatively cheap to maintain. Instead, engineer Jean-François de Verville insisted on works constructed entirely of the more expensive and more brittle masonry. They consisted of two large bastions, the King's and Queen's, and two half bastions, the Dauphin and the Princess, facing the landward front, with two bastions, the Maurepas and the Brouillon, facing the sea.

The problems associated with masonry fortifications were soon apparent. Construction materials, tools, mills, craftsmen, and a larger work force all had to be imported from France. Costs soared throughout the 1720s and 1730s, giving rise to the story that Louis XV in France said he expected any day to see the walls of Louisbourg rising above the horizon. To make matters worse, the damp climate of Louisbourg, with its violent temperature fluctuations, caused mortar to crumble and stone to tumble into the ditches. Wooden revetment had to be placed all along the seaward front of the Fortress to keep the stones in place, and considerable money was spent on replacing lost stone.

Though construction of the Fortress presented a great number of difficulties, the French remained confident. Louisbourg's landward front faced a bog which attackers could only cross through superhuman effort. Moreover, except for the area within range of the seaward bastions, the nearby shore was rocky and dangerous, which would discourage troop landings. The Fortress should do its job.[6]

Louisbourg prospered enough to justify its great expense. True to prediction, the fishery became the life blood of Isle Royale. Fishermen lived on the island or returned annually to make their catch. The wet fishery was practiced: fish were caught and salted aboard ship and carried immediately to France, where they enjoyed wide sale. On the other hand, the resident fishermen salted and dried their fish ashore. This longer-lasting dried catch could be shipped long distances, such as to the West Indies.

This combination of resident fishermen and seasonal fishermen allowed France to exploit a broad market. The French soon outclassed the English fishermen of Newfoundland and New England, and dominated the markets of southern Europe.[7]

With ascendancy in the fishery came commercial power. Isle Royale was strategically located on the Gulf of St. Lawrence. French merchants, wishing to send their wares from France up the St. Lawrence to Québec, could avoid the long, arduous trip by leaving those wares at Louisbourg for transshipment. The time saved could mean a trip to the French West Indies with a shipment of fish, and a voyage back from there to France with tropical produce. The same applied to Québec merchants who could send their goods to Louisbourg for shipment on to France when a large enough load was assembled. Louisbourg was thus an entrepôt—a gathering place for the further shipment of goods.

It was as a transshipment centre that Louisbourg was surprisingly successful, and it was not long before the inhabitants took advantage of this asset. Many who had begun as fishermen became merchants. It was an easy step for someone who was carrying his yearly catch from Cape Breton to Canada or the West Indies to bring back goods like furs or rum for shipment to France. International trade accounts for the huge variety of exotic products found in later excavations at Louisbourg—Chinese porcelain, Dutch delftware, German stoneware, and New England food, lumber, and dishware. Many fishermen made the complete transition to merchant; others retained the dual role of fisherman-merchant.

By 1744—the year to which the modern Fortress of Louisbourg has been restored—the original hamlet of perhaps 100 fishing people had been transformed into a busy commercial port. The quayside was particularly active, full of people in summer.[8] The wharves were crowded as ships were being loaded and unloaded, carters hauling away goods; there were street sales taking place on the spot. Taverns along the waterfront were packed with people eating and drinking with friends and new arrivals, enlivened by the occasional fights among intoxicated fishermen. On fine days, children played games and the sounds of music brightened the atmosphere. At one end of the quay was the *carcan* or pillory for those accused of crimes—held there sometimes for a few hours or for a day, perhaps being chided by passersby. In the 1750s, grimy coal piles were located at one end of the quay. But above all, the smell of drying fish permeated the air, since "king cod" was spread to dry wherever convenient.

Proximity to the fishing banks gave Louisbourg fishermen

an advantage over their European-based countrymen and New England counterparts. More and more fishermen settled permanently near Louisbourg and thousands more joined them each year on a seasonal basis. These fishermen lived just outside the Fortress in the Dauphin Faubourg, and around the north shore of the harbour—the site of wharves, storehouses, and flakes. A local fisherman or *habitant pêcheur* could fish by himself. More often he employed from a few to as many as 60 fishermen per season. The lesser fisherman lived very simply indeed, in a small house with his few possessions in a trunk, drinking home-brewed spruce beer.

The wealthier fisherman presented a different story. He likely lived in the town in a better house of half timber or of stone. He enjoyed more social mobility. Antoine Paris had been a fisherman in Plaisance, Newfoundland. He moved to Louisbourg at its birth and began fishing with his wife, elder son, and one assistant. When he died he owned six chaloupes —small sailing vessels—employed about 30 men, and owned property in the Dauphin Faubourg and in the town, which he rented out to merchants and innkeepers. His son became a ship captain, and three of his daughters who began as *coutourières* (seamstresses) ended up marrying merchants and surgeons.

Joseph Lartigue, another fishing proprietor, eventually became a judge and member of the Superior Council.[9]

While Louisbourg cannot be imagined without the fishery, all the ships in the harbour did not belong to fishermen. The growing population encouraged a demand for goods like brandy, tobacco, clothing, and household articles, and for services such as living accommodations, taverns, medical care, and civil and admiralty courts. In this important international trading settlement, merchants developed sophisticated trading techniques, employing agents in foreign ports and using various forms of credit to ensure smooth business exchanges. Merchandising and services were necessary not only for local needs, but also for outlying settlements such as Port Toulouse, Baie des Espagnols—the future Sydney—and Port Dauphin. This attracted more fishermen into marketing as they used their boats to transport goods. It was only a short step from there to the purchasing of goods for resale around the colony. Storehouses became the most characteristic buildings in Louisbourg. And storehouses became shops as fishermen became merchants. Parish records show fishermen serving as baptismal witnesses who, only a few years later, became *marchands* (merchants) or, even better, *négociants* (businessmen).[10]

In 1745 there were over 25 inns and taverns in Louisbourg. *Cabarets*, offering wine, rum, and some food, were often scenes of debauchery, and the administration tried to clamp down on their proliferation. In response, the *cabaretiers* began to call themselves *aubergistes*, while the *aubergistes* aspired to the title of *hotelier*. In this Louisbourg reflected a similar move that was also taking place in France.

Society in Louisbourg developed as the role of the colony of Isle Royale evolved. After 1720, Louisbourg became an armed fortress. There is little evidence to suggest that soldiers mixed outside their own social orbit. There was some marriage with civilians, but this was discouraged before 1745. Regular soldiers were thus socially apart, useful in building the fortifications, but looked down upon as untrustworthy scum. They lived up to that evaluation with frequent drunkenness, nighttime carousing, and court appearances for charges such as murder and robbery.

Military and civilian discipline, once enforced, was rigid. Some lawbreakers, such as murderers, were hanged on a gallows erected either at the *carcan* or at Black Rock on the end of Rochefort Point at the tip of the Louisbourg peninsula. Some bodies were quartered after death and left hanging for long periods.[11] Others, for lesser crimes, would be paraded through town—then chained at the ankles as prisoners bound for the king's galleys for the rest of their lives—a virtual death sentence.[12]

The military's role was significant, but secondary to that of the merchant and fisherman. The soldiers were there to defend the populace, and they usually comprised a third to one half of the town's population. By 1745 these units totaled around 500 men. These soldiers were housed in the large 365-foot-long barracks of the King's Bastion. Despite its size, soldiers were crowded, sleeping two in a bed. Quarters were cold and damp; vermin were tolerated. Bad food caused a mutiny in 1744. The ringleaders were hanged.

On the other hand, captains and higher ranks lived in relative luxury in some of the finest homes in Louisbourg. The laxity in the application of rules forbidding their participation in trade allowed them to amass sizeable fortunes.

Slaves and servants were common in Louisbourg. Slaves were sometimes captured Indians or Blacks purchased abroad and imported to do menial tasks. They were found in any type of household: governors generally had four or five servants and a few slaves; military captains had fewer of each; merchants might have a servant to help run the shop or inn; wealthier fishermen might have one as an assistant. Even the Hospital Brothers of St. Jean de Dieu had a slave and servants.

*Domestiques* were male; *servantes* were female. They generally mingled among themselves, eating together but not "powdering" themselves as did their betters. That female servants were frequently abused is indicated by the number of illegitimate births. Many servants were Acadians; there were also a few Irish. These people had no voice in local councils. They rarely appeared in court cases and they rarely married.

As the town and fortifications developed, hundreds of stonemasons, glaziers, surveyors, and carpenters were needed. Most of these artisans came for periods of 36 months to make money and return to France. It is important to remember that Louisbourg was never self-sufficient in regard to goods produced by artisans: in other words, dish makers, candlestick makers, and the like were not present. It was less expensive to import goods in this mercantile economy than to produce them locally. After 1750, as wealth and social sophistication increased, winemakers, dancing masters, and tapestry weavers found a place in Louisbourg.

The guardian of morality in this diverse society was the Catholic Church. In Québec it played a key role in government; here in Isle Royale it exercised only a small administrative role. The bishop was far away in Québec and it was difficult for the Church to maintain rigid control over such a mobile trading and fishing population. We never hear churchmen complaining about illegal trade, social scandals, or social problems.

While boys were taught the rudiments of fishing or trade by their fathers—or if wealthy were sent to France for education—girls were neglected. After frequent calls for nuns to set up proper education for girls, the Bishop of Québec finally convinced 55-year-old Soeur de la Conception along with two assistants to go to Louisbourg in 1727. She opened a school. People were delighted, and she soon had 22 students. Eventually eight or nine sisters of the Congregation of Notre Dame arrived and brought a moral tone to the town. Indeed Abbé Maillard, revered missionary to the Mi'kmaq, claimed that they were responsible for *establishing* order in the town. Their work expanded and, after a particularly virulent outbreak of smallpox, they took in orphans.

The few Recollets who acted as parish priests were overworked. So were the Hospital Brothers who ran a vital facility in a place where diseases like smallpox could break out at any time, where falls from the parapets due to drunkenness meant fractured limbs, and where hernias plagued soldiers and artisans working on the construction and maintenance of the fortifications. They drew the line at treating venereal disease since it was considered a sinful affliction. For remedy, one would have to go to France or visit the town surgeon who had frequent run-ins with the brothers over this and other treatments.

Since the colony pretty well ran on its own, local officials became the authority at Isle Royale. While Isle Royale was officially subordinate to the government in Canada, in reality France sent orders directly to Louisbourg which was in turn responsible directly to the French King at Versailles.

THE SECOND LARGEST SETTLEMENT on the island after Louisbourg was Ingonish, where there was an important year-round fishery. Nicolas Denys' grandson, Louis Denys De La Ronde, reported that the codfish were abundant at St. Ann's and Ingonish, "where the cod fishery began earlier than any other part of the island."[13]

According to historian Ken Donovan:

Along this three-mile stretch of coast, there were 100 dwellings (including outbuildings) and a total permanent population of 741 people [by 1737].... The cleared French lands of Ingonish continued to provide hay well into the 19th Century. During the summer of 1800 John Girvois was paid 15 pounds for the carrying of 12 tons of hay from Ingonish to the coal mines at Sydney Mines. [That same year] Patrick Kehoe was paid 12 pounds for a "voyage to Ingonish with my sloop to carry men to cut hay."[14]

Numerous fishing ports sprang up all around the seacoast and in the Bras d'Or Lakes. The two long-standing settlements at Port Dauphin (St. Ann's) and Port Toulouse (St. Peter's) continued as fishing and local administrative centres. At these places, regional judicial and other legal affairs were settled.

Port Toulouse was especially crucial. The fishery on nearby Isle Madame was valuable, particularly at Petit-de-Grat and Nérichac (Arichat). As well, Port Toulouse continued as a gathering place for Mi'kmaq and a place of refuge for Acadians from the British-held mainland.

All along the south coast, harbours long known to Europeans became permanent settlements with fluctuating populations dependent on the fishery. St. Esprit, Fourche (Forked Harbour or Fourchu), Gabarus, Baleine, Little Lorraine, and Scatarie Island were often used as temporary residences during the summer season when their populations could swell to over 300 people. Framboise had the added advantage of pasturage for cattle production. Along the east coast, settlements at Ingonish, Port Dauphin (St. Ann's), L'Indienne (Lingan), Baie de Mordienne (Morien Bay), Spanish Bay, Mira Gut, Main-à-Dieu (Menadou) existed mainly for the fishery, with some farming and animal production—especially at Spanish Bay and Morien.[15]

The most unusual settlement on the coast was on Isle de Verderonne (Boularderie Island) at Petit Brador (Little Bras d'Or), since it was a throwback to the earlier monopolistic concessions made by the Crown to individuals. As a reward for services at Port Royal, in 1719 Louis Simon de St. Aubin Chevalier de la Boularderie was granted Boularderie Island and adjacent territory, with the intention of meeting the crucial agricultural needs of Isle Royale. So much attention was paid to the more lucrative fishery that there was fear of food shortages. The attempt to lure Acadians to Cape Breton from their lush farms in Nova Scotia had failed. Boularderie was therefore obliged to bring out farmers from France.

These farmers experienced some success raising wheat, peas, and dairy cattle. A sawmill and flour mill were erected, and by 1737 there were 32 people living at what is now Little Bras d'Or. The following year Boularderie died. His son lacked his father's organizational ability, so the little settlement failed to reach its potential and Cape Breton Island remained dependent on outside food supplies.[16]

Due to lack of good harbours, there were few important settlements on the west coast of Cape Breton, today's Inverness County. Chéticamp was used as an occasional fishery station. There were small outposts at Judique and Isle aux Juste-au-Corps (Port Hood Island) which furnished quarried stone for the Fortress. There were a few temporary encampments along the Strait of Fronsac (Strait of Canso) where goods were smuggled between Isle Royale and the British-held mainland. Baddeck was the principle French centre on the Bras d'Or Lakes, with a small lake fishery.

By the 1740s the population of Louisbourg with its suburbs was close to 4,500 while the island as a whole was home to 10,000. Almost all of today's principal centres on Cape Breton Island can trace their origins to the French pioneers of the 17th and 18th centuries.

WHILE THE FRENCH WERE FORMING settlements on the island, the Mi'kmaq preferred to retain their migratory way of life. They travelled between the British mainland and Cape Breton and even on to Newfoundland, trading, hunting, and fishing. However, an important threshold had been crossed in the 17th century when they became dependent on European trade goods like guns, fishing gear, and metal utensils. They could get these items from either the French or the British since both sides wanted their support. They used this advantage to obtain as much as possible from both. The Mi'kmaq met regularly with officials and demanded that friendship be shown in trade goods. Treaties would have lapsed without a dependable supply of European trade items.

On the other hand, the Mi'kmaq were concerned that their homeland would be swallowed up by European settlement. Sensing this, one French official wisely commented, "If we do not admit or pretend to admit their right to the country they occupy, they will never be induced to take part in any war for the defense of this same Country."[17] The French were less of a menace to the Mi'kmaq than the British since there were fewer of them and, at least in Isle Royale, their fishing settlements and scant farms left most of the land to the natives. The British were expanding their mainland settlements and encouraging further immigration. Also, as Roman Catholics, the Mi'kmaq felt more at ease with the French, who supplied them with missionaries. France, of course, took advantage of this and used the missionaries, including those stationed in British territory, to further her imperial ambitions.[18]

The Mi'kmaq persisted in travelling back and forth across the Strait of Fronsac until around 1723, when skirmishes with the English drove them to remain in Cape Breton. France wanted them to settle in one location, easily reached for military assistance and the diplomatic gift exchange. The Mi'kmaq agreed and settled around Mirliguèche (Malagawatch) at the entrance of River Denys Basin on the western shore of the Bras d'Or Lakes, not far by canoe from their ancient route through Port Toulouse. The French government financed the building of a church where they could have access to missionaries.

The Jesuits who had left the island in 1641 were replaced by Recollets. Only five Recollets worked with the Mi'kmaq, but they had great influence—particularly the first, Father Antoine Gaulin (1674-1740) and the last, Father Pierre Maillard (c. 1710-1762). Mirliguèche remained the Mi'kmaq headquarters until 1750, when Maillard set up his mission at Île de la Sainte-Famille—today's Chapel Island, still the site of the annual pilgrimage in honour of St. Anne—ten kilometres northeast of Port Toulouse. The land was better there and its proximity to Port Toulouse made it easier for the authorities in Louisbourg to keep in contact with the natives.[19]

The missionaries played a role in the liaison between the French and the Mi'kmaq, ensuring mutual trust. Regarding Maillard, one visitor commented,

He has embraced all their customs, officiates at their weddings, baptisms, and burials, celebrates the Mass for them, and conducts their prayers every day. He often eats meat and fish without bread, sleeps on the snow, suffers the extreme cold, and has also adopted the savages' footwear, which is made from seal skins.[20]

Mi'kmaq numbers were not large. In 1721, Gaulin estimated that there were 36 natives bearing arms in Isle Royale. This would represent around 100 people. It is likely that during this period the population never exceeded 250, with 50 or 60 fighting men. They were supplemented by men from the mainland, but never in great numbers.[21] Yet this force was important to the French for their knowledge of the island and possible use in warfare. Without them more troops would be required from France. Indian alliances were cheaper, so every year in June or July Mi'kmaq would gather from all over Isle Royale and the mainland up to the Gaspé and Isle St. Jean—usually at Port Toulouse, sometimes at Port Dauphin—to cement the alliance with gifts which meant subsistence for the Indians and signified protection for the French.[22]

To solidify their friendship and learn native ways, high ranking French military families, like the De La Vallières with their noble connections, sent their sons to live with the Mi'kmaq for long periods of time.

LOUISBOURG SOON NEEDED all the help it could get. The Treaty of Utrecht in 1713, which had resulted in the establishment of the Colony of Isle Royale, had ushered in an unusual 30-year period of peace between France and Britain. This perhaps lulled the French into neglecting their fortifications which, in 1745, displayed glaring weaknesses. No outer works had been erected to prevent cannon installations in the nearby hills; some of the walls were in poor condition; and the militia was poorly trained. But continuing trade between Isle Royale and Boston implied good future relations and calmed any fears of war.

It took the outbreak of the War of the Austrian Succession in 1745 to throw the North American Colonies into conflict. When word reached Isle Royale in April that England and France were at war, privateers quickly set out from Louisbourg to raid enemy shipping and take booty. An expedition took the New England fishing port of Canso on the nearby mainland and an unsuccessful attack was made on the British capital of Nova Scotia at Annapolis Royal. These attacks alarmed New Englanders who soon resolved to take the Fortress to eliminate the dangers it posed to their safety and commerce.

Governor Shirley, before the General Court of Massachusetts, did not mince words: "Gentlemen of the General Court, either we must take Louisbourg or see our trade annihilated.... What say you? Is Louisbourg ours or not?"[23]

The answer was yes!—and following the leadership of Shirley, an expedition of over 100 ships under the command of Lieutenant-General William Pepperrell, a prosperous Massachusetts merchant, set sail and arrived at Gabarus Bay 11 May 1745. The French Governor, Duchambon, sent out from the Fortress a force of 80 men to prevent a landing—but after only a brief skirmish they fled, allowing the New Englanders to land at nearby Freshwater Creek.

The French force comprised 1500 men of the Compagnies Franches de la Marine and several companies of the Swiss Mercenary Regiment de Karrer. The morale and discipline of this relatively small force was low following a mutiny over inadequate provisions the year before. There had also been a recent rebellion against Duchambon's authority.[24] And to make matters worse, Commander Peter Warren, commanding British naval operations in American waters, had ships sent to Isle Royale from the West Indies while he took command of the New England fleet in order to cut off any help France might try to send.

The First Siege of Louisbourg is a story of the encirclement of the Fortress. The seemingly impossible was accomplished when the New England colonials managed to drag their cannon over the marshy land on specially constructed sleds, and set them up on the nearby hills. They began the bombardment of the Fortress below. The French were stunned by this accomplishment, not only demoralized but terrified. When it seemed the New Englanders were going to assault the Royal Battery which guarded the inner harbour, they quickly fled, failing to properly spike the cannon left behind. The New Englanders could not believe their good fortune. They promptly took the deserted battery, repaired the cannon and turned them on the Dauphin Bastion. It was soon in ruins.

Meanwhile, the French elicited the aid of the Mi'kmaq who were observed to be "very brave and warmly attached to the French."[25] They were particularly effective in fighting in the outlying settlements.

By the end of May the food supply in the Fortress was running low. Hope lay in a rupture of Warren's naval blockade. France had sent out the 64-gun man-of-war, *Le Vigilant*, manned by 500 sailors and carrying ammunition and supplies. The British captured the *Vigilant* after a heavy battle. Morale in the Fortress plummeted—only to rise again when a New England attack on the Island Battery defending the entrance to the harbour failed, with many New Englanders killed. The New Englanders answered this loss by erecting a battery at the nearby lighthouse from which they bombarded and all but silenced the Island Battery. This opened the harbour and allowed the British fleet to enter. The French realized their position was untenable. The starving population, the uncertain loyalty of the military, and breaches made in the walls by the hill batteries, all convinced Duchambon to sue for surrender.

On 28 June 1745, the 47-day siege was lifted. The French had suffered 50 killed and 80 to 95 wounded; the New Englanders had 100 killed, with 30 more dying of illness. We have no numbers of the New England wounded, but the statistics for both sides are incredibly low. Though the British guaranteed there would be no looting, their guards could not prevent the exuberant New Englanders from pillaging, much to the anger of the French.[26] The New Englanders, on the other hand, complained the French were allowed to take away so much that there was little to plunder.[27]

The victory of the amateur and poorly disciplined New

Englanders over the reputedly strongest fortress in America surprised the world. In hindsight, the poor location of the Fortress, and British sea power which blocked help from reaching its beleaguered inhabitants, spelled doom from the very beginning. After all, a fortress is a defensive mechanism that can hold out only as long as supplies can be sent in or until the siege can be broken with outside help. Neither came, and the Fortress fell.

British raiding parties attacked and destroyed the other French communities on Cape Breton, finally loading the sad inhabitants onto 11 transports bound for France in early July. The Mi'kmaq also suffered. One French observer wrote,

> The same year, 1745, several bodies of savages, deceased, and buried at Port Tholouze, were dug up again by the Bostoners, and thrown into the fire. The burying-place of the savages was demolished, and all the crosses, planted on the graves, broken into a thousand pieces.[28]

When word reached New England that Louisbourg was taken, rejoicing knew no bounds.

The New England soldiers, on the other hand, could not return home to rejoice until regular British troops could come to relieve them. Waiting resulted in near mutiny that fall, as the colonial troops faced a long winter in Louisbourg. The winter ravaged the New Englanders far beyond the damage done during the siege. They suffered from dysentery, called the "bloody flux," and scurvy raged. Pepperrell wrote to Shirley on February 8, 1746, "from the last of Nov. to this date we have buried 561 men, and have at this time 1100 sick."[29]

That terrible winter, 890 men died, many times more than died in the siege. Bodies were buried in random shallow graves. Often the occupiers did not have enough strength for burials,[30] and bodies were tucked in under the floorboards. One third of the garrison of around 2,000 was constantly sick. Matters were made worse by the mess in the Fortress, with garbage and ruined buildings blocking the streets. Fuel was hard to come by since nearby woods had been burned, and bad weather made life even more miserable. All were "in want of almost all the necessaries of life, clothing of all sorts more especially, great numbers of the people almost naked."[31]

Despite the suffering and homesickness, the troops had to stay, for the fight over Louisbourg represented only one aspect of the War of the Austrian Succession. It continued elsewhere. And Cape Breton was too valuable to the French to be given up that easily. They set about to recapture it and even attack Boston. In July 1746, the Duc d'Anville was put in charge of a massive force of 20 frigates, 11 line-of-battle, and numerous transports to attack Louisbourg—the largest fleet ever to sail westward across the Atlantic! The Fortress might easily have been retaken had not the Atlantic hurricane season destroyed the fleet. The 3,000 troops were reduced to two shiploads that crawled into Chebucto (Halifax) Harbour. To make matters worse, pestilence broke out among the survivors. The Duke, overcome by grief and in poor health, reportedly committed suicide.[32] His body was eventually buried in the chapel at Louisbourg, where it remains today.

The Fortress stayed in British hands and, as the War of the Austrian Succession dragged on, the conquerors made numerous repairs to the town. Buildings were reconstructed, walls rebuilt, prefabricated buildings were even shipped from New England.[33] Shirley wanted the British to keep Cape Breton as the seat of a prosperous colony. The English did all they could to retain the island, even considering the exchange of Gibralter for Cape Breton.[34] France's Louis XV was willing to give up the Austrian Netherlands and Madras, India—where his armies had been victorious—but his negotiators were instructed to conclude no peace deal without the return of Cape Breton. The British had to give in.

It was with deep bitterness, therefore, that the New Englanders and Englishmen alike learned that at the peace negotiations at Aix-la-Chapelle in 1748, Isle Royale was returned to France. The decision was met by a flood of pamphlets attacking the treaty. After all the loss of life, besides the investment that had gone into it, Louisbourg was to be abandoned. All the British could do was to found a new port on the Nova Scotia coast to act as a counterweight to Louisbourg. This was Halifax, founded in 1749, immediately after the peace treaty was signed.

SHORTLY AFTER THE PEACE, the French rushed to resettle and fortify Isle Royale. Transports with settlers and 500 troops arrived at Louisbourg in late June 1749, and the French officially took possession 23 July.[35] Battalions of the Artois, Bourgogne, Cambis, and Volontaires Étrangers, along with two companies of artillery and 24 companies of 50 men each of Canadian troops, were added. The militia was reorganized and was supported by natives. Five ships of the line protected the harbour. A total of 219 cannon and 17 mortars manned the ramparts with 44 pieces in reserve.[36]

Settlers who had taken refuge in Canada and France soon returned, and within a short time the population of the colony was back in place. Port Toulouse and Port Dauphin also received troops and increased in population. Indeed, most fishing settlements grew after 1749, with the exception of Ingonish which became a seasonal fishery. Many of the new settlers were Acadians who were encouraged to leave Nova Scotia, where increasing tension between them and the British was making their lives untenable.[37]

Louisbourg's fishery and trade flourished even more than it had before 1745. Hoping for a more balanced economy, Governor de Raymond (1751-1754) encouraged the growth of agriculture to end the colony's dependence on food supplies from New England. He expanded coal production which the French had tentatively undertaken at Mordienne (Port Morien) as early as 1720. Food production did increase in areas around the Mira River and at Baie des Espagnols (Sydney), opening the prospects of a more diverse economy.

However, another period of protracted peace for the colony like that between 1713 and 1745 was unlikely. Warfare between England and France continued in the colonial borderlands. British fears of an insurrection in Nova Scotia led to the deportation of the Acadians in 1755. Some Acadians managed to escape to Isle Royale where they swelled the population of earlier settlements in the island's southeastern corner on Isle Madame.[38]

With the increasing prospect of another war, the fortifications needed immediate attention, "recognizing the errors which have been made and by taking measures to rectify them as soon as possible." The chief engineer, Louis Franquet, wanted outerworks erected near the hills overlooking the Fortress, which the New Englanders had used so effectively.[39] In this he was unsuccessful, though the rise at Black Rock on the tip of the Louisbourg peninsula was lowered to prevent artillery from being mounted there.

As a result of the failure to improve the fortifications, however, the Fortress was still vulnerable to attackers. When formal hostilities broke out again in 1758, Louisbourg was no stronger than it had been in 1745.

The proximity of the newly-founded Halifax, from where their fleet could easily set sail, ensured British control of the sea. General Geoffrey Amherst took supreme British command and a great expedition was planned to take Louisbourg once and for all. A land force of thirteen thousand, with 23 men-of-war and many other ships, set sail in May 1758 to lay siege. The French in the meantime had 3500 soldiers and 400 militia on hand, and 10 gunships carrying around 400 cannon. This time, France had warships in the harbour to prevent an attack from that quarter, and fortified entrenchments with 2,500 men at Gabarus Bay to prevent a landing. General James Wolfe led the British attack there and was forced to retreat by the strong French defense. Then—a small ridge outside the French line of fire was spotted, permitting a landing. Other troops followed and overwhelmed the French defenders who fled into the Fortress.

After pursuing the French back to the Fortress, the British set up camp near a stream about a kilometre and a half from the Fortress, in the same spot the New Englanders had occupied in 1745. They erected blockhouses and earthworks in order to protect the camp from Indian attacks. A town of eventually 20,000 troops grew up, a base of operations. Meanwhile, trenches above Rochefort Point were dug closer and closer to the Fortress.

What followed was, in many ways, a repeat of the First Siege, though matters were carried out far more effectively. Cannons were positioned in the hills, the harbour was surrounded, the Lighthouse Battery captured. This in turn destroyed the Island Battery. The French ships in the harbour prevented the British fleet's penetration there and kept up a valiant resistance. But a number of them caught fire, resulting in huge explosions which further damaged the harbour fortifications.

With the Fortress now in flames, Governor Drucour had to accept humiliating terms, surrendering himself and his garrison as prisoners at the discretion of the enemy—26 July 1758.[40] Once again the French refugees were rounded up from all over Cape Breton and sent to France or to the islands of St. Pierre and Miquelon—all that was left to France of her North Atlantic Empire.

With the Treaty of Paris in 1763 Isle Royale, now Cape Breton Island, and her sister Isle St. Jean, came under British rule.

52

# 3

# "A Little Republick of Our Own"

## Cape Breton County and Colony
## 1760-1820

"The most avaricious will be satisfied,
& the most diffident be emboldened."[1]
— Samuel Holland

LOUISBOURG WAS A RUIN. Nothing was left standing but a few houses, the hospital, and part of the barracks. Three hundred soldiers of the 59th Regiment were stationed in the town.

In 1760, Prime Minister and Minister of War William Pitt, determined to break French sea power and prevent their reestablishing a rival fishery in America, decided "that all the Fortifications of the Town of Louisburg, together with all the Works, and Defences...be forthwith totally demolished, and razed."[2] The site was pillaged, the bell from the King's bastion going to Montreal, carved stone and chimney pieces to Halifax, Boston, and Charleston. In years to come, quarried stone would be hauled to Sydney for the foundations of houses in its North End and to build its first churches, St. George's and St. Patrick's.

In the summer of 1760, one hundred sappers and miners were sent to Louisbourg. They drove 47 galleries beneath the walls,

53

filled 45 chambers with powder—and vast explosions flung debris into the air.[3] The destruction was almost complete; yet the remains would fascinate visitors for the next two hundred years. Historian Francis Parkman, visiting in the late 19th century, could only ponder that "this grassy solitude was once the 'Dunkirk of America'; the vaulted caverns where the sheep find shelter from the rain were casemates."[4]

THE DESTRUCTION OF LOUISBOURG, and Britain's determination to retain Cape Breton, inaugurated 25 years of neglect and steady decline which left the island backward despite her natural riches. Halifax replaced Cape Breton as the guardian of the northern sea lanes, and in 1763 a Royal Proclamation united the island to Nova Scotia.

Britain was reluctant to follow through on its promise in the Proclamation to offer free land in Cape Breton to veterans, at least until she had a better idea of the island's resources. To this end, in 1764 Samuel Holland, an expert and level-headed craftsman, was commissioned to survey the new conquests, the Islands of Cape Breton and St. John (after 1800 called Prince Edward Island). A native of Nijmegen, Holland, Samuel Holland had served under Wolfe at Louisbourg and made a valuable sketch of the town after its fall, before travelling with Wolfe to Québec and the 1759 battle for Canada on the Plains of Abraham.

As surveyor general of the Northern District of America, Holland was put in charge of the survey and description of Cape Breton, its people, and its resources. He travelled to Cape Breton and came up with a vision for its development. Looking forward to settlement, he divided the island into manageable town and county units, and named or re-named nearly every part of it with decidedly British names. He called the island "Cape Britain." And he wrote in 1768:

It is very certain; from the Situation; from the Climate; & above all from the concurrent Attestations of all who have long resided, & tried the Possibility of it, that this Country is capable of being improved to a very high Degree of Cultivation. The soil is in general good, nay in some Places luxuriantly so; the Woods afford a great Quantity of excellent Timber; the many Rivers, Rivulets, Creeks, Lakes, Coasts & sea, abound with Fish; the Game that resorts here, at different Seasons, thro' the Year is inumerable; these are such Inducements that with little Encouragement would invite Numbers to become Settlers, especially when it is considered, that in raising of Corn, Vegetables, Hemp, & Flax, in Lumber, Potash, but above all in the Fishery; there are such inexhaustible Funds to reward the Industry of the Pursuer, & all so humanly speaking, sure of Success; the most avaricious will be satisfied, & the most diffident be emboldened.[5]

About coal, Holland said, "There are such a Number of Veins...that they could supply the whole Continent of America." He uses the word "encourage" again and again. But William Knox in the British Colonial Department worried:

If the coal mines of Cape Breton should be wrought and the coal sold, the Americans would supply themselves from thence and work up their own [industries] and we should lose that trade.[6]

To prevent such development in competition with their own coal resources, the British government decided to close Cape Breton to all settlement. It forbade permanent land grants.

The only exceptions to this closed-door policy were lumbering for masts and ships' timber for the Royal Navy, and the fishery, since neither called for extensive areas of settlement. But how would the fishery be carried out?

After the fall of Louisbourg, Cape Breton was practically depopulated. When word reached Acadians at places like Port Toulouse (St. Peter's) and Isle Madame that their settlements might once again be pillaged by the British and that they could be banished like their brethren on the mainland, many fled to the woods in places like the interior of Isle Madame. Others simply left Cape Breton for St. Pierre and Miquelon or even France. Those who stayed led a nomadic existence until it was safe to return to the coast after the signing of the Treaty of Paris in 1763.

The population of the Acadians on Cape Breton, which had been estimated at 550 in 1752, dwindled to less than 200.[7]

The Acadians' fear of the British was paralleled by that of the Mi'kmaq. After all, the natives had fought beside the French in both sieges of Louisbourg, serving as scouts and auxiliaries, especially during the First Siege in 1745 for which the French were so ill prepared. They had even engaged in hand-to-hand combat at the Royal Battery.[8] In the Second Siege (1758) the Mi'kmaq were better prepared, and reinforcements were sent from mainland tribes. The garrison listed 500 Indians not including those established along the coast. In order to keep their friendship, the British allowed the Mi'kmaq in the Fortress to depart before the formal capitulation.[9]

With the French gone, the Mi'kmaq felt deserted and open to British reprisal. The Royal Proclamation of 1763 had not promised the natives any protection.[10] The only hope they had was the memory of a treaty signed on the mainland in 1761 giving them protection of the British King.[11]

Accordingly, some withdrew from Cape Breton, going as far as St. Pierre and Miquelon, and to Newfoundland itself. A 1774 census showed only 23 natives on Cape Breton.[12] With the decline in Mi'kmaq numbers, Abbé Maillard left the mission at Île de la Sainte-Famille—today's Chapel Island—which the British burned to the ground.

Fear and dislike of the Protestant English conquerors kept the Mi'kmaq close to the Acadians hiding in the interior, whom they supplied with food and intelligence of British movements, and with whom they sometimes intermarried.

The Acadians received some relief when in 1764 the British allowed the Philip and Charles Robin firm of the British Channel Island of Jersey, located off the coast of France, to establish a fishery on what became known as Jerseymen's Island and then on Isle

Madame at Arichat, which the French and Mi'kmaq called Nérichac. These Jersey businessmen were British subjects officially of the Anglican faith. Their loyalty to Britain was unquestioned, while their ability to speak French—and the security they offered as buyers and suppliers—encouraged the Acadians to bring them their catch, which the Jerseymen then exported to the British West Indies and to Europe. A fishery similar to that of the Louisbourg era was soon established. Shipbuilding followed, allowing a measure of security and prosperity to the 270 or so Acadians living in Isle Madame.[13]

Besides the Acadians, the largest number of inhabitants on Cape Breton lived around Louisbourg. A British garrison of 300 remained there until 1768 as a deterrent to any hope the French might have of returning. The presence of the troops attracted merchants and fishermen from Newfoundland, many of Irish origin who settled among the ruins. Names common in Louisbourg today, such as Tutty, Kehoe, and Kennedy, date from this period. Some members of the garrison also settled in the vicinity of Louisbourg; their descendants bear names like Bagnell, Townsend, and Martell.

Before the troops were withdrawn, Louisbourg had a civilian population of around 145.

IN 1763, Cape Breton became part of Nova Scotia. In 1765, it was recognized as the County of Breton. The following year the people in Louisbourg sent John Grant and Gregory Townsend as representatives to the House of Assembly in Halifax. They were refused admission on the grounds that there were no freeholders—owners of land—on the island and therefore no one was qualified to elect representatives.

The Louisbourg region's population was enraged, feeling they were being taxed without having direct representation. They petitioned the British authorities, complaining that they were neglected by the distant mainland capital from which they received no help and by which they were

oppressed by the most grievous impositions on almost every necessary commodity, and charged exorbitant rents for the liberty of dwelling in the wretched ruins of the town of Louisbourg; that they had no courts of justice...; that they had in vain applied to the Governor of Nova Scotia for absolute grants of land: and that spiritous liquors, so essential in carrying on the fisheries 'in this *intemperate* climate' were highly taxed by the legislature of Nova Scotia.[14]

In his *Description of Cape Breton Island*, Samuel Holland was very critical of the Nova Scotia government's treatment of the island, expressing the view that its taxes hurt the island's fishery and other exports. He was a voice for separation, and felt Cape Breton would be better off free of its "dependency" on Nova Scotia.[15]

Despite Holland's valuable report, the authorities in Halifax had only slight knowledge of Cape Breton. George Cottnam, a Halifax government agent, was sent to Louisbourg as magistrate to enforce the laws of Nova Scotia and to collect customs tax, especially on rum. The local citizens ignored him. In effect Cottnam and the few troops stationed there could do little to wrestle with the absence of law and order. Fishing stages were being torn down; coal smuggling was rife, particularly at the old French mine at Port Morien (or Cow Bay) and at Spanish Bay (Sydney Mines). The British authorities stationed troops at both places not only to prevent smuggling but to dig coal for the garrisons at Louisbourg and Halifax.[16] Despite some prosecutions, organized smuggling of coal continued, to places as far away as Boston.

When the garrison was withdrawn from Louisbourg in 1768, George Cottnam was even more powerless. The inhabitants who had depended on the troops for their livelihood and protection became desperate. When the Government of Nova Scotia tried to raise a tax to defray the cost of maintaining a provincial militia, which had no presence on the island, the people refused to pay.[17] Governor Legge declared the inhabitants of Cape Breton "lawless

"Mi'kmaq Encampment," watercolour by H. N. Binney, c. 1790

"Fort Sainte-Anne, 1629," researched and rendered by Jean-Luc Chassé. Portrait of Nicolas Denys, a detail from a painting by Lewis Parker. Map of St. Ann's Bay called "Plan du Port Dauphin et de la Baye de Ste. Anne dans L'Isle Royalle," c. 1740.

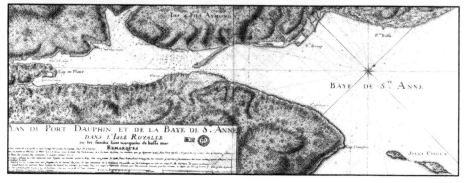

A PLAN of the CITY & FORTIFICATIONS of LOUISBURG.

The Spur
A Boom to preserve the French Ships
The Key Curtain
POND
BEACH
Burying Ground
Line Kiln
A New Battery Erected since 1745

Hospital
Parade
Brouillan Bastion

Queens Bastion

The Profile

Scale of Feet

References.

a. Glacis .......... l. Chapel
b. Cover.W. .......... m. Barracks
c. Traverses .......... n. Powder Magazine
d. Ditch .......... o. Fortification House
e. Parapet .......... p. Arsenal & Bakehouse
f. Rampart .......... q. Ordnance Stores
g. Talus or Slope of .......... r. General Storehouse
  the Rampart .......... s. Fredricks Gate
h. Casemate .......... t. Maurepas Gate
i. Guard House .......... u. Queens Gate
k. Governors Apartment .......... w. Piequet Line rais'd during the Siege in 1745.
  .......... x. Circular Battery
  .......... y. Dauphin Gate

1. Glacis .......... 4. Countrescarp .......... 7. Banquet
2. Banquet .......... 5. Ditch .......... 8. Rampart
3. Covert Way .......... 6. Parapet .......... 9. Talus

The de la Plagne house, Fortress of Louisbourg National Historic Park

The de Gannes house

Landing of the New Englanders at Louisbourg during the First Siege, 1745, said to be by John Stevens, a rare example of contemporary portrayal of the event.

"Founding of Sydney, 1785" by Lt. Wm. Booth

Rev. Ranna Cossit and
Cossit House, Sydney

Lt.-Gov. J. F. W. DesBarres

DesBarres' "Plan of the Town of Sydney"

The Old Barracks, Victoria Park

Details from DesBarres' *Atlantic Neptune*: Richmond Isle, Strait of Canso; entrance to Port Hood Harbour; view of Gabarus

Left, St. George's Anglican Church; above, St. Patrick's Catholic Church (now a museum); left below, Acadian church at Le Platin, and the Aspy Bay United Church, built 1878.

Fr. Pierre Fiset

Inside Église Saint-Pierre, Chéticamp, built 1892; a Robin store, main street, Chéticamp; Christ's Church, called the Jerseyman Church, Point Cross, built c. 1894; painting of Charles Robin by Lewis Parker; Major E. Sutherland's "Sydney from Hardwood Hill," 1853.

The *Breadalbane*, 224 tons, built in Baddeck, 1854, one of six ships that carried Cape Bretoners to New Zealand in the wake of Rev. Norman McLeod; Rev. McLeod; surviving passengers of the ship *Margaret* at the 1903 reunion, Waipu; left: John Munro, St. Ann's merchant and shipbuilder.

Drying cod fish on Ingonish Beach.

Glendyer Woolen Mills and its founder, Donald MacLean MacDonald; the *Aspy* leaving Englishtown, heading Down North; workers at the North River Lumber Company; and below, the sidewheeler *Marion*, a lake boat, in the St. Peter's Canal.

At the start of construction, Cape Breton Railroad, Point Tupper on the Strait of Canso, 1901

Grand Narrows Bridge, Iona

Handpick miners opening mine at Port Morien, 1880

Lobster Factory Crew, White Point

rabble" who caused Cottnam "continual apprehension of danger whenever he puts the laws in execution." The conflicts broke Cottnam's health; in 1774 he left for Halifax where he died six years later.

The withdrawal of the garrison dealt a hard economic blow to Louisbourg. Without customers, the few merchants departed, leaving behind, according to the acting lieutenant-governor of Nova Scotia, the "dregs of the English and French garrisons."[18]

One of the merchants who left was Laurence Kavanagh, a native of Waterford, Ireland, who had come to Louisbourg via Newfoundland in 1760. The most prosperous merchant in the area, he had 42 fishermen working for him. He ran a flourishing farming industry with cattle, horses, sheep, and pigs. After the withdrawal of the garrison, he moved his enterprise to St. Peter's which was located near the traditional portage between the Bras d'Or Lakes and the mainland—where the St. Peter's Canal would eventually be built.

On a trip to Halifax in 1774 Kavanagh died in a shipwreck, leaving his considerable interests to his sons James and Laurence, Junior. James set up in Halifax while Laurence soon became the wealthiest merchant in Cape Breton, expanding his business from St. Peter's to Main-à-Dieu and Arichat. After 1770, between the Robin Company, the Acadian fishermen, Kavanagh, and other merchants, the southwest region showed the greatest development on the island. By 1774 most of the population had shifted there from Louisbourg. It was estimated that there were 532 settlers living in St. Peter's-Isle Madame and only 420 on the rest of Cape Breton.[19]

At the outbreak of the American Revolution in 1775, New England privateers began raiding shipping and settlements along the Nova Scotia coast. With only a single British ship of war stationed at Canso, privateers like the infamous John Paul Jones sacked and destroyed the Robin establishment on Jerseymen's Island. Jones also sank fishing vessels there, but fled on the approach of a British ship of war.

Coal smuggling led to an even worse intrusion in July 1781, when five small British warships sailed into Spanish Bay, escorting a flotilla of little vessels which had come to pick up coal at present-day Sydney Mines. As the ships approached Low Point, two large French warships with 44 guns each came into sight. The French were smuggling coal. The British coal ships managed to reach the inner harbour safely, but the "Battle of the Coal" between the warships raged through the night. By morning the British had lost 19 sailors, including the captain, and 35 wounded—the largest sea battle fought in Nova Scotia after the fall of Louisbourg.

Cape Breton was an easy prey for smugglers and privateers since, except for a few places along its south coast, it was deserted of Europeans. With the exception of summer fishing camps, there were no permanent settlements at all in the north—even at Ingonish, which had been an important fishery during the French Regime. This point is brought home from the sorry tales of ship-wrecked people, like that of Saint-Luc de la Corne on the *Auguste*, driven ashore in Dingwall harbour in November 1761. Of 121 aboard, only seven survived. From De La Corne's narrative, we have the terrible image of his struggle to escape the battered vessel, a child under each arm. The children died. Then De La Corne and six others walked southward in winter, following the coast through trackless northern Cape Breton. More died along the way. The survivors were finally rescued at Jersey Cove Beach, near to-day's Englishtown Ferry crossing—rescued by Mi'kmaq who then took De La Corne to St. Peter's.[20]

Perhaps an even more harrowing adventure took place 20 years later in December of 1780, when the brigantine *St. Lawrence* went aground in a storm somewhere near Margaree Island. Ensign Walter Prenties, a survivor, described how he and his companions with dwindling supplies first sailed a leaking boat they'd sealed with ice and then continued on, walking the steep western coast over the northern tip of Cape Breton, past what had been the bustling fishing settlement of Ingonish, and then south along today's North Shore. Again, they saw not one soul until they too were met by Mi'kmaq who saved them at Jersey Cove Beach, St. Ann's Bay. An old Mi'kmaq lady remembered De La Corne and the *Auguste*, and was "exceedingly affected" as she recounted the misery she had witnessed almost 20 years before.[21]

NEARLY DEPOPULATED, with permanent land grants frozen, collieries neglected, troops withdrawn, her coasts pillaged by privateers, her Mi'kmaq abandoned by the French and the Catholic Church, generally lawless and without representation in an imperial Halifax, Cape Breton Island's prospects seemed hopeless.

Significantly, and striking a theme of an independent Cape Breton that will run throughout its history, Samuel Holland wrote:

Should a separation [of Cape Breton from Nova Scotia] ever be thought necessary it would be at an Emulation between the then two Colonies as would insure success in all their measures, and would perhaps be the most effectual method of preventing all ill judged Taxes and Imposts.[22]

These opinions were supported, elaborated, and carried into reality by Joseph Frederick DesBarres who in 1785 became the first lieutenant-governor of the Colony of Cape Breton. A brave, headstrong, hands-on organizer, DesBarres was born around 1720 in France or Switzerland—he was always purposely fuzzy about his background. He was educated in Switzerland but moved to England around 1752. He became a cadet at the Royal Military Academy at Woolich and sailed to America in 1756 as an engineer with the Royal American Regiment. Two years later, he served as assistant engineer at the Second Siege of Louisbourg. After the fall of the Fortress he obtained charts of the St. Lawrence River from defeated French officers. While he was working on the charts in Halifax, he met Captain James Cook, and helped Cook work up a large scale map of the St. Lawrence River. This map became a tool in the attack on Québec in 1759, and DesBarres was present at the defeat of the French on the Plains of Abraham.[23] He was then sent to Halifax to draw up plans for the defense of that town and its dockyard.

In 1763 DesBarres undertook a work "of national importance": *The Atlantic Neptune*, his memorable survey for the Admiralty of all the harbours of the east coast of America, including Nova Scotia and Cape Breton.[24] The actual surveying took ten years under the most trying circumstances, "frequently (being) wrecked with the loss of...necessaries and instruments, and... suffer(ing) great personal hardships."[25] We can only imagine the problems of trying to triangulate headlands from a small boat, the sea swell a constant menace and, as DesBarres put it,

exploring among rocks and shoals, the channels of safe pilotage into the numerous excellent harbours...as well as...ascertaining the soundings and navigation of the coast until then unexplored.[26]

When the survey work was complete, DesBarres spent the next ten years supervising a staff of 20 to 23 in preparing the charts for publication. Ten more years! He was in charge of selecting, correcting, and adapting not only his own surveys but those done earlier. Then he supervised the engraving, printing, and publishing. DesBarres drew with exquisite sensitivity to colour both the seascapes and the towns with their harbours, among them Louisbourg, Arichat, and Port Hood. In 1783 *The Atlantic Neptune* was acclaimed not only for its usefulness but also for its artistic excellence.

Historian J. C. Webster claimed,

The work must be regarded as one of the most remarkable products of human industry which has been given to the world through the arts of printing and engraving.[27]

Holland and DesBarres surveyed the Maritime colonies at the same time, DesBarres concentrating on the hydrographic aspects while Holland was more concerned with the topography. While the two men hardly corresponded, much of the *Atlantic Neptune* was based on Holland's work—particularly for Cape Breton, Prince Edward Island, and the Magdalen Islands—and DesBarres acknowledged the debt in the published *Neptune*.[28] DesBarres was well aware of Holland's attitudes about the political and economic future of Cape Breton.

Meanwhile, Cape Breton Island continued its neglected existence. Nova Scotia treated it as a preserve rather than as an integral part of the province.

A proclamation was issued 26 August 1775 ordering that infantry companies be raised throughout Nova Scotia. One thousand men were needed and Cape Breton was expected to raise one fifth of the troops, while the remainder of Nova Scotia, with at least twenty times the population, would raise the rest.

In December, though Cape Breton had no representation in the House of Assembly, a tax was imposed for the payment and support of the Nova Scotia militia, and three commissioners were sent to Cape Breton to make the assessment.[29] At the same time William Campbell, governor of Nova Scotia, exploited the coal on the island, allowing Halifax merchants to take what they wanted so that his government could tax the coal to build a road to the Bay of Fundy. When the home government—ever fearful of coal finding its way to New England and competing with Britain's own product—got wind of this, they stopped Campbell in his tracks.[30] Once again, Cape Breton's resources seemed to be just waiting for exploitation.

THE DEFEAT OF THE BRITISH in the American Revolution (1783) got things moving, as United Empire Loyalists began streaming out of the Thirteen Colonies into Nova Scotia and Québec. By 1782 so many people had entered Québec that General Haldimand, then in charge there, was worried that all the good land along the St. Lawrence would soon disappear. Samuel Holland convinced Haldimand that Cape Breton would make an admirable "Asylum for the Refugees from the Sea Coasts of the Northern Provinces."[31] Holland pointed out that, going back to the days of Louisbourg less than 30 years before, there was prosperity in Cape Breton; it had been a booming French colony. Haldimand discussed this possibility with an inspector of refugee Loyalists, Abraham Cuyler, a former mayor of Albany, New York. Cuyler was typical of a breed of Loyalist who had held high positions in the American colonies, and who now sought new posts in the remaining British colonies.

Cuyler became convinced that Cape Breton offered him golden opportunities. He was willing to lead a group of Loyalists and disbanded soldiers to settle there. He sought out fellow Loyalists from New York. Soon he was certain that over 3,100 people were willing to go with him to Cape Breton.[32] With characteristic verve, he prodded the governor of Nova Scotia, John Parr, for permission to settle,[33] and even dispatched Captain Jonathan Jones, another New York Loyalist, to scout out the island.

Later in 1783, despite Haldimand's pleas that he wait for Jones's report on Cape Breton, Cuyler left for England to obtain a quick decision on reimbursement for his losses in the American Revolution, and to get permission to lead a settlement in Cape Breton.

While Cuyler was on his way to London, British officials— aware of Haldimand's problems in settling the flood of land-hungry Loyalists—realized that Cape Breton would have to be opened to settlement. By the time Cuyler arrived in London early in 1784, there were rumours that Home Secretary Thomas Townsend, Lord Sydney, was planning a new political division of the present Maritime region that would make Cape Breton a colony separate from Nova Scotia. Cuyler assured Lord Sydney that Loyalists were ready to settle there.

Lord Sydney's only reservation lay in the cost of financing the colony. Britain had just fought a series of wars, so she was broke. She had to pay the Loyalists who had lost property in the United States and were seeking compensation from the British government.

Lord Sydney turned to DesBarres, who assured him that the government of a colony in Cape Breton could be run for less than £2,500 per year, and that the sale of coal to nearby garrisons would provide a good income for the operations of that colony. At the same time, a government established there would cut down on coal smuggling.

The idea of settling Loyalists cheaply appealed to cash-strapped Britain and led to the establishment of the separate Colony of Cape Breton. In turn, Cuyler was given permission to bring his Loyalists from Québec to the island.[34] But when it came to deciding who would be in charge of the new colony, officials saw this as an opportunity to pay off their debt to DesBarres for his completion of *The Atlantic Neptune*. They offered him the post of lieutenant-governor—a reasonable decision since he probably knew the island best.

So the Colonial Office cleared their debt to DesBarres. Plus, they paid off Loyalists with land grants in Cape Breton—200 acres each, free. And they gave Cuyler the job of secretary of the new colony, a good-paying position.

Since it was already June of 1784, Cuyler rushed to obtain supplies, while Lord Sydney ordered Haldimand to load vessels with Loyalists and stores for the voyage to Louisbourg.

Cuyler reached Louisbourg before the others and must have been shocked when on 28 October three small vessels, the *Liberty*, the *Sally*, and the *St. Peters*, arrived with only 140 people aboard—he had expected 3,100! When the rest had not heard from Cuyler before summer, they feared he had failed to obtain permission to settle Cape Breton, so they had decided to stay in Québec. One ship landed its cargo at Louisbourg, the others turned westward along the coast to St. Peter's.

Only four houses remained at the Fortress, and since trees

had long been stripped from the area it was practically impossible to build shelters or obtain a reliable fuel supply. Governor Parr of Nova Scotia, who claimed he did not even know that Cuyler was going to Cape Breton, could offer only "locks and hinges."[35] Small comfort for the tiny group of Loyalists about to face a stormy, damp winter among the ruins of Louisbourg.

The summer of 1784 also saw DesBarres stocking up the 600-ton ship *Blenheim* in England's Portsmouth harbour, and rounding up 129 settlers composed of Loyalists, disbanded troops, and English immigrants. In October DesBarres sailed to Halifax, while the *Blenheim* departed for the new colony in Cape Breton. She arrived at Louisbourg on 5 November. Her passengers must have been appalled at what they saw—Cuyler's people were in very bad condition—because after one week the *Bleinheim* left for Spanish Bay (today's Sydney Harbour), the spot DesBarres had chosen for his settlement.

Spanish Bay seemed ideal. Holland had said that it was the perfect place, because it was free from fog, surrounded by relatively fertile soil, well-wooded, and on the north side of the deep harbour there was coal for fuel and export.

But the season was late, and as the *Blenheim* entered the harbour a blinding snowstorm began to rage. In the confusion supplies were lost or ruined, but temporary huts were thrown up near the coal mines. Finally, stores were landed near Point Edward, possibly at Crawley's Creek, between the north and south sides of the harbour.[36] Later that winter, Cuyler and his people joined them, realizing that Louisbourg was not going to be the capital.

Despite the winter weather, DesBarres left Halifax, arriving at Spanish Harbour on 7 January 1785. He held the first meeting of his executive council on 21 February 1785, where he was proclaimed lieutenant-governor in a formal manner and the first minutes of the new colony were taken. We date the founding of Cape Breton Colony from that meeting.

IN MAY, WHEN THE DRIFT ICE was likely just out of the harbour, a permanent settlement was established on the peninsula on the south side of the harbour, to be called "Sydney" in honour of Lord Sydney, the home secretary.

DesBarres, his son William, and Florida Loyalist David Tait—the colony's provost marshal who had a background in surveying—drew up plans for a beautiful capital, with a water-side esplanade, wide avenues, parks, a large commons area, circular plazas where statues would presumably go, a place for the government house, and a large area at the north end for the military, which we call Victoria Park. Sydney was to be modeled after Bath, England—an 18th century city with elegant curved lines.

They got down to work, staking out what is now called the North End of Sydney. A member of the military, Lieutenant William Booth, visiting from Halifax that August, painted the portrait of the founding of Sydney, so we know what the *Blenheim* in the harbour looked like. DesBarres even named a street after himself.

Then, to his new capital city, DesBarres brought the military. In July 1785, six companies of the 33rd Regiment, under the command of Lieutenant-Colonel John Yorke, arrived and settled at the north end of the peninsula. Clearing of the woods began in earnest and settlers began crossing from the coal mines to Sydney.[37]

DesBarres drove the troops mercilessly. Stone had to be carried for foundations, roadways had to be cleared. By December 1785 a barracks, a hospital, a mess house, carpenter shop, governor's quarters, bake house, provision store, and jail were in various stages of completion.[38] While Loyalists continued to arrive from mainland Nova Scotia, DesBarres—probably with more enthusiasm than truth—reported: "New Settlers are flocking in from all parts, the value of property in this Island must in a very little time far exceed that of any other in America."[39] He even estimated that the population of Cape Breton was between three and four thousand by September 1785.[40]

The reality of carving a new settlement is revealed by another visitor, Lieutenant William Dyott in 1788, who described the town by then as consisting of about 50 houses,

surrounded to the very sides of the buildings by an almost impenetrable wood. There is a narrow path from the barracks just to keep up a communication.... The barracks are shamefully bad; the troops have cleared a good parade and made themselves as comfortable as their situation would allow. The officers had no rooms in the barracks, and were obliged to build huts and log-houses.[41]

Meanwhile, in the spring of 1785, many from the two shiploads of Loyalists who had landed at St. Peter's went inland and, under Captain Jonathan Jones, established themselves on the Baddeck River. Jones was made magistrate for the Baddeck area and received 2,000 acres.

Other Loyalists came independently, some directly from the United States. Captain David Smith came in his own ship from Massachusetts with his wife, one daughter, and six sons. He soon drowned, but this family formed the backbone of a settlement at Port Hood in western Cape Breton. Others stopped first in Nova Scotia before moving on to Cape Breton, such as Jacob Sparling who had received land in Shelburne County and did not arrive in Cape Breton until 1808, settling first at Aspy Bay and then at North Sydney.[42]

While most of the Loyalists clustered around Baddeck and eventually the North West Arm of Sydney Harbour, smaller groups settled near Ingonish, Port Hood, and the Gut of Canso. It is difficult to estimate the number of Loyalists who came to Cape Breton, but using references in the Colonial Office Records, early Cape Breton censuses, and militia returns, it seems that less than 500 came to the colony.

DesBarres used all of his considerable inventiveness to attract settlers. He realized the potential value of a flourishing fishery off

Cape Breton, which Samuel Holland claimed had employed 20,000 French before 1758.[43] So DesBarres sent a merchant, Captain Thomas Venture, to Nantucket, Massachusetts, with a proclamation promising land and good anchorage to fishermen willing to settle in Cape Breton.[44] The entire project was a disaster. Fishermen did not come and, on the return voyage, Venture's ship was blown off course to England where he was imprisoned for debt.

While DesBarres tried luring settlers again and again, it seems that the number of those who left, unable to take the hard life, was at least equal to those who arrived. Undaunted, he continued giving Loyalists land grants, and set up a farm near the coal mines where he raised sheep and cattle and on which he erected the colony's only sawmill, freeing Cape Breton from dependence on lumber from Halifax. He paid settlers who worked on this land in money or supplies.[45]

ALTHOUGH THE COLONY OF CAPE BRETON was granted the right to a house of assembly, it was not to be called until the colony had a population large enough to support it. As a result Lieutenant-Governor DesBarres, who ruled on the advice of an executive council, was responsible directly to London. There the Colonial Office had followed Holland's suggestion and ordered that "nothing be passed or done that shall in any way tend to affect the Life, Limb, or Liberty of the Subject, or to the imposing of any Duties or Taxes."[46] In other words, only a Cape Breton assembly could directly tax the colonists. Lacking such an assembly, the British home government had to raise money through customs duties in Cape Breton and, in turn, send the funds back for the colony's operations.

Moreover, the absence of a sitting house of assembly seems to have been a prime factor in the divisiveness which began during DesBarres' regime. Since the colony's assembly was not yet called, the Executive Council became a forum for debate. DesBarres was not an ideal governor. He was a visionary, creative, enthusiastic, and ambitious for the colony, but his military background had not prepared him to deal with opposition to his plans. Lieutenant William Dyott on his visit in 1788 referred to him as "a most eccentric genius."[47] The Executive Council, on the other hand, was composed of strong-minded Loyalists—who, after all, were Americans used to representative government with its arguments and counter arguments. Abraham Cuyler had been mayor of Albany, New York, and clearly wanted power and privilege. David Mathews, a proud individual seeking high office, had been mayor of New York City. Other members—William Smith, surgeon for the 33rd Regiment, and Benjamin Lovell, their chaplain— opposed DesBarres' uncompromising attitudes.[48]

This group quickly formed an opposition to DesBarres. DesBarres' chief supporter, Richard Gibbons, had been attorney general of Nova Scotia but had fallen out with Governor Parr. He was then chosen by DesBarres as chief justice of Cape Breton.

The Executive Council became an immature quarrelling arena. They squabbled over control of supplies and everything else, splitting the settlers into two rival groups, leading to the establishment of political factions.

Cuyler, supported by other Executive Council members, drew up a petition calling for DesBarres' removal, claiming he was an autocrat whose conduct was "painful to British-born subjects."[49] Lord Sydney at the Colonial Office, faced with a whole series of largely false accusations against DesBarres, called him back to England in 1787. Once he had him there, Lord Sydney did not dismiss DesBarres formally but appointed his replacement—Lieutenant-Governor William Macarmick. DesBarres would never see Cape Breton again.

Before DesBarres had departed Cape Breton, he had unofficially sanctioned the formation of a volunteer militia, mainly for his supporters' protection against Yorke and the troops. Chief Justice Richard Gibbons[50] used this group as the nucleus of a "Friendly Society" composed largely of settlers who had arrived from England on the *Blenheim* and which, according to the new Lieutenant-Governor Macarmick, "held regular meetings of the lower order of men."[51]

Cuyler's ally, Attorney General David Mathews, formed a group made up of "all the principal people" opposed to the Friendly Society—which Mathews called "the Mob."[52] Macarmick tried to steer a middle course.

Not all of the Loyalists were followers of Cuyler and Mathews. Generally speaking, those who arrived with Cuyler formed a united group, but those who arrived after 1785 either were not admitted to Cuyler's clique or were won over by DesBarres and his followers. Among these were Ranna Cossit of New Hampshire, the first Anglican minister in Sydney, and William McKinnon who was a Carolina Loyalist. After the removal of DesBarres and the death of Richard Gibbons, Ranna Cossit became leader of Mathews' enemies. For six years, between 1794 and 1800, these two Loyalists fought for political and social control of the colony. Council was the scene of constant conflicts, and the Colony of Cape Breton was the despair of its administrators.[53]

Despite his good intentions, William Macarmick also fell into the habit of quarreling, especially with Mathews and Cuyler. This hurt the town of Sydney whose population declined within a few years to 121, then to 95—all clustered at the north end of town. The mines were not producing enough coal, and a new level had to be dug at Indian Cove. Meanwhile, most of the troops which kept the liquor trade alive—the Sydney merchants' chief form of livelihood—had been withdrawn.

The situation was aggravated when, during the winter of 1788-89, a boatload of starving Irish convicts landed in Sydney. In 1784 the lord lieutenant of Ireland had been authorized to send convicts to any destination outside Europe, and in 1788 a Captain Debonham sailed from Dublin with a cargo of 126 convicts bound for the backwoods of Canada—meaning Québec. In horrible conditions, 46 died during the seven-week crossing. On December 11 the ship reached Cape Breton, where the captain decided to save return time by dumping the convicts at a headland near Main-à-Dieu, now known as Convict Point. The prisoners were forced onto boats at gunpoint. Striking the rocks, some drowned or froze to death in the surf. When the last of the half-clad men, women, and children stumbled onto the shore, they huddled together, losing six more of their number—one of whom, an old man, was robbed and killed by two of his fellow convicts.

Some of these convicts finally found their way to the home of Charles Martell, the local justice of the peace and veteran of the Second Siege of Louisbourg. Martell had them taken in and he sent out a search party to find the rest. He informed Macarmick of the situation, and the convicts were sent to Sydney. They were put up in a large house and in the town hospital where some died. There was fear that infection might spread from sick convicts, so they were banished to 11 kilometres outside of Sydney. Others were allowed to wander at will.

Macarmick had the killers of the old man tried, but they escaped hanging by fleeing. Faced with having to feed the convicts and cut off from help in Halifax by the winter weather, Macarmick finally allowed the convicts to go free. Some went to work as servants and others disappeared into the backwoods.[54]

This incident had two important repercussions. British Home Secretary Lord Grenville was so shocked when he heard the story that he wrote the lord lieutenant of Ireland, "you are not to direct or authorize the Transportation of Offenders to the Colonies...or to any other part of His Majesty's Dominions [other] than the Coast of New South Wales."[55] Thus it was that an event in Cape Breton influenced the history of Australia.

Of more importance locally was the problem of a tiny settlement of 100 people having to feed so many interlopers in the middle of winter. It gave yet another excuse for bickering. Macarmick felt these people must be fed. Cuyler claimed the convicts should be abandoned or the colony would starve. An argument ensued which Macarmick won, but as the winter wore on conditions were so bad that Macarmick had to let the prisoners go. Cuyler blamed him for the near starvation of the town, causing a rift that grew until finally, in 1795, Rev. Ranna Cossit and his followers managed to gain Macarmick's support and, despite Mathews' and Cuyler's protests, backing of the Executive Council as well.

Cuyler left Cape Breton and, soon after, Macarmick decided to return to Great Britain and rejoin his wife who had been captured in France during the French Revolution. Although he left Cape Breton in 1795, Macarmick retained his position of lieutenant-governor until his death in 1815, receiving half pay from the military and the rest as official lieutenant-governor. In the interim, the Colony of Cape Breton was run by administrators who had the same powers as a lieutenant-governor.

Controversy extended to every facet of island life. With no house of assembly—no forum for political debate—arguments erupted at every gathering. At a vestry meeting at the garrison church, St. George's, the Loyalist Scot William McKinnon challenged A. C. Dodd to a duel. The duel concerned a remark Mrs. McKinnon had made concerning Dodd, alleging that he had accused Ranna Cossit of robbing the church in Halifax, and of being guilty of sacrilege. Dodd refuted the story and referred to Mrs. McKinnon as a most "infamous liar" and to McKinnon as a "Damn'd Scotch Highland brute."[56] The duel was averted only by the interventions of Reverend Cossit.

This was the situation which greeted General John Despard when he arrived to take over the Colony's administration in 1801.

News of Sydney's political climate was shocking even in other strife-torn colonial capitals. The lieutenant-governor of Nova Scotia, John Wentworth, wrote to the powers in England that there was "no semblance of law in Cape Breton,"[57] and that the situation there was "too bad to describe" since all was "in disorder, & party confusion."[58]

The strife played into the hands of the Halifax officials who were looking for an excuse to re-annex Cape Breton to Nova Scotia.

John Despard had already had a long military career when he arrived in Sydney. He had fought in twenty-four engagements, had two horses shot from under him, and had three times been shipwrecked. His experiences helped prepare him to be the administrator of Cape Breton—perhaps the battle of his life.

The Sydney he found was a strange capital. Despite DesBarres' great plans, it had not developed. The Esplanade, Charlotte, and Great George Streets were the only north-south streets cleared of stumps. Charlotte veered toward Great George near present-day Falmouth Street, and together they formed a path leading toward the Mira River and Louisbourg. Cross streets included DesBarres, Amelia, Yorke, and Dorchester. They ran up from the harbour only to Great George Street. On the other side of Great George Street was swampy land already fancifully called the Louisa Gardens, perhaps after one of DesBarres' daughters. St. George's Church was standing—but it had no pews or pulpit, no bell or steeple.

A. C. Dodd lived on the Esplanade at Dorchester Street, and Cossit's house still stands on Charlotte. Merchants and tavern keepers had their shops on Charlotte and the Esplanade. The lieutenant-governor's house was about 250 feet back from DesBarres Street, between Charlotte and present-day Campbell Street—a drafty government building which also served as a meeting place for the executive council. The troops lived at the barracks north of DesBarres Street. People considered "of quality" lived at Point Edward, near Crawley's Creek, or at Point Amelia.

And outside Sydney? Farms were scattered along Sydney River and the North West Arm. The Loyalist Captain William Cox, living at what is now Coxheath, had cleared more than 100 acres of land. Visiting Bishop Charles Inglis praised this as the best farm he had seen, remarking that "the barns, the stables for cows and sheep are extensive, neat and very convenient. As is also the Dairy.... Here we had field strawberries of an uncommon size." Cox also grew a large crop of turnips on the farm, which likely found a ready market in Sydney. Nearby on Sydney River, Philip Ingouville, a native of Jersey, had a large farm specializing in red and white clover for dairy and honey production.[59] Ingram Ball, previously co-chief justice of Cape Breton, farmed with his large family at the creek which bears his last name. The Rudderhams, who were Englishmen, lived at the lime kiln on the west side of Point Edward. John Rudderham was one of the colony's best carpenters, as was his friend John Muggah at today's Westmount, who also did a bit of shipping on the side.

Beyond this was the forest. To the south was the shrunken Louisbourg with few families; only four decent homes stood there. French cannons rusted on the harbour's shores, and ribs of French ships still protruded from the water.[60]

Those who were there before the Loyalists arrived—Lorways, Spencers, Skinners, and Kennedys—must have faced cold damp winters in the foggy ghost town. Two prominent inhabitants had already deserted Louisbourg. Charles Martell had lived near the ruins of the old French hospital but moved to Main-à-Dieu, where he was justice of the peace in 1787. Laurence Kavanagh had moved to St. Peter's where he was a merchant to the 600 or so French, Acadians, and a few Irish in the region. Nearby Arichat, dominated by Jersey merchants, was by far Cape Breton's largest town, with around 200 people who fished and now saw their catch shipped to Spain, Jersey, Barbados, and even Majorca. The Robin firm's ships brought in most of the foreign imports the island received, such as molasses, tobacco, and sugar, including its favourite, black rum.

The Bras d'Or Lake shores were virtually uninhabited except at Baddeck, where Jonathan Jones and 20 or 30 Loyalist families were scattered, farming near the Baddeck River. An insight into the simple, lonely, but determined life of a settler is painted by Jones in a letter to his brother, Dr. Solomon Jones, living in Augusta, Upper Canada:

I believe I told you that I am settled here intirely alone Thirty Miles from any soul with a white face, Except one Family 2 Miles from me and 3 or 4 single men Honest Old soldiers that have small farms near me, you will ask how we Pass away our Time in Long winter Evenings, I will Tell you, I get a Book in my Hand and then I am satisfied, my wife always at work, spining niting or sewing, Kittey Do niting or sewing Billey up stairs with a Book, sometimes writing...Ditto Ditto sometimes ciphering, Salley Reading and writing, Prentice Boy ditto ditto. Now this is the sum total of our Winter evenings Amusement, Except sometimes when the ice is good, the young Gentlemen from Sydney pay us a visit, and stay a few days, which has been the case three or four times this winter. I pity the young folks but don't tell them so—I am always troubled with Rheumatism tho not confined this winter, keep Trudging about I don't like to idle, you would laugh to see me attending a Little grist mill, not much bigger than a Pedlers Box, but its no Matter, it makes good flour, and plenty of it, and thats enuff for me, i have to learn to be content with Little things—you want me to say something about the childen, they are all well and with me, and I am Happy to have it in my power to Tell you they Constitute the Principal Part of the pleasure I enjoy...my coming here when they were so young prevented my giving them such Edducation as i could wish, but by the assistance of there Eldest brother Billey they have got a Little and they continue to improve Themselves as Mentioned in there Evening Amusements.... You see how we live seperated from all the world, a Little Republick of our own, I sometimes think we are as happy as Tho we were in the hurrey and Bustle of company, at Least I strive to make the young folks think so, tho there is Nothing I wish for more than a little good Society but i see no prospect of getting it soon.[61]

Along the Gut of Canso and in the present-day Port Hood area lived a scattering of Loyalist families. The first group of New

England Loyalists arrived at Port Hood in 1786—Captain David Smith, his wife Rebecca, and their children.

They were soon joined by the families of Matthew Hawley and Hugh Watts, who were to make up the backbone of the first permanent settlement.... In the 1790s a number of Catholic Highland Scots arrived at Port Hood.... Some enterprising young Irishmen were also drawn to Port Hood—men like the entrepreneur Edward Hayes and the brothers James and Dennis Murphy.... By 1818...there were nearly 170 people living in the area."[62]

Judique held a few Scottish squatters who had crossed from Prince Edward Island or mainland Nova Scotia. To the northeast was Chéticamp, where about 100 refugees arriving from Saint Pierre and Miquelon during the French Revolution—people who did not want to live under the irreligious republican regime of the Revolution—fished for the Robin Company when it expanded from its home base at Arichat. The only other significant cluster of permanent settlers was at Ingonish, where immigrants from New-foundland and a few Loyalists fished and eventually grew hay to feed horses at the mines.

The Mi'kmaq people still hunted and fished freely in Cape Breton, and in 1800 around 450 of them lived on the island. The population numbers were fluid. It was much easier for them to live in Cape Breton than in Nova Scotia, where the controls were tighter—reservations were already in place. Of this number, 130 were able hunters who used the bow and arrow, but who could also hurl a tomahawk with great precision. They remained Roman Catholics, served by missionary priests. With the small population on the island they were hardly disturbed by the new arrivals.

Altogether, the Colony of Cape Breton held no more than 2,500 people in 1800, many of whom were poor and illiterate. Connecting roads were non-existent, the mines were poorly maintained, and Sydney, the capital—immersed in bickering—was in decline and out of touch with the rest of the colony. Houses, as quickly as they were deserted, were used as firewood by their neighbours.

ADMINISTRATOR JOHN DESPARD took the reins of office in this stagnant little colony on 16 June 1801, accompanied by his wife and daughter, together with his nephew William, who served as his private secretary. Government House must have brightened up considerably after the bachelor days of the previous administrators.

Despard turned his attention to the land situation. Like everything else in Cape Breton, it was in confusion. When DesBarres arrived in 1785, he had given free land grants to Loyalists; non-Loyalists had to pay, but those who could not afford land were given leases which expired at the lessee's death. This policy backfired; it dissuaded urgently needed colonists from coming to Cape Breton. Despite this, some settlers were content with leases, but many decided simply to squat without paying any money. To make matters worse the British government, in an attempt to recoup financial losses, had frozen leases and demanded land purchases only, discouraging settlement even further.

Despard noticed that a good deal of land granted by DesBarres had never been improved or settled, particularly 100,000 acres around the Mira River. So in 1802 Despard set up an Escheats Court which was empowered to take over land from those who had never actually settled there.[63] This huge acreage in Cape Breton thus became available just at a time when most of Nova Scotia's best land was settled and Prince Edward Island's land was locked up by absentee landlords. Cape Breton alone of the eastern Maritime colonies now had good land available.

But Cape Breton needed more than land. To attract settlers she needed roads, bridges, mills, doctors, and teachers. To get them required money. Yet, in a colony without a house of assembly, taxes could not legally be collected.

Despard solved the problem. He noticed the colony consumed around 10,000 gallons of rum per year. A tax of two or three shillings per gallon could build roads all over the island.[64] To convince the colonial authorities, he said that if Cape Bretoners did not supply money for roads, then the British taxpayer would have to foot the bill. This argument carried, and the constitutional illegality of taxing people in a colony without a sitting house of assembly was simply overlooked.

The tax was to be collected in the form of a duty, which by adding to the cost of spirits would, it was fondly hoped, cut down on consumption and serve "as a measure calculated to preserve the Health and Morals of the Inhabitants of Cape Breton."[65] While it is not recorded whether the tax actually affected Cape Bretoners' morals, their island improved as a place to live. The tax money flowed in, land became available, and the mines were producing more coal. Cape Breton was ripe for new settlement.

# 4

# The Hebridean Connection and the Roots of Discontent

"When one is made to toil and strain on the spot where he was born, his attachment to that spot is absurd and foolish. You are sensible it is foolish; oppression taught you by degrees to overcome it. Your brethren now abroad have overcome it."[1]
— "A Minister of the Gospel"

ON AN AFTERNOON IN EARLY AUGUST in 1802, a 245-ton ship, *The Northern Friends*, sailed into Sydney Harbour with 415 Scots aboard. They had heard, perhaps from their relatives squatting on lands around Judique, that good land was available in Cape Breton.

Despard was overjoyed. He quickly rounded up councillors, none of whom was in town that day, so unexpected was the event. Council agreed to use the money available from the liquor tax to "prevent their [the Scots'] farther Emigration to A Foreign Country."[2] Hence 40 shillings were lent—in reality given—to each man, 30 shillings to each woman, 20 shillings to each child over twelve, and 15 shillings to each child under twelve.[3] Such fast action encouraged them to stay. The new settlers were given property near

Mira and Sydney, and by September they were already clearing land.

Despard's action was a turning point in Cape Breton's history. The entire racial character of the island would have been different without the Hebrideans. The Scots sent word back to Skye, Harris, Uist, Benbecula, Barra, and Lewis that Cape Breton would welcome more Scots and assist them to settle in a home much like their own.

It is not difficult to understand why the Scots first came to Cape Breton. Numbers of them began arriving in the New World after the defeat at Culloden in 1745, when the English began the destruction of their ancient clan system. Deprived of livelihood, many joined the British forces and some actually served at the fall of Louisbourg in 1758. One of these was Donald Og MacNeil of Barra, who decided that Cape Breton would be the ideal place to settle. His clansmen eventually came to Caolas nam Barraich, Barra Strait, in today's Grand Narrows and Iona areas—places with glorious, Scotland-like vistas.

However, the vast majority of Scots left Scotland because they were driven from their homes. By the 1760s and 1770s the Scottish clan chiefs were being absorbed into English society, educating their children in England and feeling distant from people living on their former clan lands. With the advent of the agricultural and industrial revolutions, it became more profitable for chiefs to clear their lands for sheep-raising than to have tenants scattered about their holdings. Wool was sent at a good profit to the new factories in England. More and more, the ordinary clansmen, mere peasants now, were evicted from their land.

In the 1770s, a wave of Scots began leaving home, in what James Hunter refers to as "The People's Emigration"—the period when they *chose* to leave Scotland as against the later time when they were driven out. In 1773 a group landed at Pictou on the ship *Hector*. Over the next few years, boatloads of them began settling in present-day Antigonish County and Prince Edward Island. The P.E.I. experience was not satisfactory, since the land there was owned by absentee landlords in England and Scotland, a situation the new arrivals were trying to escape.

Cape Breton was nearby with land they could own. By 1775 early Scottish settlers are recorded around Judique, having crossed from Prince Edward Island. And in 1802, as we have seen, the first boatload arrived in Cape Breton *directly* from Scotland.

Cape Breton was the nearest point to Scotland with arable land and therefore the cheapest place to reach. When they arrived, they really didn't have to pay for their land since much of it was unsurveyed and they could simply squat. Colony Surveyor Captain Thomas Henry Crawley[4]—appointed around 1805 or '06—was sympathetic and felt new settlers should be allowed to stay in Cape Breton until they could purchase secure titles. The Scots could fish as they had in the Hebrides and the virgin soil, once it was cleared, was productive.

The first arrivals tended to settle around water, particularly along lakes and streams. Hence the Mira River below Marion Bridge, the Margaree Valley, and the Bras d'Or shores were filled up early. Later settlers had to go inland. The migration reached a peak between 1817 and 1820; the flow continued, and the last arrivals came around 1850.

Families followed families, with the people of one area or island settling next to their former neighbours from Scotland. This segregation by settlement tended to keep people of opposing religious views apart. Hence, we find a heavy concentration of Presbyterians from North Uist around Catalone, while around Grand Mira South the population was Roman Catholic from South Uist. Boisdale and Iona are made up of Catholic Barramen or people from South Uist. Scots settling in Orangedale and along the North Shore—between Englishtown and Ingonish—were Presbyterians from North Uist, Lewis, and Harris.

Since land was difficult to obtain in Scotland, the new settlers tended to amass large quantities of property. Joseph Howe noted in 1830 that, when money came their way, instead of improving their holdings the Scots purchased more land. This tended to keep farm production down. However, most of these settlers were not interested in exporting food for profit; they were aiming at self-sufficiency. They planted potatoes and turnips in the burnt ground among the tree stumps, feeding themselves and newly-arrived relatives. Later, stumps and stones were removed—the piled monuments to that work stand to this day—and grain was grown to feed themselves and their oxen, cows, and horses.

Scots, like the Loyalists and Acadians, brought their surplus produce, mainly by water, to the Jersey merchants at Arichat or Chéticamp, and to Laurence Kavanagh at St. Peter's. They bartered for exotic goods—tea, rum, sugar, and molasses. Settlers often imported sheep with them, and as the flocks grew they were shipped along with cattle and other surplus to Newfoundland and to towns like Arichat and Sydney.

Those Scots living along the water fished, built ships, and cut timber for lumber. A simple but self-sufficient existence was carved from the island's resources.

Comfort and encouragement from Presbyterian Scotland was supplied by societies worried about the spiritual well-being of settlers in the New World. The Edinburgh and Glasgow Ladies' Bible Associations sent bibles and ministers to the Cape Bretoners. Early Catholic Cape Breton was within the Diocese of Québec. The first priests were merely visitors to the island, but the need for Gaelic- and French-speaking resident clergymen led to chapels and permanent priests in various parts of the island during the later years of Cape Breton's colonial period.

To encourage homestead production, Administrator John Despard gave the new settlers money for communal, water-driven grist mills to replace the stone querns each farm used to grind its grain. Food production rose dramatically. Land petitions increased quickly as the Scots, who had never owned their own land before, were willing to accept leases, permitted after 1816. These petitions preserve the reality of their achievement—as they detailed what the settlers had accomplished in the first years on the land.

We read of Dougald MacDonald, who arrived in Cape Breton at the age of 25, having first settled in Prince Edward Island. By 1811 he set out to build a grist mill near East Bay, to the delight of his neighbours.[5] We can barely imagine the stamina of Murdo McCaskill who had lost to flood the two grist mills he had built near Antigonish and at the age of 40 had to start over again at St. Patrick's Channel.[6] Mary McRae at the age of 56, a widow, came to Cape Breton two years after her husband died in Scotland and with six children cleared a farm at St. George's Channel.[7] As to Mary McKinnon of McKinnon Brook—husband Hugh set out for Sydney to obtain a land grant; enroute he fell through the ice in the Bras d'Or Lake and drowned. Despite this, Mary banded together with fellow Barramen living nearby, obtained the land grant, and set up a farm for her family.

By 1805, the growing population brought about new optimism in Sydney. A marketplace was built for the peddling of local produce.[8] For the first time, Cape Breton could feed itself without relying on extensive imports. St. George's Church was finally completed—£300 was allocated for pews and a steeple.[9] A new surveyor general, Captain William Cox, was appointed to mark out urgently needed land boundaries; he replaced the colony's first surveyor, who had been absent for fifteen years![10]

In 1803 A. C. Dodd, now chief justice, began travelling to Arichat by canoe to hear court cases involving the growing numbers of people in the western part of Cape Breton. In 1806 the Executive Council met in Arichat for the first time, with Job Bennett Clark, A. C. Dodd, and Thomas Crawley present.[11] Understandably, land questions dominated proceedings. The island was now officially divided into Eastern and Western Districts, as Scots crossed in growing numbers from the Nova Scotia mainland to enter the River Inhabitants, Judique, and Port Hood areas.

In the five years after 1802, the colony's population doubled to nearly 5,000. Cape Breton was now multilingual: French, English, Mi'kmaq, and Gaelic, with Gaelic gaining on French as the majority language, particularly from Margaree Forks to Port Hood.

The Scots quickly fitted into the life of the island. Before the arrival of the Scots, Jerseyman Philip Ingouville had built ships near Wentworth Creek, in the area of Sydney that is now called the Shipyard. Shipbuilding began among the Scots in what is today Margaree Harbour, Mabou, and Port Hood. Between 1800 and 1805, the number of Cape Breton ships under sail increased from 217 to 267.[12] Most were small shallops or schooners, which took coal from Sydney to Halifax and Newfoundland. With Cape Bretoners carrying their own coal, money stayed on the island, benefitting local businessmen.

DESPARD LEFT FOR ENGLAND in 1807. The Sydney he left to his successor, Nicholas Nepean, was showing signs of hope. The first hurdles of settlement were past, pessimism melted away. Despard's steady, hard-working, honest disposition shows him to have been a man of great ability—after DesBarres, one of the few administrators in Cape Breton's 36 years as a separate colony of which Cape Breton can be proud.

The year 1807 is significant in the history of Cape Breton not only because of the departure of John Despard, but because of the passing of the Embargo Acts by the United States. Napoleon was blockading sea trade with Britain; Britain replied by attacking any ships trading with France. The Americans as neutrals were hurt by this move, and in retaliation passed the Embargo Acts which forbade American merchants from trading with Britain.

The hope was that Britain, which was now dependent on American products and shipping for her carrying trade, would end its attacks on U.S. shipping. This plan backfired. Instead, Britain turned to the Maritime colonies to transport goods to her shores, while New England—which opposed the Embargo Acts—was happy to smuggle goods to the Maritimes for shipment on to Great Britain. This resulted in a considerable economic expansion for the Maritime region, and reinforced the connections between the Maritimes and the eastern United States.

Although Cape Breton did not participate directly in this trade boom, the increased prosperity of Nova Scotia and New Brunswick led to their buying more Cape Breton coal and fish. On the other hand, inflation also increased in Cape Breton as miners demanded higher wages, left for more prosperous areas, or joined the British Navy.

On the whole, the period after 1807 was one of relative prosperity. In the southwestern part of the island, fishing expanded quickly. Indeed, the increased population of the area led to its establishment as a separate judicial region in 1808, with its capital at Arichat.

The growing population also meant that more rum was imported, increasing the Cape Breton Colony's revenue. In 1812 alone, £2,142 was collected. This led to more public improvements, including a new main bridle road with a few bridges built from Sydney to Isle Madame via St. Peter's—present-day Highway 4. A road from Baddeck to Margaree was also begun, as well as the Lingan Road and one to Bras d'Or via the north shore of Sydney Harbour.

In Sydney, schoolmaster James Hill's salary was increased to £50 per year, a new dog pound was constructed, and a ferry service was inaugurated between Sydney and Sydney Mines.

When Despard left in 1807, there were only two officers and 40 soldiers in Sydney. By 1811, as British and American relations worsened, the garrison was increased to 168, with the local militia numbering another 150. Some of the rum revenue was used to rebuild a redoubt or defensive earthworks at Battery Point on the tip of the Sydney peninsula, and barracks near the mine and at South Bar. During the summer of 1812 American privateers, sailing along the coast, threatened fishing and navigation near Arichat. That area was almost defenseless since there were only two British warships protecting all of Cape Breton's coasts.

After the War of 1812, the island continued to progress. Mail delivery—by Indian carrier—was inaugurated with the mainland, and more roads were cleared near Baddeck and D'Escousse, with bridges at places like Muggah Creek near Sydney, and Baddeck.

In 1813 there were 5,975 people on the island; in 1817 there were 7,000. By 1819, with a population of 9,000, the island's numbers surpassed the French regime, over 60 years before. Population growth led to the building of a new Anglican chapel at Point Edward in 1818. Roman Catholic priests were located permanently at Chéticamp, Arichat, and Judique.

Besides coal, gypsum quarried around the shores of the Bras d'Or Lakes was also being shipped out, with a small royalty going to the colonial treasury. To ensure that revenues were properly collected, customs stations were established at Arichat and Port Hawkesbury, as well as at Sydney. The new lieutenant-governor, George Robert Ainslie, who arrived in 1816, was once again allowed to make permanent land grants. These had been forbidden since Lieutenant-Governor Macarmick's tenure, which formally ended in 1815.

CAPE BRETON'S POLITICAL ATMOSPHERE remained charged and volatile, due mainly to Richard Gibbons, Junior, who dominated the island's politics after the departure of John Despard. Gibbons' life had been difficult and this perhaps accounts for his uncompromising behaviour. Back in 1792, he had left Cape Breton for London with his father, the chief justice, when the latter went to defend himself in the wake of DesBarres' dismissal. The French captured their ship on the return voyage and his mother, father, young Richard, and their maid were imprisoned in Nantes, where he saw his father die. After 22 months in jail, Richard and his mother escaped to England, where he studied the law.

In 1796, the young man returned to Cape Breton with hatred for his father's political enemies. When Ranna Cossit left the colony for a posting in Yarmouth in 1805, Gibbons replaced him as leader of his political faction.

Gibbons became the chief advocate for the calling of a house of assembly as a constitutional right. Gibbons declared that Despard's rum tax—the tax that had done so much to help the island's development—was nonetheless unconstitutional. That tax had been appropriated with no recourse to a house of assembly. Gibbons used these arguments to invigorate and provide an ideology for the political faction whose members had previously been followers of Ranna Cossit. He was opposed by A. C. Dodd, the chief justice and former follower of Abraham Cuyler and David Mathews.

John Despard managed to ignore Gibbons' initiatives. However, his successor Nicholas Nepean (1807-1812), a weak-willed individual who probably received his appointment because his brother had been under-secretary of state for the colonies, fell under the indomitable will of Gibbons. By 1812 Gibbons had convinced Nepean of the necessity of calling a house of assembly. In June of that year, Nepean suspended the rum tax and wrote to the new colonial secretary, Lord Bathurst, asking for a Cape Breton House of Assembly.

With the Empire in the midst of a struggle with Napoleon and the United States, Bathurst could hardly be less interested in the island's constitutional woes, and instead of complying with Nepean's request, he had him replaced by the single-minded Brigadier-General Hugh Swayne.

Swayne—administrator of the colony from 1812 to 1816—

saw his mission in Cape Breton as military: to protect the island during the War of 1812. When he arrived, he found that Nepean had suspended the rum tax, and consequently the colonial treasury was almost empty.[13] Swayne immediately sided with A. C. Dodd, who told him that not only did the lack of tax keep the coffers bare, but Gibbons and his followers were demagogues who wanted a house of assembly so they could gain control of the colony.[14]

Swayne re-introduced the rum tax. Oddly, he had popular support, since he had lowered it to a penny per gallon, which was not high, and the revenue was used for much-needed public improvements. Gibbons, however, continued to attack the legality of the entire constitution of the Colony of Cape Breton. Swayne replaced him as attorney general with Richard John Uniacke, Junior, a Halifax lawyer and son of the attorney general of Nova Scotia.

But Swayne did not last. He was replaced by Colonel Jonas Fitzherbert—but only on an interim basis. Swayne's permanent replacement was to be George Robert Ainslie who, following the death of William Macarmick in 1815, was to assume to the full title of lieutenant-governor and not merely administrator.

Ainslie however took over a year to arrive on the island. And during this interim Gibbons, who never gave up, in collusion with Ranna Cossit, Junior, his chief supporter, precipitated a constitutional crisis. He convinced Cossit, who was assistant rum duty collector, to suspend collection of the duty—again on the grounds that the tax was unconstitutional. Fitzherbert threatened Cossit with the loss of his job, so he once again began collecting the duty, including back taxes covering the period of its suspension.

Messrs. Ritchie and Leaver—entrepreneurs who were operating the coal mines—refused to pay the taxes.[15] Instead they decided to go to court. And they employed Richard Gibbons to represent them.

Gibbons' case was a brilliant attack on the legality of the colony's constitution. When the matter came before Dodd and the grand jury, 15 November 1816, Gibbons argued for the island's right to a house of assembly based on the fact that the King had relinquished his privilege to tax or withhold an assembly in 1763. According to this reasoning, when Cape Breton was conquered in 1758 the island fell under direct royal power for the King to do with as he pleased, which included the imposition of taxes. However, when the Royal Proclamation of 1763 annexed Cape Breton to the government of Nova Scotia, the colony had been conferred a constitution, along with the right to legislative representation. This constitution replaced the royal prerogative in Cape Breton, meaning that the island could not return to direct royal control. Furthermore, Gibbons contended that the King—by allowing John Parr, the lieutenant-governor of Nova Scotia in 1784 "from time to time as need shall require to summon...General Assemblies" for Cape Breton and Prince Edward Island—had strengthened the colony's right to representative government.

In other words, once it conferred representative government on a colony the Crown could not remove it. The validity of this argument had been proved in 1765 in the case of Campbell *versus* Hall, when the King tried to remove the legislature from the Island of Grenada. This was declared unconstitutional since the King, by granting Grenada a constitution, could no longer exercise his prerogative powers over that island.

From this precedent, Gibbons deduced that the King-in-Council, and hence the lieutenant-governor-in-council, had no right to tax Cape Breton. Only a colonial legislature or the House of Commons could do this. Gibbons reasoned that "the authority was given to the Commander in Chief in Cape Breton to call a House of Assembly." Therefore, Gibbons argued, he should do so immediately, because the King was constitutionally bound to approve.

The attorney general and Crown prosecutor, R. J. Uniacke, could hardly counter this sophisticated argument. He weakly pointed out that the copy of the Proclamation of 1763 had to be shown under seal to be admitted as evidence, and that

The Instructions to the Lieutenant-Governor of Nova Scotia which are positive, state in the 153rd Sec[n], that such is the situation, & circumstances of Cape Breton, that at present, it will not admit of a House of Assembly being called. It is therefore manifest, that no such Instructions, as the Defendants (*sic*) wish to make out, were ever given.[16]

Uniacke's argument missed the point. It did not matter if the King decided the island was not ready for an assembly. *The King had no right to refuse legislative representation to Cape Breton*, and Section 15 of the governor's instructions was unconstitutional.

Even Dodd—who disliked Gibbons, later referring to him as the "Robespierre of Cape Breton"[17]—had to agree with his argument, and charged the jury to find that "the Prerogative over this Island was given up" in 1763. The jury found the tax illegal and it was suspended.

And of course a new lieutenant-governor—Ainslie—arrived in the midst of the ensuing constitutional crisis. Unfortunately, he was hardly the man to handle such a situation. In his previous appointment in Dominica he had fought with and dismissed his entire executive council. He seems to have been determined to follow the same policies in Cape Breton in not allowing democracy of any kind to develop. As a result, he fell out with every official in Cape Breton, and was perhaps the island's most unpopular administrator. The feeling was mutual, since he disliked Cape Bretoners and their island, and was determined not to allow the granting of a house of assembly.

Ainslie fed the Colonial Office what little knowledge they had of Cape Breton. He had nothing good to say about the people, calling them "the refuse of three kingdoms"—England, Scotland, and Ireland. Gibbons was just as adamant, and stood by Dodd's decision that taxation without representation was illegal.

In 1816 the need for money reached crisis proportions when a famine struck the island. This is known as the "summerless year" when frosts struck deep into the American south and snow fell in June. The cold weather was caused by the 1815 eruption of Mount Tambora, Indonesia. The sun was blocked by ash. In Cape Breton the unusually cold weather caused starving field mice to eat the crops of the newly-arriving settlers. The cold weather even affected the fishery, which failed that year. People were starving and needed financial aid to purchase supplies. Without income from taxes, the few dollars in the colony's contingency allowance were soon exhausted.

Ainslie wrote begging the Colonial Office to come to a decision on the tax. The reply came that it would not institute a house of assembly. Instead, it would annex the island of Cape Breton to Nova Scotia.

Ainslie was secretly informed of the decision and he quietly prepared to leave the colony. When the people in Sydney heard of the decision they were dismayed and sent a petition to the Colonial Office begging for a house of assembly so that tax could be collected. They feared annexation to the larger colony, claiming distance and conflicting interests would prevent a harmonious union.

Fears were confirmed when it was discovered that most officials' jobs would be transferred to Halifax. By 1819 property values in Sydney were dropping drastically. No longer a colonial capital, Sydney had been dealt a blow from which it would not recover for many years. The lieutenant-governor of Nova Scotia, Sir James Kempt, turned down any proposals for a special supervisor of Cape Breton affairs. He issued a Proclamation on 9 October 1819, annexing Cape Breton to Nova Scotia.

# 5

# The Forced Marriage with Nova Scotia

## 1820-1851

> "I...declare that the island of Cape Breton is, and
> from henceforth shall be and remain, a several and
> distinct county of the Province of Nova Scotia,
> to be called the County of Cape Breton"[1]

WITH JAMES KEMPT'S PROCLAMATION, Cape Breton was once again part of Nova Scotia.

Politically, the island was now one county divided into three districts: the Northeastern District, roughly the present-day Cape Breton and Victoria Counties; the Southern District, or present-day Richmond County; and the Northwestern District, today's Inverness County. Each district held Courts of General Sessions of the Peace dealing with litigation on the island. One court sat at Sydney in the Northeastern District, one at Arichat in the Southern District, and one at Port Hood in the Northwestern District. However, the island as a single county formed only one judicial circuit, which meant that there was only one judge and one sheriff for all three districts. These districts were further subdivided into townships: Sydney, St. Andrew, St. Patrick, Canseau, Port Hood, Ainslie and Margaree. Townships were unequal divisions with no power except to hold annual meetings for the support of the poor.

At annexation, all officeholders were dismissed by the provincial government except for the surveyor general, Thomas H. Crawley. They needed him because he knew the island and he knew the Mi'kmaq. But no Cape Bretoners were appointed to the Legislative Council of Nova Scotia.

Lucky for Cape Breton that Crawley remained. He brought a rare attitude of flexibility—even humanity—that helped to people the island.

Judge A. C. Dodd—who had accepted Richard Gibbons' argument that the rum tax was illegal, thus precipitating the crisis which led to Cape Breton's annexation—was retired and replaced by John George Marshall, a former MLA (Member of the Legislative Assembly) from mainland Guysborough County. A stern man of strict religious principles, Marshall was largely responsible for successfully maintaining law and order over his huge circuit, which included the whole of Cape Breton Island. Marshall never liked Cape Breton, even begrudged the rugged routes he had to travel to do his job.

Since this was the first time "Cape Bretonians"—as they were then called—had enjoyed representative government, this was largely a period of learning and adjustment. Nova Scotia was beginning to mature politically. Like Cape Breton before 1820, it had an appointed lieutenant-governor responsible directly to colonial officials in London, as well as an executive council. However, Nova Scotia also retained an appointed legislative council and an elected legislative assembly—the coveted House of Assembly that Cape Breton never had.

Party government was just beginning to evolve in Nova Scotia. Nominally, members of the legislative assembly were independent of party control. However, two main groups were evolving: the Conservatives and the Reformers.

Generally the Conservatives favoured the status quo whereby the lieutenant-governor appointed his executive council from favoured individuals in the legislative council or legislative assembly. He and the executive council ran the colony and were not accountable for their actions to the assembly. Before 1848 there was no real departmental government, in which individual ministers would be responsible to the house of assembly.

The Reformers, eventually under the leadership of newspaperman Joseph Howe, promoted a new approach whereby the government would be arranged into departments headed by ministers who would be members of the elected legislative assembly and would be responsible to the assembly for their department's activities. If the assembly did not agree with the way the minister administered his department, he could be dismissed. In such a scenario, the lieutenant-governor would have to choose his executive council from the house of assembly and would therefore have to govern in accordance with the wishes of that elected assembly. In effect, he would be responsible to the house of assembly—and not to Britain—for his and his executive council's actions.

Thus, the colony of Nova Scotia was moving toward Responsible Government.

The Conservatives felt that the largely uneducated electorate, with no great stake in the economy of the colony, could not be trusted to choose responsible representatives. They favoured the continuation of control by a dozen or so powerful interests who had the ear of the lieutenant-governor. The lieutenant-governors in turn appointed their supporters to public office, thus controlling patronage, the tool by which they maintained their power.

Because of the electoral laws, it was difficult to change this situation. In 1820 voters had to be non-Roman Catholic landowning males over 21 years of age. In Cape Breton, due to the influx of settlers—many of whom were poor Roman Catholic squatters unable to buy their land—most people were not qualified to vote. In 1842 a Cape Breton newspaper, *The Spirit of the Times*, estimated that out of a population of 20,000, there were only around 600 qualified freeholders on the island![2]

As a county of Nova Scotia, Cape Breton Island was allowed two representatives in the 41-member House of Assembly.

The island's first election lasted the entire month of November 1820. With only two polling stations—Arichat and Sydney—voters from all over the island had to travel to meet candidates and vote. Running in pairs, there were four candidates. Edmund Murray Dodd, son of the former chief justice, ran with Richard Gibbons, who was a loyal subject of the British Crown but a rabid Cape Breton separatist. Laurence Kavanagh, Junior, the most powerful merchant in the Southern District—to whom many people were in debt—ran with Richard John Uniacke, former solicitor-general of Cape Breton. As there was no newspaper yet, we don't have the tasty details of this campaign. We know that the majority of the vote went to Kavanagh and Uniacke since they carried the more populous Arichat region.[3]

But the election of Laurence Kavanagh presented a significant problem because he was a Roman Catholic. Though religious equality had been declared in Nova Scotia in 1787, Roman Catholics could not sit in the House of Assembly. This impediment could be waived if they took an oath against transubstantiation—against the belief that, at the Mass, bread and wine are changed into the body and blood of Christ. Since in effect this would deny a chief tenet of his faith, Kavanagh refused to take the oath. The Assembly debated the point, suggesting to the lieutenant-governor that the British government modify this outdated rule. Kavanagh was willing to take the standard state oaths swearing loyalty to the Crown, but not an oath against transubstantiation. Both houses agreed that Roman Catholics could act as members "without evil consequences." So the House of Assembly passed a bill allowing Roman Catholics to sit in the assembly after taking the oath of loyalty.

On 3 April 1822, Kavanagh "The Emancipator," as he was

thereafter known, was admitted to the House of Assembly. Henceforth Catholics could fully participate in democracy—they were freed, as it were. Cape Breton had made its first contribution to the political life of Nova Scotia, three years ahead of a similar reform in Great Britain.[4]

Uniacke and Kavanagh retained the seat in the elections of 1826 and 1830. Kavanagh died in 1830 and was replaced by his son, yet another Laurence.

With only two members, Cape Breton remained seriously under-represented in the House of Assembly. With one-tenth of the province's population, the island should have qualified for four representatives. To make matters worse, the island had no representatives on the appointed legislative council. This situation, together with the continuing bitterness in Sydney against forced annexation, led to the development of a long-lasting separatist movement, particularly in eastern Cape Breton.

Not only did Cape Bretoners feel they did not have a fair number of representatives. They also felt there was not enough money spent on their roads and bridges; that the distance to Halifax was too great for travel to the House of Assembly; that a reversion to local rule was needed; and that Halifax was not really interested in the island's problems. And there was the whole legal aspect: according to British law, the King had no right to annex the island to Nova Scotia.

The economy of Sydney, with a population of only around 300, suffered from annexation. No longer capital of a colony, Sydney's property values plunged, people hoarded their money, and a number of educated officeholders left.[5] Trying to avert the annexation before it could be proclaimed, a petition signed by 94 men was drawn up in the Sydney area and sent to Britain, begging for an assembly, since "in Nova Scotia our voice will never be heard;...Cape Breton's interests which can never have anything in common with those of Nova Scotia, will be neglected...." The petitioners insisted that these conditions would see the island becoming a "burdensome dependent on her elder Sister."[6]

The petition failed, and many former officeholders in Cape Breton Colony became separatists. Richard Gibbons was the most vocal, supported by Charles R. Ward, who had held numerous positions in the former government of Cape Breton. In 1830 Ward became publisher of the island's first newspaper, the *Cape Bretonian*, which he used as a separatist sounding board.

In 1823 money was raised to send Richard Gibbons to London, where he managed to have the illegality of the annexation brought up in the House of Commons. As ringleaders, Ward's and Gibbons' efforts did not stop. Numerous petitions with this theme were sent to London during the first 25 years after annexation. A mass meeting in Sydney in 1833 raised funds to hire a counsel in London to keep the matter alive there. Even Lord Durham was approached during his investigation of the governance of British North America.

The British government was in a bind. Lord Stanley, the colonial secretary, saw the justice in islanders' arguments but remarked that dissolving the union would be very "inconvenient" since Cape Breton's coal mines were becoming a valuable source of revenue to Nova Scotia, guaranteeing that it could pay the costs of self government. By the 1840s the British Government, including Lord Stanley, agreed with Joseph Howe's Reformers that Nova Scotia was ready for Responsible Government—but only if it were self-supporting. This in turn depended on the revenue from the Cape Breton coal mines. A formal decision on the status of Cape Breton was thus essential—should it be a separate colony or a part of Nova Scotia?

In April 1846 the case was brought before the British Privy Council which decided that annexation should stand. No reasons for the decision had to be given, but the political and economic consequences for Nova Scotia—especially the coal revenues—give a clue.[7]

The decision by the Colonial Office was final. It was a practical solution just like Despard's rum tax, which was illegal and unconstitutional but did the job.

The Cape Breton separatists were now without peaceful recourse and, though the formal separatist movement waned, from now on islanders' unhappiness with their political and economic situation would invariably be linked to the issues of separation which, in turn, were fed by a growing sense of being "Cape Bretonians"—in their hearts a people apart.

THE RACIAL, HISTORICAL AND ECONOMIC interests of Cape Bretoners were too divergent before 1850 to permit a unified sense of themselves and the place. The Acadian population far from Sydney were not warm separatists and it is doubtful if their sense of "Cape Breton" was as strong as their religious and racial affinities. This would be true of the Mi'kmaq as well. And the largely Gaelic-speaking Scottish population were just arriving during the first half of the nineteenth century. It would take at least a generation for their sense of island identity to begin to emerge.

The divergent interests of islanders is shown in the election of 1832, known as "The Great Election." By that time the island had three seats in the House of Assembly—one each in Sydney, Arichat, and a new riding simply called "Cape Breton," which included the rest of the island. The candidates for the first election in this new riding were Scottish-born, reform-minded William Young, and the business-oriented and more conservative Richard Smith, an Englishman and manager of the coal mines in eastern Cape Breton.[8]

Smith represented the coal mining interests while Young demanded that provincial coal royalties be increased. The election was fought between the "monopolists"—Smith's people—and the "patriots"—Young's constituency. Young's support came from his fellow Scots countrymen in the Northwestern District while Smith, insisting that higher royalties would curtail mining development, drew his votes from the Northeast. Open voting was still the rule—which meant that everyone knew where everyone else stood.

The voting lasted throughout December. As the votes were tallied, the results threatened to be close. When the polls in the Northeast closed, Smith's "bully boys"—hired to intimidate voters—prepared to meet Young's ruffians in the Northwest. The contenders were in a dead heat with the last poll at Chéticamp. Both groups marched there—1,500 for Smith, 2,000 for Young. The sheriff supported Young and tried to keep Smith's backers from voting.

The election culminated in a riot, with Smith's supporters beaten back from the polling house. When Smith tried to intervene, he was tossed out of the house and beaten. Extra votes supporting Smith were then stuffed into the ballot box. Still, Young was elected—but the House of Assembly unseated him and installed Smith. All in all, the election revealed the island's need for more ridings to represent its divergent interests in the House of Assembly.

Indeed, inadequate representation was a strong factor in island separatist sentiment. By 1837, Richard Smith was responsible for prodding the assembly into increasing Cape Breton representation to five seats in a House of 49. The Reformers in the House supported increased representation from the island since they usually received strong support there. Cape Bretoners had few ties with the Conservative Halifax elite, and many still harboured resentment over annexation.

Behind the gain in seats was the island's new division into three counties: Juste-au-Corps, the former Northwestern District; Richmond, the former Southwestern District; and Cape Breton, the rest of the island, which included the present Cape Breton and Victoria Counties. Each county was given a seat which was added to the existing seats of the townships of Sydney and Arichat. Cape Breton's rapidly increasing population left it still under-represented since with one-fifth of Nova Scotia's population, it had only one-tenth of the seats. In 1847, for example, Cape Breton County with 25,000 people still had only two representatives, while mainland Nova Scotia's Shelburne with 6,000 people returned three.[9]

Under-representation was due not only to the island's rapidly growing population, but to a number of slower-growing mainland counties who feared losing influence. This was the case of the Annapolis Valley and other regions where farming interests feared fishing concerns would predominate in the House. Even within Cape Breton there was a continuing clash of interests where Richmond County, long the most populous area, feared the loss of seats to the two other more quickly-growing counties. To avoid this, Richmond urged that Cape Breton County be divided.[10] Consequently in 1851 Victoria was established as a separate county with two representatives, increasing Cape Breton Island's representation in the House of Assembly from six to eight.

Since the period before 1850 was a time when Cape Bretoners were still learning the ropes of democracy and many did not speak English, they were frequently represented by mainlanders. The first Scottish representative to the House of Assembly born in Inverness County (formerly Juste-au-Corps) was not elected until 1868.[11] And Acadians were not represented by an islander until 1874.[12]

The chief exception was Sydney Township where Murray Dodd (1797-1876), son of former Chief Justice A. C. Dodd, was Conservative representative from 1822 to 1848. Like his father— who had generally supported David Mathews before annexation— he was the closest Cape Breton came to having a member of the Family Compact, a largely Halifax-dominated elite who were generally Anglican, with deep influence over the operations of the colonial government.[13] Murray Dodd was a member of the executive council 1838-1848, and solicitor general from 1844 until 1848. After the establishment of Responsible Government, he left political life to become a judge of the Supreme Court, 1848-1873. Though he professed to be a separatist, partly to woo the voters of the Sydney region, he generally supported the Halifax elite and controlled local patronage, assuring his retention of power and the support of Sydney's "aristocracy."[14]

As the move toward Responsible Government grew, members of the House of Assembly from Cape Breton tended to support the Reformers. Nova Scotia's Lieutenant-Governor Lord Falkland could see this and even went so far as to hope that separation in Cape Breton would triumph, ridding the Colony of Nova Scotia not only of Reformers but of Roman Catholics! Falkland meanwhile tried to govern through a coalition of Reformers and Conservatives. This failed when the Reformers walked out. Shortly afterwards, Britain's newly-elected laissez-faire Whigs, who felt colonies should run their own affairs, appointed Sir John Harvey as lieutenant-governor for Nova Scotia with instructions to allow the party with the majority of support in the Assembly to form the government. When a subsequent election was held in February 1848, the Reformers gained the most seats and were called to form a government. Cape Breton had elected three Reformers, two Conservatives, and one undeclared member. Dodd, who was a Conservative, agreed to resign as solicitor-general to make room for a Reformer, thus assuring the principle of Responsible Government.

A by-election in April 1848 returned a Reformer to Dodd's Sydney riding, giving the island four Reformers, one Conservative, and one Independent in what was Canada's first Responsible Government. Though no cabinet members came from Cape Breton, the speaker, William Young, represented Inverness County.

Between 1820 and 1867, Cape Bretoners adapted to political life as part of Nova Scotia, while influencing the growth of democracy in the province. Interestingly enough, the island's political alignment during the time was rooted in pre-annexation partisanship. The problems of accommodating its economic and political aspirations to the new marriage would bear a direct influence on its attitudes toward the coming union with Canada.

# 6

# "The Epidimical Fury of Emmigration"

## Settlement in the 19th Century

> "In the evening the company danced as usual. We performed, with much activity, a dance which, I suppose, the emigration from Sky has occasioned. They call it 'America.' Each of the couples, after the common involutions and evolutions, successively whirls round in a circle, till all are in motion; and the dance seems intended to shew how emigration catches, till a whole neighbourhood is set afloat."[1]
> — James Boswell

WHILE POLITICIANS JOCKEYED for position in the colonial government that played out in Halifax, the people of Cape Breton were building the foundations of the rural world which would eventually define pre-industrial Cape Breton.

The four decades after 1810 witnessed rapid population growth on Cape Breton Island. To the previously settled peoples—the Mi'kmaq, French, Irish, and Loyalists—was added an overwhelming number of Highland Scots.

Throughout the 19th century the Mi'kmaq, despite government attempts to settle them, remained primarily migratory. As European settlement grew they moved between the fringes of white settlements and their hunting and fishing encampments, selling handmade wares like baskets and moccasins. While the island was a separate colony, little was done to interfere with their freedom, but after 1820 the Nova Scotia government's native settlement policy—developed to assimilate the natives and prevent clashes over property rights with settlers—came into effect.

Just before Cape Breton received separate colonial status, in 1783 the government of Nova Scotia issued settlement licenses to Mi'kmaq for lands on which they wanted them to live. One of these grants was near today's Chapel Island at the present Barra Head. Even though there were no longer at that location any full-time missionaries dedicated to their needs, Chapel Island continued to be the annual gathering place for the Feast of St. Anne (26 July) for natives from all over the Maritimes. The island's sacred character probably went back far before the chapel established there by Abbé Maillard in 1750.[2]

The early Protestant governors of Cape Breton tried to get priests for the natives. In 1792 Father François LeJamtel led to the St. Peter's area a group of Acadian settlers from St. Pierre and Miquelon; they were fleeing the anti-religious French Revolution. LeJamtel began ministering as well to the natives—but on a limited basis. Shortly after his arrival, and probably hoping for LeJamtel's visits, two Mi'kmaq, Francis Bark and Chief Tomma Michael, were given permission to build a new chapel on "the island of Villemoi" (Chapel Island).[3] Still, LeJamtel was too busy with the needs of the Acadians and Irish at Isle Madame, and the Mi'kmaq were neglected. When Bishop Plessis visited in 1812, the Mi'kmaq complained:

We live like dogs, left to die without sacraments. Our children are ignorant of religion. No priest speaks our language. Our old people have not heard a sermon in fifty years. What have we done that we should be abandoned in this way?[4]

Without priests, the Mi'kmaq relied on their keptins—captains or local chiefs—for religious guidance, and for leading the prayers Abbé Maillard had left them in ideographic writing based on an orthography that priests had earlier noted in use among the Mi'kmaq.[5] The people performed rituals learned before the fall of Louisbourg, such as kneeling and crossing themselves, singing hymns, and using rosaries and crucifixes.[6]

The Mi'kmaq had always venerated the grandmother—as they do to this day—with the daughter Mary and the son Jesus venerated to a lesser extent. Hence, the annual St. Anne's mission at Chapel Island. Elements of Mi'kmaw life were woven into Catholic practices, such as the giving of everything—the sharing of everything—that had belonged to the dead. With the return of the priests, this practice was modified into today's auction, which includes cash to pay the costs of burial—but the "giving" remains a fundamental part of Mi'kmaw life incorporated into Catholic practice.[7]

THE NATIVES SEEMED TO LIVE without much interference until just after annexation in 1820. In the face of wholesale Scottish immigration into the island, the best land was being gobbled up and natives who persisted in "trespassing" were being driven away by new settlers. Many of the Mi'kmaq retreated to Halifax or to the outskirts of Sydney, begging or peddling baskets, quill work, and even toys.[8] The provincial government had inaugurated an Indian policy to keep the natives on land away from the non-native settlements. It was hoped this policy would induce them to take up agriculture so they could be gradually assimilated.

To guarantee the natives at least some land and to try to get them to settle, Henry W. Crawley, Commissioner of Crown Lands, was ordered by the Halifax government to map out protected reserves for native settlements. In 1834 six sites were set aside, all adjacent to the Bras d'Or Lakes: Wagmatcook (Middle River), Whycocomagh, Malagawatch, Margaree (Indian Garden), Eskasoni, and Chapel Island, totaling 12,205 acres—this on a Cape Breton Island of over 2,500,000 acres. The natives ignored the policy and continued to roam through most parts of the island, hunting and fishing and peddling their crafts, pretty much at will.

This "settlement" policy continued until Confederation in 1867, and was supplemented by a system of financial relief which was probably rooted in the French and British policies of giving gifts to the natives in return for their military support. The Mi'kmaq also remembered the treaty signed 1 July 1761, when they had been received into the protection of the British King. A century later the natives felt this treaty still applied, and that relief grants were simply "testimonies of respect" and compensation for the land and fisheries they had lost, and that they need do nothing in return.[9] Provincial authorities, on the other hand, regarded this as a form of welfare. As money was distributed, the need for administration grew, and white Indian Agents were appointed to oversee the reserves and to disperse "relief."

Due partly to government inefficiency, the Mi'kmaq continued their habits of seasonal migration. They were not trained in agricultural methods. One year seed potatoes sent to them arrived late for planting, so the Indians ate them and reverted to their usual fishery. Besides, the reserve lands were generally poor. Those of good quality—such as at Wagmatcook (Middle River) and Whycocomagh—were encroached upon by white settlers. Whycocomagh, at the western head of the Bras d'Or Lakes, was becoming a trading point for goods coming east or west, from eastern Cape Breton or from the Gut of Canso—that is, stores and warehouses were established by white merchants. Settlers intruded on the reserve, some claiming they were renting land from chiefs. Others just moved onto the empty lands.

To the Scots, vacant land was wasted land and waste was a sin. To the natives, Whycocomagh was one of their ancient points of departure for hunting and fishing trips all along the shores of the Bras d'Or Lakes. In the protection of their rights the Indians were at a disadvantage; they did not own land individually and they could not vote. The settlers on the other hand controlled the political system and could act individually to appropriate native lands.

A notorious example of land encroachment, known as the Cape Breton Land Dispute, occurred between 1830 and 1832 when a group of Scottish settlers took up native land at the juncture of the Southwest and Northeast branches of the Margaree River at Margaree Forks. Though the land was commonly known as Indian Garden, the Scots refused to move on the grounds that the land was lying unused. Crawley took them to court and the Scots were told to move. They refused, and eventually took all but 700 of the 4,500-acre Indian Garden. Nothing further was done to defend the Mi'kmaq. For their protection, H. W. Crawley—now also an Indian Agent—suggested that the natives be given the vote, but his plea fell on deaf ears. In despair, he resigned as agent in 1852.

In 1859 a legislative committee suggested that the encroached land be sold to the non-native violators. It was thought that the longer they were on the land, the more expensive it would be for government, presumably because they had made "improvements" on it—improvements for which they would expect compensation! The legislative committee suggested the money raised be used for grants to the Indians engaged in agriculture or for the relief of their sick.

The Mi'kmaq of Cape Breton, on the other hand, petitioned the lieutenant-governor that a survey of the reserve lands be made showing "the names of the parties trespassing...and the damages they have done." They asked that these parties be made to pay compensation for this damage "for the benefit to the tribe."[10] Their petition was ignored. Within a few years even the payments stopped coming. The angry natives, in turn, prevented surveyors from coming near their land. This kept trespassers from settling there and forced the government to stop selling the land.[11]

The result of these events was the loss of a great deal of native land and, as important, continued deterioration of their faith in the white man's laws.

The Mi'kmaw population in Cape Breton stood at only 473 in 1842.[12] Though some married Acadians, the Nova Scotia government's policy of settlement and assimilation failed, and in their frustration they considered the natives to be "uncivilizable"—that is, unwilling to accept European values.

In the 1840s Chief Louis Benjamin Pemincut, a mainland chief, wrote to Queen Victoria:

Madame...my people are poor. No Hunting Grounds—No Beaver—no Otter—no nothing. Indians poor—poor forever. No Store—no Chest—no Clothes.... Let us not perish.[13]

Nova Scotia's approach to the natives was a complete failure. As the Indian Commissioner for Nova Scotia reported in 1848:

Almost the whole Micmac population are now vagrants, who wander from place to place, and door to door seeking alms...they are clad in filthy rags.... The half famished mother and her squalid infant and naked children, the emaciated bodies of the aged, the frightful distortions of the infirm, and the unrelieved sufferings of the sick, concealed in the forest beneath a few pieces of bark or a thin shelter of boughs, have a real but almost unknown existence.[14]

THE ISLAND'S ACADIAN POPULATION continued to pursue the fishery at Isle Madame and the adjacent shores of Cape Breton, working for the Jerseymen. In 1770, the Jersey merchants established a second fishing centre at Chéticamp on the west coast of Cape Breton, which attracted Acadian fishermen. Starting with two families in 1782, by 1790 Acadians from Prince Edward Island and the islands of St. Pierre and Miquelon off Newfoundland had settled in and around Chéticamp, bringing the number of Acadian families there to 26.

Acadians who had tried to settle in Prince Edward Island experienced "odious exploitation." They were often permitted to establish themselves and clear the land, only to have English-speaking owners show up at harvest time and claim the fruits of their labour. They had a choice between serfdom or exile. "As early as 1787, a dozen of the heads of Acadian families from Fortune Bay...complained of never having obtained the promised leases...in October a large number of these Acadians emigrated to Cape Breton."[15]

In 1790, a group of Acadians from Chéticamp, known as "Les Quatorze Vieux"—the fourteen original settlers—were granted a charter by Cape Breton's Lieutenant-Governor William Macarmick for 7,000 acres of land, which they in turn parceled out to their fellow settlers at Chéticamp. By 1798 the first chapel was built at Chéticamp. By 1809 settlement was spreading to nearby Petit Étang, Grand Étang (St. Joseph du Moine), Le Plateau, and Chéticamp Island.

As the century advanced, the population spread south into the nearby Margaree Valley, where Acadians intermarried with Irish living there. As the settlement and the fishery continued to grow, Chéticamp's population reached 2,500 by 1879, with lesser but steady growth in nearby Acadian communities.[16]

The first settlers in the area lived simple lives indeed. Anselme Chiasson describes a house of the period as typically built of axe-squared logs.

The house isn't finished on the inside. The floor itself is of squared wood, sometimes even of smaller round logs or *rollons*. The furniture is very rustic, a dining table made of planks, no chairs, just benches for seats. Against the wall there is a *dorsoué* (sideboard or shelving) for the dishes.[17]

He goes on to describe beds as simple sleeping couches doing double duty as room dividers.

While springing from the same root as their Isle Madame brethren, the Chéticamp Acadian population emerged as another distinct Cape Breton people. Because of the Jersey merchants' control, and given the climate, they concentrated on fishing to the detriment of the expansion of agriculture. And since they were left to their own devices through the winter—most years, all of the Jerseymen returned to the Channel Islands—they preserved and created distinctive cultural elements, often expressed in their songs and storytelling.

MANY IRISH FISHERMEN left the British Newfoundland colony and crossed to Cape Breton where they found work in the French fishery at Louisbourg in the 1740s and 1750s, thus enjoying freedom from anti-Catholic persecution. Couples even visited from Newfoundland to have their marriages blessed.[18] Already long-settled near Louisbourg and St. Peter's, they continued to migrate to Cape Breton after the fall of Louisbourg, many travelling on to the Margaree Valley, which offered them sumptuous fertile land and rich salmon rivers—besides the ocean cod fishery.

A further influx of Irish settlers occurred following the Napoleonic Wars after 1815, when economic depression drove many from Ireland. Some of these found their way to Margaree and to Ingonish in northern Cape Breton, sometimes by accident. We have already seen the political effects of the Irish convicts abandoned on the shore of Main-à-Dieu in 1788. In 1834 the brig *Fidelity*, bound for Québec from Dublin with 183 immigrants, ran aground at Cape Breton's Scaterie Island. They all got ashore but three died before being rescued by the inhabitants of Main-à-Dieu.[19] In 1835 the barque *William Ewing* from Londonderry was wrecked in fog off Scaterie with 250 emigrants aboard, all of whom were saved.[20]

Despite their often inauspicious arrivals, *Freeman's Journal* wrote of the Irish: "The dregs of our society are bound for Nova Scotia, where many of them may, at a future day, become useful members of the British Empire."[21]

Cape Breton, however, never became a major haven for the Irish. They tended to settle in larger urban centres like Boston,

Saint John, and Halifax. Since they preferred living close together, they favoured fishing to farming. We can see this in settlements like Rocky Bay, Louisbourg, Main-à-Dieu, and Ingonish. Some were attracted to the coal mines near Sydney: James Miller, an Irish geologist who was responsible for the first corporate mining efforts in Cape Breton in the 1780s, enticed a number of Irish colliers to Sydney Mines. Some of these moved further along the coast as new mines opened—to Lingan and Low Point. Enough Irish settled in that area that it became known as the "Irish Grant."

A number of these people in turn moved to coastal locations such as Ingonish, Pleasant Bay, Aspy Bay, and White Point, where they fished in summer, living in shacks, joined by fishermen from Newfoundland. In the autumn, in a process known in Ireland as "booleying," they moved back to the nearby interior valleys where their more substantial homes were located, driving the cattle before them. There they harvested crops they had sown in spring and settled down for the winter, before returning to the coast the following spring.[22] Well into the 20th century, fiddler Winston "Scotty" Fitzgerald was able to say,

> Between 15 and 20 families would move down [to White Point] in May. Move back in October, after the summer fishing. That would leave us local people [about 12 families] by ourselves for the winter.[23]

Sometimes the fishermen and their families were brought to Cape Breton deliberately and in groups, to fish for a certain merchant, as when the Scottish MacLeods of Baddeck brought people from Newfoundland's southwest coast to Hungry Cove, renamed New Haven, in Victoria County. It is said that they even dismantled some of the houses and brought them across on deck.[24]

By the 1820s a number of Irish, such as the Ryan, Tompkins, Murphy, and Coady families, found their way into the Margaree Valley. Some Scots-Irish merchants from the mainland made their way to the Mabou area (William McKeen), Little Judique and Port Hood (Edward Hayes and Peter Smyth), or nearer to Margaree

(William Frizzle). These people bartered with farmers and fisher-men for local produce like dried cod and fruits and vegetables in exchange for imported goods such as molasses, rum, tea, and sugar, which arrived from the Caribbean and Europe via Arichat, Hali-fax, and Newfoundland. Though the Scots-Irish were relatively few in number, they wielded substantial economic and social power by extending credit to the cash-poor settlers. Moreover, their abil-ity to speak sophisticated English—unlike the Gaels, Acadians, and Mi'kmaq—greatly enhanced their influence, both locally and in the wider world.[25]

Another group who spoke English were the Loyalists. Most had arrived by 1793, and tended to remain in their original areas of settlement: Sydney, Baddeck, near Middle River, Port Hood, Hillsborough, and the Gut of Canso region. They often intermar-ried, keeping their distinctness alive throughout the 19th century. Although Loyalists are often considered in popular culture to have been people of high rank, most were farmers or fishermen.

THE FUNDAMENTAL CHARACTER of Cape Breton Island was established with the settlement of the Highland Scots. Their great numbers caused a major change in the population of Cape Breton and ultimately set the tone for the island.

One of the factors that had kept people in Scotland's coastal Highlands and the Hebridean islands was the slim opportunity offered by the kelp industry. This seaweed was abundant and, when burnt, yielded an alkali or potash that was used as fertilizer and in the manufacture of glass and soap. Although a higher quality of potash was being imported from mines in Spain, the Napoleonic Wars upset this trade, and manufacturers in the Scottish Low-lands and England were forced to rely on the Highlands for their potash. The lords realized the value of this trade and declared their sole right to manufacture and sell kelp. Their "tenants" could no longer work at kelping on their own, selling to the highest bidder.

Now they were forced to kelp for the landlord at a low wage.[26]

When a temporary peace was signed with France in 1802-1803, and French patrols which had blocked shipping were lifted, 7,000 people left the Highland region. At least 400 of them came to Cape Breton. They were the first of a huge migration that began to pick up steam after the Napoleonic Wars ended in 1815. With peace, Spanish potash again entered the market, imperiling the Scottish kelping industry—and a flood of emigrants left for Cape Breton. These people could afford decent passage with money from kelping and the sale of their cattle, and they decided to leave for North America for a more secure life.

The poorer Highlanders who remained behind eked out a living from kelping; but by the late 1820s that industry was gone and their crofter economy fell apart. The people could not pay the rents. To make more money, the lords introduced sheep farming, evicting the tenants. The lords were so anxious to be rid of their tenants that in some cases they cancelled their debts. By selling all their possessions these crofters scraped together enough money to buy passage to Cape Breton. The Cape Breton "land rush" peaked between 1815 and 1838. The numbers of immigrants declined after that time—but by 1850 over 30,000 Scots had arrived on Cape Breton's shores. And the complexion of Cape Breton was fixed for the next hundred years.

The poorer Highlanders came to Cape Breton because it was the closest point to Scotland with cheap arable land. As Charles Dunn wrote, "How the settlers decided which portion of land to head for in the tree-covered wastes will always remain somewhat of a mystery."[27] Certainly some had been aware of the possibilities of settlement on the island since the middle of the 18th century, when Scottish soldiers serving with British forces at the attack on Louisbourg—notably Donald Og MacNeil, Donald MacNeil, and Finlay Glas MacKenzie, all from Barra—had sailed through the Bras d'Or Lakes hunting down French settlers and burning their homes—and at the same time noting the land's potential, particularly at Grand Narrows. Their reports were not forgotten, and large numbers of Barramen eventually settled in that region. Today's Grand Narrows and Iona "are peopled by descendants from the kinsmen and friends of the three soldiers."[28]

Indeed, the Bras d'Or Lakes were among the first regions to which the Scots headed after 1802. Along the south shore of the Lakes, settlement quickly spread toward St. Peter's and over to Grande Anse and Grand River. By the teens and twenties of the 19th century they were moving into River Inhabitants and in a half-moon along the River Denys basin. Presbyterian settlers from North Uist and Skye attracted others who spread out toward St. Esprit and L'Archeveque. By the late 1820s and 1830s settlement spread onward to the recently discovered Loch Lomond.

We can use the Loch Lomond settlement as an example of the experiences of many newcomers. In 1828 a group of Scots settled there who were led by a man identified by his grandson Johnny Allan MacDonald as the "Big Carpenter." As Johnny Allan put it:

This Big Carpenter—he called a meeting [in Scotland]—you know, during the Clearances—he called a meeting of his relatives and friends.... And he suggested that they all sell whatever they could get along without—whatever little they'd get for it, to sell it.... That it was just as well for them to prepare to leave, rather than to be driven away.... They did away with whatever they could get along without.

The group sailed to Sydney where some went on to the Mira area between Albert Bridge and Catalone, the rest to Big Pond and Irish Cove and eventually to Loch Lomond. When they arrived there, they quickly built log houses on stone foundations—and there was plenty of stone.

They slapped [the log houses] together,...they'd notch them down with an axe.... And they used to level them off and then plant the end of the logs...together.... But they'd take moss and...chinking between the logs, to keep the wind out, the storm.

Floors were slabs of stone.[29]

The Big Carpenter was right about the value of preparation. Later settlers forced from their lands suffered on their arrival. People often arrived with nothing. A group from Uist landed at East Bay and walked to Ben Eoin, leaving children so hungry that they ate the seed potatoes they had planted, while the men walked all the way to North Sydney for flour, carrying it home on their backs.[30]

The tale of settlement of the first Scottish people at Grand Narrows tells of their coming face to face with an angry group of Mi'kmaq approaching in 80 canoes. The natives made it quite clear that they resented their land being taken. However, when they realized that the settlers were Catholic—perhaps a frightened Scot made the sign of the cross—the chief was interpreted as saying words to the effect that "Oh, then we all same brothers," and the natives left with no further problems.[31]

The few American-born settlers, often called "pre-Loyalists," who had settled on the shores of the Mira River and Mira Gut between the fall of Louisbourg and the arrival of DesBarres in 1785—Americans like the Protestant Huntingtons, Spencers, and Leys—helped the first Scottish settlers there to clear the land and build cabins. Most of these Scots were Roman Catholics from Loch Morar, and their farms extended further up the river to Grand Mira. Their numbers were increased by fellow Catholics, largely from South Uist, who spread inland to French Road, eventually linking up with Catholics from Moidart and Loch Morar on the shores of East Bay on the Bras d'Or Lakes. Between 1807 and 1829, the region along the St. Andrew's Channel of the Lakes was also settled, first by people from Grand Narrows spreading west toward Iona as far as Ottawa Brook and eastward to Christmas Island and Boisdale. Most of these Roman Catholic settlers came from the islands of Barra and South Uist.

On the other hand, the west end of St. Ann's Bay to South Haven and North River became home to Protestant Dissenters from Gairloch, Cromarty, and the Isle of Lewis. They were led by the Reverend Norman McLeod, the fiery backbone of his people, who arrived in 1820. Ruled by his iron hand as judge, teacher, and minister, McLeod's community was considered one of the most successful on the island, its inhabitants forming

the most sober, industrious and orderly settlement in the island, [who] have a pastor of their own, endowed also with magisterial authority, to whose exertions and vigilance the character of the people is not a little indebted.[32]

Fortified by new arrivals, this settlement spread during the 1830s to Middle River, Baddeck, and the north shore of Boularderie Island. South Side Boularderie was likewise populated by Presbyterian Scots to the tip of Kempt Head.

The area near Port Hawkesbury and particularly around Port Hood and Judique had been settled since the late 18th century by Roman Catholic Scots who had crossed to Cape Breton from around Antigonish and Prince Edward Island. By the late 1820s, settlement there was reinforced by new arrivals whose holdings were eventually established as far as seven kilometres back from the coast.

The territory between Whycocomagh and Port Hood was settled inland from Port Hood branching at Southwest Mabou to the Mabou River then extending along both sides of Lake Ainslie, eventually reaching Whycocomagh on the Bras d'Or Lakes. Those on the west side of Lake Ainslie were Catholics from the Isle of Mull, Moidart, and the adjacent mainland of Scotland. Protestant Scots settled on the east side of Lake Ainslie extending north to Kenlock and Strathlorne and south to Whycocomagh. The west coast of Cape Breton, from Cape Mabou to Margaree Harbour, including the backlands behind Broad Cove, were settled during the 1820s by Catholic Scots.

Generally speaking, settlers arriving after 1830 had to settle for backland areas, up the sides of lofty hills where soil was poor.

In 1832 alone, 300 settlers from South Uist arrived in the backlands of East Bay, Catalone, Hillside, and Gabarus Lake, while the backlands of the Mira River were settled by Presbyterians from North Uist after 1830. Settlement took place in the 1830s and early 1840s in the interior of Boularderie Island, Loch Lomond, the Creignish Hills, and finally the rock-laden "North Shore" of Victoria County, which was receiving settlers as late as the mid-1840s and even the early 1850s. While not strictly backlanders, the North Shore settlers overcame poor soil with a combination of farming and fishing.

Whether it was pride or reality, there were also those who were so grateful for the land that the backlands were their heaven. As Charles Dunn wrote:

> This partisan devotion to the native soil could be illustrated by count-less Gaelic songs of varying literary merit.... [The parents of Donald MacDonald] came from Moidart to Cape Breton and settled on a moun-tain top in what is known as "the rear" of South-West Margaree.... In later years he had to leave "the rear" and work for a season at "the shore," as the rival area was called. Here he found life, nature, and the people different from what he had known out back, and in every respect dis-tinctly inferior. His prompt response was to compose a song, *Moladh a' Chuil agus Di-moladh a' Chladaich* (Praise of the Rear and Dispraise of the Shore).[33]

Donald's exaggerated disgust about life at "the shore" invited a response. And his neighbour Duncan MacLellan responded with *Moladh a' Chladaich agus Di-moladh a' Chuil* (Praise of the Shore and Dispraise of the Rear), offering opposing images.[34]

BY 1850 THE CHIEF SETTLEMENT PATTERNS of the is-land were clear. The areas around Chéticamp and Isle Madame were largely Acadian with a sprinkling of Irish, principally in the Margaree Valley, and near Sydney and Louisbourg. The Loyalists remained near Baddeck, Sydney, Port Hood, and the Strait area, and the Mi'kmaq homes could be found reasonably close to their designated reserves. Otherwise, Highland Scots populated the island, with whole regions either Catholic or Protestant depending on their place of origin in Scotland. Approximately 40 percent of the Scots were Presbyterian or at least Protestant, and the rest were Roman Catholic.

An estimate would put the population of Cape Breton at 10,000 in 1820; 18,700 in 1827; and 37,278 in 1838.[35] Cape Breton County, which still included the present-day Victoria County, numbered at least 15,000. So did Juste-au-Corps or Chestico, which was called Inverness County after 1837. The once most populous but relatively infertile Richmond County had only 7,500 inhabitants in 1838.

The later the settlers came, the poorer they were. Likewise, the earliest settlers got the best land. After 1830 the best lands around the Bras d'Or Lakes and Western District—generally speaking, today's Inverness County—were gone, and people decided to settle in the "Indian hunting territory," a phrase used by Samuel Holland to describe uplands remote from the coast and probably unsuited to farming. Freehold lands were available after 1817 and 200 acres could be bought for three to five pounds—still well beyond the means of most settlers.

As a consequence, when the government began raising land prices, the poorer Scots became squatters. In sympathy with their plight, Provincial Surveyor H. W. Crawley simply ignored the problem and let them settle.[36] After a time prices fell, but by then squatting had become endemic. By 1839 it was estimated that half the population of Cape Breton was settled without permanent land title.[37] As late as 1857, the deputy surveyor of Cape Breton reported that two-thirds of the residents of Cape Breton County were squatters living on holdings of between two and three hundred acres.

Scots coming to Cape Breton brought with them a propensity for raising cattle and cultivating the potato. In the Scotland they had left behind, the land was damp and marginal, with lush pastures suitable for black cattle. During the mid 18th century they began to grow potatoes which flourished even in poor soil. Oats and barley were also grown, but were neglected for potatoes. These immigrants to Cape Breton sometimes brought their cattle with them, and were given seed potatoes by the government.[38] When they arrived, they cleared the forest, using the trees to build their first homes. They burned the undergrowth, enriching the soil with potash. On good land, potatoes or wheat could be grown between the tree stumps, and the swelling potatoes helped loosen the stumps. The following year, this land was allowed to go to meadow for cattle grazing while new land was cleared. The cattle manure further enriched the meadow, which could then be stumped and plowed under for the planting of oats. Stumping was a tedious process. Generally, farmers built bonfires over the stumps and exposed the roots to ensure they too burnt. After this, stumps could be levered or pried out of the ground with the help of oxen roped to the stump. Often, however, oxen were not available, and only the slow rotting of the stump cleared the land.[39]

Because of their ease of cultivation, potatoes continued to be a popular crop on the island. In 1827 an estimated 468,607 bushels were harvested.[40] Certain more fertile areas—like Mabou, the Margaree River, South Side Boularderie, Loch Lomond, Lake Ainslie, and River Inhabitants—produced a variety of surplus crops and cattle for early export.

There is, however, controversy over Scottish farmers. One school sees them as lazy, disinclined to improve their land, and content with inefficient methods of farming.[41] They were accused of being satisfied with their lot: "never having known prosperity, they did not miss it."[42] It is alleged that they did not favour agriculture and were quick to abandon it for other ways of making a living.[43]

On the other hand, there are indications that many of the Cape Breton Scots adjusted to an agricultural way of life, especially if they were located on good land. Though people lacked capital, they showed an interest in improvements, and petitioned for grist mills to grind their grain. Government-supported agricultural societies were encouraged by John Young, MLA for Inverness County, and in the early 1820s spread quickly throughout the settled parts of the island. These societies were responsible for the diffusion of new concepts in farming and agricultural improvements such as the use of fertilizers, the planting of new and varied strains of crops, and cattle husbandry. Agricultural societies largely disappeared when government withdrew its support of them, but they reappeared in the 1850s after the terrible famine. Their advice was accepted, particularly by farmers on good "frontlands," and cattle, sheep, and crop production continued to rise in the 1830s.

One chief problem, however, was that while earlier settlers progressed, newcomers, uneducated and poor, were pouring into the remote backlands. In their huts, they lived a marginal existence in those rugged uplands, susceptible to natural or economic disruption. Their miserable situation after a series of crop failures is depicted in this 1835 account by the Rev. John Stewart, an itinerant preacher in what is now Victoria County:

I have baptized the child of a parent lying on a a pallet of straw with five children in a state of nudity, I have baptized where neither father, mother or children could venture out in their tattered rags. I have seen dwellings where six or eight of a family lived for five weeks on the milk of a cow without any other food.... There are children in abundance who, covered with rags, lie stretched all night alongside the fire on the floor from having no bed clothes to cover them, and a person starts up every other hour to throw a log on the fire.[44]

In this particular case, when word of this situation reached Sydney, the General Mining Association sent six teams loaded with provisions up the Bras d'Or on the ice to Baddeck for distribution to the needy.[45]

An incident like this reveals how precarious an existence many of the poor, newly-arriving settlers lived in mid 19th century Cape Breton.

# 7

# "Poverty, wretchedness, and misery"

## The Great Famine Reshapes Cape Breton

"...running continually from door to door, with the
ghastly features of death staring in their very faces"[1]
— Reverend Norman McLeod

T HE GREAT FAMINE was a disaster waiting to happen.
It began in 1845 with a potato blight that destroyed the potato crop for seven years running. The blight was a virus that attacked potato growth above ground level and turned the vegetation black. Potatoes rotted even in storage. Newly arriving settlers
brought infected potatoes from Ireland and Scotland where the
rot was already causing famine. Cape Breton was vulnerable since
it was still in the pioneer stage; settlers depended heavily on this
staple. Previous crop failures in 1816, 1832, and 1833 had threatened food shortages, but the potato blight caused genuine famine
in Cape Breton between 1845 and 1851.

The backlands—most recently settled—suffered the worst,
but no part of the island was spared. Homesteads in the Mira
River region were badly affected in 1847 and 1848; but a more
vigorous infection extended from there westward to the recently-
settled lands around Red Islands and Loch Lomond, particularly
in 1848. Isle Madame's worst year was 1847, when both the po-

121

tato harvest and the fishery failed. In 1845 the backlands near the Gut of Canso, and even further eastward at Broad Cove, were quickly infected. The following three years saw repeated infection and crop loss. In 1848, the whole region from Baddeck to St. Ann's Bay to Middle River and Margaree was badly hit. Sydney suffered most in 1847 and 1848.

When the blight first struck in 1845, some farmers hoped to feed the infected potatoes to their cattle, but the animals died. Surviving cattle had to be sold off to purchase feed and seed. In 1845 alone, the Margaree area exported 440 head of cattle and 600 sheep to Newfoundland, decimating herds. Newly settled backland areas, however, could not fall back on this expedient. When cattle and sheep had eaten all the grain, they were slaughtered to preserve some seed grain for the next season. If these crops failed, starvation loomed.

The year 1849 was drier and the rot was not as extensive—but the wheat fly attacked that crop and continued to do so in 1850 and 1851. 1852 saw both rot *and* the wheat fly.

The province had never faced destitution on such a scale and of such a duration. Incredulity greeted the first alarming reports from Cape Breton. *The Nova Scotian* newspaper in Halifax speculated that stories of the loss of the potato crop in Cape Breton had been circulated to drive up prices. As late as 1847 the paper felt that stories of famine in Cape Breton were exaggerated. The Central Board of Agriculture calmly reported that "no real distress, it is believed, will be produced by [the potato rot] except, perhaps, among a few of the inhabitants of Cape Breton."[2]

While it is true that frontland settlements and ports like Arichat and Sydney could obtain food supplies, remote areas were neither aware of the arrival of supplementary food nor able to reach it. Groups of people walked as far as 80 kilometres begging for a bit of flour or meal, only to find supplies at the ports exhausted. W. J. Ousley, a retired colonel living in Sydney, noted that there were "families in the back woods that are hardly known by those in the front settlement.... There are a great many settlements completely shut out, the inconvenience of travelling being so great."[3]

All over Cape Breton starving settlers were begging for food. As the Reverend Norman McLeod so graphically described it:

"The general destitution has made it impossible, even for the most saving, to shut their ears & eyes from the alarming claims and craving of those around them, running continually from door to door, with the ghastly features of death staring in their very faces."[4]

No specific records were kept of those who died from actual starvation among the newer settlers and the Mi'kmaq, or of those who perished from debilitation or disease developed in bodies weakened by hunger, but between 1845 and 1851 many reports indicated that people were in a "state of starvation." A poor man, for example, starved to death at Cow Bay (now Port Morien), and a short while later a coroner's inquest found that a Mi'kmaq had died "from the affects of cold and want of food."[5]

Starvation would certainly have been worse had people not foraged for berries and wildlife, shared food, or fished if they were near rivers or the coast. However, even the fishery failed in 1848 and 1849. A Committee of Relief finally reported in 1848 that "Poverty, wretchedness, and misery have spread through the Island of Cape Breton,"[6] which was described as the "Ireland of Nova Scotia."[7]

The situation was made all the worse because no one understood the cause of the rot. Some thought it was "atmospheric; others that it is insectile. Some able chemists suppose it to arise from an excess of moisture, or from excessive cultivation. The Indians are of the opinion that the Great Spirit has got angry with the earth for the wickedness of its inhabitants." *The Presbyterian Witness* journal claimed the crop failure to be traced to the "direct interference of the Almighty," as punishment to man for giving "undue prominence to the Potato," and "the ease with which (it) was cultivated and the indolent habits thereby induced."[8] Rev. Norman McLeod from his settlement in St. Ann's Bay also felt the blight was "retribution" for his neighbours' "unthriftiness and offensive violence; who can well feed and flutter, dress and dandle, and carelessly chafe away with toddy and tobacco."[9]

Such words did not feed people. The province finally realized that food dissemination was essential. However, it perversely decided to put the people to work on road building. Commissioners in each county would distribute supplies which individuals had to repay with work. The amount of money set aside for roadwork soon proved inadequate. In the early winter of 1847, when the magistrates of Cape Breton County met, 400 heads of families came begging for supplies. This drained all local resources.[10]

Moreover, the idea of roadwork in payment for seed or supplies proved unsatisfactory, largely because there were no roads in the most remote areas which were hardest hit and in greatest need. In areas where roadwork was done, records were poorly kept, causing confusion, while the hungry people resented the work, which in turn was poorly done. Local politicians, under pressure from their constituents, preferred to just hand out supplies. Provincial officials were loath to do this, fearing it would lead to what they called a "relaxation of moral principle."[11]

The principle on the other hand was whether the settlers should pay at all. *The Nova Scotian* wondered why counties should be penalized with poorly made roads for their efforts to ameliorate starvation.[12] The MLA for Inverness County wondered why the settlers should pay, since the government had recently given £1000 in emergency aid to Barbados and Québec without demanding repayment. Mi'kmaq as well had been given free food and supplies.[13]

Merchants like Gammel and Christie in North Sydney, McKeen at Mabou, Kidston at Baddeck, and Smyth of Poor Hood, all imported large quantities of food for starving settlers. They expected payment in cash or credit, and although many settlers were consequently indebted to them, some all but worshipped these merchants for saving their lives.[14]

Though the blight continued after 1851, its effects diminished as new crops like turnips, carrots, rye, corn, buckwheat, beans, and peas were introduced by the newly-resurrected agricultural societies in the 1850s. These societies encouraged people to plant oats and pressured the provincial government to erect oat mills and kilns on the island. As a result, even though the potato crop of 1850 was a failure, disaster was averted by an abundant oat crop. The wheat fly's effects were also mitigated simply by delaying the sowing of early wheat. So after 1852, crop diversification, better planting practices, the use of machinery, chemical manure, the use of turnip and rutabagas as a supplement to hay for animal feed, and finally the decline of the blight, put agriculture on a surer footing.

Things had improved to the extent that in 1852 the *Cape Breton News* could finally report that though there was poverty on the island due to past crop failures, "there is...no probability of any suffering from want of food this winter even amongst the poorest of our farmers."[15] The Presbytery of Cape Breton appointed 28 October as a Day of Thanksgiving.

THE GREAT FAMINE had even deeper effects on Cape Breton. The merchants—largely non-Gaelic speaking Scots-Irish or Lowland Scots, some from the mainland—gained even greater power than they had previously wielded. Many settlers were deeply in debt to them and had to pay with their land. Furthermore, some like McKeen and Peter Smyth, as members of the legislature, combined political and economic power. They controlled local patronage like roadwork, and amassed land from people who could not pay.

The famine ended large-scale Scottish immigration to Cape Breton. In 1846, the widespread distress on the island due to the potato blight induced the province's lieutenant-governor, Sir John Harvey, to write the colonial secretary, Earl Grey, begging that he discourage "pauper emigration" to the island.[16] Grey in turn instructed emigration officials to distribute copies of Harvey's plea to all emigration and customs officials, and newspapers.[17] This curbed not only Scottish emigration, which veered toward Australia and New Zealand, but also that of the Irish, who headed for Halifax, Boston, and Saint John. By 1850, large-scale Scottish immigration to Cape Breton had ended.

Not only that, but emigration *from* Cape Breton grew. Near the end of the famine, in 1851, several hundred newly settled Scots left the Broad Cove-Margaree Valley area for the fertile Codroy Valley of southwest Newfoundland. They took their Gaelic culture with them—still apparent there today in architectural styles and music, refreshed in later years by tunes they picked up "across in Cape Breton or via the Sydney radio station."[18]

At the same time as Scots left for the Codroy Valley, Cape Breton's most famous emigration occurred when nearly 900 Scots left the St. Ann's Bay area to head for Australia and New Zealand. As mentioned earlier, in 1820 the Rev. Norman McLeod had led a group of Scots to St. Ann's where he organized a settlement which he ruled. The Normanites flourished until the potato blight struck. Norman's son Donald had previously left for Australia and had sent home glowing accounts of that colony. As the destitution increased, McLeod's followers became restless to leave. The final blow came in 1850 when McLeod's own potato crop was wiped out while that of his neighbour was spared. McLeod saw this as a divine call to leave Cape Breton, and the following year, 28 October 1851, he and 130 people, calling themselves "Eòin a' Chuan" (The Sea Birds), sailed away to eventually pioneer again in New Zealand.

Not all of the St. Ann's area settlers were followers of Norman McLeod. As the years passed and favourable reports of life in New

Zealand reached Cape Breton, many decided to join their relatives there. Hence we read: "With the exception of a few from St. Ann's and Big Harbour, most of the [ship] *Breadalbane's* passengers were from Boularderie."[19]

In all, six shiploads of Cape Bretoners sailed for New Zealand. A thriving Presbyterian community was established, and their Cape Breton connection is maintained to this day.

Emigration from Cape Breton was not a new phenomenon. In the 1820s, for example, during a crop failure, a number of Acadians left to settle on the west coast of Newfoundland.[20] However, the main cause for emigration lay in overpopulation on poor land. Generally, the settlers living on the backlands, often high up on the rugged and infertile hills in tiny clearings, raised some livestock, oats, and potatoes, with only a small surplus. They often depended on working for the more affluent settlers living on the frontlands, generally near the water or closer to denser settlements. This work might include plowing, fence mending, or even helping with shipbuilding or fishing. As Neil A. MacKinnon later reminisced, "The Rear area where I was, and beyond, were only a sort of hewers of wood and drawers of water for the front people."[21] This created a floating population who were able to hire themselves out as opportunities arose.

However, after the famine, along with the re-organization of agricultural societies and new agricultural techniques, came mechanization of farming, with the introduction of tools such as horse-drawn mowers and reapers. Farmers would often share equipment and labour, reducing the need for the backlanders' help. Backlanders either had to find other employment or emigrate.

DESPITE AN IMPROVING ECONOMY in the 1850s and '60s, emigration continued. Generally speaking, young men and women left first for other places in the Maritimes, like Halifax or Saint John, where shipping and lumbering offered opportunities.

Adventurous types found interesting and unusual ways to supplement incomes. In the 1840s and '50s, some left for gold fields in California and Nanaimo, British Columbia, and ended up as sealers in Alaska. Some became soldiers serving on both sides in the American Civil War.

The eastern United States, however, was the most popular goal, particularly Massachusetts, which was the destination of 60 percent of emigrants going to the U.S.[22] The connection to Boston, strong since the time of the Fortress of Louisbourg, continued when coal and fish were shipped to colonial Boston, and was strengthened in the 1860s when steamers began sailing there on a regular basis. Young women left for domestic work after seeking employment in Sydney or Halifax; many faithfully sent money and clothing home. They retained a longing for the island, often marrying fellow Cape Bretoners in the "Boston States," and sometimes returning home.

Despite this population drain, the island's numbers continued to grow, rising from around 37,000 in 1838 to 63,000 in 1867, and to 75,500 in 1871. As we shall see, expansion of agriculture, fishing, shipbuilding, lumbering, and mining provided increasing opportunities for those who remained.

# 8

# The 19ᵗʰ Century Economy

"No part of British America is richer in natural resources, and all those elements necessary to create wealth and prosperity; but unfortunately for Cape Breton, its progress has been retarded by the want of capital."[1]
—John Bourinot

**M**OST OF CAPE BRETON'S BUSINESS enterprises were small, and the consequent lack of capital continued to limit the growth of local industry. Boat building, mills, tanneries, carriage making, and small-scale mining operations depended on local investment, which rarely had the resources for large-scale manufacturing. Consequently, mining and other major industries came under the control of outside interests, first from Britain or Halifax, then from the United States. After the inauguration of the National Policy in 1878—a system of high tariffs to protect Canadian manufacturing—Canadian investors became serious players. By the 1880s, the demise of boat building, grist mills, and tanneries left outside interests virtually in control of the Cape Breton economy. By then railroads, fired by outside capital, had kindled the economic revolution which would eventually transform the island's way of life.

The 30 years following the famine, roughly from 1853 to the mid-1880s, witnessed a steady increase in agricultural productivity. One factor in this growth was security of land tenure. During the land rush of the first half of the century many immigrants had obtained only leases for their holdings; the resulting insecurity of ownership kept them from improving their land. In 1850, the provincial government declared that anyone possessing a Crown lease in Cape Breton would henceforth own the land.[2]

Another factor in growth was that as the second generation of Scottish farmers became better informed by agricultural societies and improved communications—telegraph and phone, faster mail—they were more able to gauge changing markets. Starting in the 1820s, many farmers were shipping excess produce like cattle, pork, potatoes, and butter to Newfoundland. It soon became difficult to compete with Prince Edward Island in potato exports, so they shifted to the small but growing local market. The same applied to cattle. Livestock was driven to gathering points across the island for shipment to Newfoundland or Halifax. After 1870, competition from large beef shippers from the Canadian West led to a switch to milk cattle; milk was shipped to the rapidly growing market in Cape Breton County.[3]

Still, the vast majority of holdings in 19th century Cape Breton were small subsistence homesteads which gradually emerged from the pioneer period after 1850. Small farms were the rule, particularly in coastal areas where people fished as well as farmed. This was especially true of the Acadian regions around Isle Madame and Chéticamp. Along the North Shore of Victoria County, where people typically owned 160 acres, the portion used for farming was small, the soil often poor and rocky. Richmond County farms were tiny compared to those in Inverness and Cape Breton Counties. In 1871, out of 1,817 farms in Richmond County, 532 contained less than 10 acres. In Inverness, there were 3,259 farms with only 212 of them under 10 acres. Cape Breton County had 406 such small farms out of 3,106, a higher percentage than Inverness due to the proximity of larger settlements which provided an opportunity for the production of more specialized crops like turnips and other vegetables.[4]

The rural nature of the island's population meant that small farmers, particularly in the backlands, lived in relative isolation. They supplied their own needs as much as possible. Everyone, including women and children, played a role. Men plowed, harrowed, and seeded, but women worked with the men in preparing the sheaves; they raked and stacked the hay, tramped hay in the mow, they cleaned out the stables, they carried water and made the soap—an onerous and often dangerous task preparing the ashes, firing up the boiler beside the brook, tending it for hours, adding a dipper of cold water now and then to keep it from boiling over. Women raised lambs, sometimes sheared sheep, washed and dyed the wool in boiling vats by a brook and, in the wintertime, wove the wool.[5]

Women often benefited by marketing eggs or milk on their own account so they could buy clothes, underwear, or little luxuries.[6] Generally, however, most surplus production was exchanged for other products with neighbours, keeping a local trading network alive, particularly important in times of crop failure. Butter, eggs, cheese, and hides were taken to local store owners for barter, the real basis of exchange in the rural economy of Cape Breton until the end of the 19th century. Goods thus obtained were shipped by the merchants to larger settlements for cash, which the average person rarely saw.

Despite their isolation, connections were maintained by church activities and the occasional "frolic," when people gathered to help families in distress, or simply to get work done. "Planting frolics," for example, played a valuable role in the welfare of the families run by widows, when boys and girls spent the day planting her family's crops. "There would be more frolics for the fencing, the harvesting, the plowing, and the cutting of the winter's wood."[7]

Though we can hardly call rural life in 19th century Cape

Breton a "golden age," with its hard work, distance from medical care, and its long cold winters, yet as one writer put it:

> These simple people lived a wholesome but primitive life close to the soil. Their wants were elementary and necessary and their thinking direct and concise.... They were rough and ready but kindly at heart. They looked for no favors. They would prefer to give rather than receive. They were well equipped to care for themselves in the world they knew.[8]

The Margarees, Middle River, the Mabou-Whycocomagh corridor—particularly the more fertile intervale lands—supported larger farms and agricultural societies.[9] Productivity rose steadily in these areas. As early as 1829 oats, butter, salt beef, pork, and even wheat were being shipped to places like St. Pierre and the West Indies, as well as to Halifax and Newfoundland. In 1830 alone, 25,105 bushels of potatoes were exported, together with 3,485 bushels of oats and 556 sheep.[10]

Sydney and Arichat were the main shipping ports, the latter shipping most of the agricultural produce. In 1828 Sydney was declared a free port; this eliminated landing fees and shipments increased quickly. By the 1850s other ports grew rapidly. Cattle were shipped primarily from Baddeck, Whycocomagh, and Big Bras d'Or, as well as Port Hood, which sent them on, primarily to Newfoundland.[11]

Another sign of productivity is the output-per-person of population. Inverness was Cape Breton's leading agricultural county throughout the 19th century. In 1871, the average size of families there was 6.77 members. Using this ratio, Inverness was one of the most agriculturally productive areas in Canada. Indeed Cape Breton as a whole surpassed Canada in the per capita production of winter wheat, barley, oats, potatoes, hay, and butter.[12]

There were, however, challenges. In the last 30 years of the 19th century, as new areas opened up not only in North America but in Australia and New Zealand, the mass production of agricultural goods and the consequent increase in efficiency and pricing cut into the markets of local farmers. For example, imported clothing lessened the demand for sheep. Sheep production peaked in Inverness County in 1871 with 45,556 sheep, and in Cape Breton County in 1881 with 23,649, Victoria with 16,716, and Richmond with 15,212.[13] After that, the overproduction of sheep in Australia and New Zealand resulted in a drastic drop in prices and a decline in Cape Breton production. As the Canadian prairies opened in the 1870s and 1880s, the island's wheat suffered the same fate. Farmers had to shift production more and more to the local market; if they were unable to do so, particularly if they lived on land only suited for sheep, potatoes, or wheat production, they had to seek supplementary income or give up farming.

FORTUNATELY, THERE WERE ALTERNATE livelihoods. By the 1830s, next to farming, the fishery involved the most workers in Cape Breton, and it was growing. The number of fishermen increased from 2,700 in 1851 to 8,000 in 1890.[14] Many fishermen were also farmers seeking a supplementary source of income in the face of changing markets.

The Cape Breton fishery continued to be divided between offshore, inshore, and lake fisheries. The offshore fishery was carried out by larger vessels. Schooners could remain at sea longer, working the fishing banks. These vessels were costly and there were never many more than a hundred of them, operating with crews of 10 to 20 men. Cod, hake, and halibut were gutted, salted, and kept in the hold of the ship before being brought ashore for export.

Once ashore the fish were dried for shipment. The following description of such an operation in the Chéticamp area would apply anywhere on Cape Breton:

There were the *graves* [stony beaches], with huge racks or trellises on poles on which the cod was laid out to dry. There was the large *chafaud* [shed] and the small *chafaud* [warehouse] to store the dried cod.... The fishermen were busy cutting their fish, transporting the gear.... The employees, especially the women and children, bustled around the *vigneaux* [flakes or drying racks] to spread out the fish, turning them again and again to let them dry out in the sun in order to pile them up in the warehouses later on.[15]

The inshore fishery required the smaller vessels, such as shallops, with crews of two or three men. Cape Breton-crafted shallops were of course far more numerous than the larger off-shore vessels, numbering more than 3,000 in 1884 and manned by over 6,700 men.[16] The Bras d'Or Lakes fishery, pursued by Scottish farmers in flat-bottomed boats, caught mainly haddock, cod, salmon, trout, bass, or gaspereaux. One observer commented, that in

winter season, the lake was generally frozen over, strong enough to bear the heaviest teams, at which period, within a few hundred yards of their own doors, by cutting holes through the ice, they could take abundance of fine cod and haddock.[17]

The seal fishery was pursued from places like Chéticamp and Neil's Harbour. Seals provided furs, and fat that was melted down for oil and shipped to the United States. Seal hunting boats went out in the spring when the drift ice arrived. This hunt was carried out along the Gulf of St. Lawrence coast and northern Cape Breton. The locally constructed boats had to be well built to withstand the crushing weight of the ice.[18]

The United States played an increasing role in the development of the fishery. After their Revolution, the Americans were given the right to catch and cure fish along unsettled areas of the coasts of the Atlantic Colonies. This of course led to the smuggling of Cape Breton coal to the United States, and rum and American-made goods to the Atlantic colonies—an illegitimate trade which was almost impossible to control given the large number of uninhabited coves. In 1818 Americans were restricted to fishing beyond five kilometres from the coast, except for shelter, repairs, and supplies. While not universally obeyed, this policy— along with the loosening of restrictive trade regulations and the

Nova Scotia government's encouragement of the fishery in the form of bounties and of public works such as wharves and roads—resulted in expanded catches for export to the United States. By the 1830s, the fishery was the centre of Cape Breton's export trade.

Of course, American fishermen often disregarded the five-kilometre limit in the pursuit of fish, especially swarms of mackerel swimming inside the limit, particularly at the Strait of Canso. While there, they purchased supplies and smuggled goods to and from the Strait area—an important part of the economy of that region. The British Government sent in cutters to try to block this trade; in 1853 alone, 162 U.S. vessels were boarded and searched.

Trade relations were finally settled with the signing of the Reciprocity Treaty of 1854, which allowed the mutual exchange of many trade items, including fish, between the United States and British North America. In 1871, the Treaty of Washington opened the American market even wider. Cape Breton's pickled mackerel and salmon found ready purchase in the United States, with expanding markets for herring in the Caribbean, Ontario, and Québec.[19]

By that time, technology was changing rapidly. The market for salt cod was being challenged as the demand for tinned and fresh fish began to grow. By the 1890s, salmon was exported in cans as well as on ice.[20] Canneries opened around the island, employing children as well as men and women, and introducing factory work. Local tinsmiths, many of whom had learned their skills in the United States, came home to set up canneries. By 1874 all four Cape Breton counties had canneries along their coasts. In 1891, there were 32 canneries in Cape Breton[21] which brought a measure of seasonal employment to coastal communities. Both fish and meat were being canned by 1870, and by 1891 there were a dozen meat-packing businesses along the island's coasts.[22]

A direct result of the opening of canneries was the growth of the lobster fishery. To that time the perishable lobster had been useless for export. Now eager New England merchants welcomed the new product, and places like Port Hood, Mabou, Judique, Neil's Harbour, Ingonish, as well as south coast locations like Fourchu, River Bourgeois, Point Michaud, and L'Archeveque together with Isle Madame, all greatly benefitted. Usually controlled by local merchants—or merchants in league with the New Englanders—the canneries in these locations brought income and helped reduce individual debt in rural communities.

The opening of lobster canneries had a profound effect on small coastal communities. An example is the Kennington Cove-Gabarus-Fourchu region. In the 1860s Gabarus was a fishing community with a small shipbuilding industry. The population of the widespread area in 1873 was around 1,780, made up of fishermen, ships' captains, carpenters, and blacksmiths.[23] Fourchu was smaller, with 200 residents.[24] Five lobster canneries were established at or near Gabarus in the last two decades of the century, so that by the early years of the 20th century the area had a population of over 3,000 people and maintained three schools, four churches, and four "large" stores. From Gabarus to Fourchu, shipbuilding expanded. Seven schooners of up to 123 tons were built at Gabarus before 1900, owned or built by wealthy merchants such as the Ormistons, the Rutledges, and the Hardys. Gabarus exported by means of a fleet of 27 large schooners to the Caribbean, Europe, and Africa. Its major import was template, from which lobster cans were made at the canning factories, and waterproof paper, with which the cans were lined. Approximately 200 fishing boats operated out of Gabarus from March to December. They were supplemented by other boats from Framboise, Fourchu, and as far away as Kennington Cove.[25]

The cod fishery—still largely controlled by the Jersey merchants headquartered at Isle Madame and Chéticamp—remained the backbone of Cape Breton's fishing industry. By the 1850s, the Jersey companies had been consolidated into three firms: Charles Robin, Callas and Company, and Decarteret and Le Vesconte. A hallmark of these companies was their extreme conservatism: they stuck to dried salt cod and persisted in exporting to the Caribbean and the south of Europe, each year bringing in their agents—bookkeepers, managers—from the Channel Islands. With time, local merchants began to compete, and fishermen sometimes banded together to purchase fishing boats and share their catch, and the returns. But most small fishermen still had to buy their supplies from the Jersey merchants and, with prices kept low, were on a tight margin of profit and constantly in debt to them.

Despite the lack of technological innovation, catches nearly tripled from 65,500 quintals (3,334,545 kilograms) in 1851 to more than 180,000 quintals (9,163,636 kilograms) by 1890, simply disguising the need for change in the cod fishery.[26] In 1890 the Cape Breton fishery supported 30,000 people. The economic spinoff from these jobs, like shipbuilding and equipment and bait supply, easily supported another 10,000 people out of a total island population of close to 100,000.

THE FISHERY AND AGRICULTURE formed the basis for numerous other Cape Breton industries in the mid to late 19<sup>th</sup> century. Chief among these was Cape Breton's third most important industry, shipbuilding, essential for the shipment of fish, farm products, and coal. There was plenty of timber on the island—pine, hemlock, oak, birch, maple, tamarack, and spruce—some of which was being exported to the English market in the 1820s.[27]

As noted earlier, by 1790 shipbuilding had begun in Sydney when Jerseyman Philip Ingouville started construction of a brig of 101 tons. Called the *Nancy*, this first vessel sailed between Sydney and Halifax with fish, timber, and coal. As the coal trade increased in the 1830s, larger ships were built. The foremost site for shipbuilding remained Arichat—including West Arichat and Little Arichat. In 1812, Bishop Plessis, on a pastoral visit to the island, noted that 40 schooners had been under construction there the previous year. In 1850, another observer noted:

I had never been in Arichat previously—and I was completely astonished at the shipping and the business prospects of the place. To give you an idea of the extent of enterprise displayed, there are now in the stocks, ready for launching, a schooner of 120 tons, owned by Mr. Simon LeBlanc; a schooner about 70 tons, owned by Mr. Crichton; a schooner of 60 tons, by Mr. Benjamin Landrie; a schooner by Mr. Francis Boudrot; a schooner by Mr. Simon Boudrot; a schooner by Mr. Francis Marmaud; a brig by Mr. Anthony Oliver; a brig by Mr. Thomas Le Noir; a brig by Mr. Alex Boudrot; a brig by Mr. Joseph Fouchier;—and at St. Peter's, Mr. Handley has a fine brig ready for launching, and the keel of a large ship laid.[28]

Smaller ships plied the coastal trade, but the brigs and schooners carried fish to Europe and coal to Halifax. By the 1860s they transported coal to the United States, Brazil, Britain and, after Confederation, to Montreal.[29]

In most cases, merchant families—such as the Archibalds of North Sydney, who employed a staff of 50 in the 1830s, Charles Campbell of Victoria County, and the Gammel family of Bras'Or—merchants, traders, investors in coal mining—either constructed their own ships or contracted master builders such as the Moffatts, the Moores, the Musgraves, the Morgans, or the Nesbitts of North Sydney.[30] Remnants of this prosperity are evidenced in the magnificent houses of North Sydney, erected by the shipbuilding families.

At St. Ann's John Munro—first at Munro's Point, later at Shipyard Point—built a variety of ships, purchasing local lumber, employing settlers, and shipping timber to Britain and butter, farm produce, and cattle to Newfoundland. Munro emigrated to New Zealand in 1856 on his brig *Gertrude*, four years after the departure of Norman McLeod. There was an important shipyard at Little Bras d'Or owned by J. S. Christie, the wealthiest merchant in that area. He also built schooners at George's River between 1878 and 1884.

Shipbuilding centres emerged all along the Bras d'Or Lakes, where excellent supplies of lumber were available. In Baddeck,

Charles Campbell became the principal shipowner in Victoria County; he carried on shipbuilding as part of the largest mercantile business there, and undertook coal mining and shipbuilding at New Campbellton. His shipyard built vessels like the *Breadalbane* which carried more of the emigrants to New Zealand.

As Captain John P. Parker writes, "our native workmen were very expert with wood tools and almost any gang recruited in Cape Breton included a large percentage of skilled carpenters."[31] Besides a work force, a blacksmith's forge was needed, as well as a steam plant to run the big saw and provide heat to soften the planks for bending.[32]

By the mid 19th century, there was shipbuilding in virtually every settled cove and port in Cape Breton. In Fourchu it was the Hooper family, in Main-à-Dieu it was the Butlers. The Mira River was home to a number of shipbuilders like Archibald Gillis. John P. Parker in his *Cape Breton Ships and Men*[33] lists 632 sailing vessels built in Cape Breton from 1830 to the 1890s.

The great shipbuilding era peaked in the 1860s when the Reciprocity Treaty with the United States and the American Civil War encouraged trade, and ended in the 1890s as nearby supplies of large timber shrank and steam and steel ships turned shipbuilding into a large-scale industry. The new metal ships were built in places like Glasgow, Scotland. In 1854, 30 wooden vessels were built in Cape Breton; by 1891, the number had dwindled to only seven, totalling a mere 165 tons.[34]

The close alliance between shipping and shipbuilding held through most of the 19th century. Shipping was stimulated by Great Britain in 1828 when Sydney and, soon after, Arichat were made free ports. This meant that ships could go directly to their destinations without a stopover in Halifax for clearance and tonnage dues. This made the shipment of goods quicker and cheaper.[35] In 1850 Britain gave provincial authorities the power to declare free ports, and Port Hood and Ship Harbour (Port Hawkesbury) were soon added to the list. Besides Sydney and Arichat, other ports shipped agricultural products, fish, coal, and small amounts of gypsum to the United States, other Maritime provinces, St. Pierre and Miquelon, and Newfoundland. By 1851 over 1,000 men were employed as sailors and captains in shipping alone.[36]

North Sydney in particular benefitted from increased shipping after the mid 19th century. Included in the term "Sydney Harbour," North Sydney—also known as North Bar—had first served as a port of coal shipment from Sydney Mines. Its importance grew from 1834, when its first coal shipping pier was completed. At that time Samuel Cunard, who had managed to win a bi-monthly mail contract from Liverpool, England, to North America, acquired land nearby and built a wharf where his ships took on supplies.[37] North Sydney henceforth became a centre of shipping as well as shipbuilding.

In 1840, a regular sailing packet service was established at North Sydney linking Halifax and St. John's, Newfoundland. The advent of coastal steamships in the 1840s and 1850s made North Sydney an essential refuelling stop. By 1855 North Sydney replaced Sydney for the Registry of Shipping, and as the local Port of Entry and Clearance.[38]

Richard John Uniacke, rector of St. George's Church, Sydney (1853-1877), described North Bar in the 1860s:

> At this place the coal from the Mines is shipped and carried off to various parts of America. A bustling scene is here presented. Some fine ships are often seen upon the stocks; and beside the ordinary colliers, which are anchored around waiting for their freight—large steamers plying between England, Central America and Quebec are often at the wharf loading for their voyage. British men-of-War (sic), and more frequently French naval steamers on the Newfoundland station, continually call in here to replenish their fuels.... This part of the [Sydney] river and its neighbourhood is often called North Sydney....[39]

By the 1870s, North Sydney was Canada's fourth port in gross tonnage, superseded only by Québec, Halifax, and Montreal. Coal shipments continued to rise, from 109,259 tons in 1879 to 913,549 tons in 1896.[40] At the same time, North Sydney became the great supplier for the 200- to 300-vessel fishing fleet from Gloucester, Massachusetts. The opening of the St. Peter's Canal in 1867 made North Sydney a centre for trade between St. Pierre, Baddeck, and Arichat. With the completion of the transatlantic cable in 1866, the area's chief Western Union office was established at North Sydney, making it a key link in intercontinental communications, a role that would grow in importance in the next century.[41]

The prosperity of the merchants of North Sydney in the latter years of the 19ᵗʰ century is seen in the fine mansions that still stand, such as those of George B. Moffatt (1867), Alexander Bertram (1875), Thomas S. Bown (c. 1868), C. Bedford Thompson (1865), and William A. Moore (c. 1867).

Though land transportation remained poor in western Cape Breton throughout the 19ᵗʰ century, good harbours such as Port Hood, and settlements along the Gut of Canso, attracted shipping and commerce. In Port Hood, the opening of coal mines in the 1890s spurred on this growth; by then four hotels, stores, a newspaper, and even a bottling company joined with several lobster canneries to add to Port Hood's role as regional municipal and economic centre. Throughout the 19ᵗʰ century, Port Hood shipped potatoes, oats, butter, cheese, salt, beef, and pork, especially to Newfoundland, competing with Arichat, Port Hawkesbury, and Sydney as a shipping port.[42]

Port Hood as well as Port Hastings and Port Hawkesbury had long supplied and traded with American fishermen heading through the Gut of Canso toward the Gulf of St. Lawrence fishery, or returning from the Grand Banks. The Reciprocity (Free Trade) Treaty of 1854 with the United States—plus Port Hood and Port Hawkesbury's status as free ports—meant that customs offices operating there facilitated commerce with the

Americans. Prosperous merchants like William McKeen and Peter Smyth benefitted immensely from this trade. Smyth's fine stone Georgian home near Port Hood still stands as witness to his wealth.[43]

Port Hastings' location on the Gut of Canso made it a natural communications centre. Ships carrying mail and passengers between Cape Breton and the mainland made it a transportation focal point. Before railways, Henry A. Archibald with a "fleet" of around 100 horses contracted to carry goods and passengers from Port Hastings to places as far away as Chéticamp, Baddeck, and North Sydney.

With the arrival of the telegraph in the 1840s, masts or towers had been erected on the top of Cape Porcupine on the mainland and at Port Hastings. Although they sagged and impeded sailing ships, the telegraph lines were a necessary nuisance. The laying of the transatlantic cable in 1866 solved this problem; a submarine cable under the Gut of Canso and the opening of a cable and telegraph office at Port Hastings made it a key link in international communications.[44]

A major shipbuilding site, Baddeck was also a shipping centre, particularly after the mid-1850s, exporting livestock to St. Pierre and Miquelon and importing wines, brandy, and manufactured products like finer clothing of French and American design.[45] In the *Cape Breton News* of 1 October 1853 we read that during that season 14 cargoes consisting of cattle, butter, lumber, barrel staves, and sheep, valued at £7000, were shipped from Baddeck to Newfoundland. Big Bras d'Or was another cattle, sheep, and produce shipping centre. In 1885 it was surpassed by Margaree Harbour, which was second only to Baddeck in cattle exports.[46]

OTHER LARGELY RURAL INDUSTRIES were closely related to agriculture. To protect the local market and stimulate local flour production, the government of Nova Scotia gave capital grants for the erection of kilns and grist mills, for drying and grinding grains. Starting in 1834, two were erected in Cape Breton. During the famine of the 1840s the government encouraged the growth of oats to replace wheat, which was prone to attack by the wheat fly. As a result, between 1851 and 1853, 21 mills and kilns were erected. The first steam grist mill in Nova Scotia was built by James Anderson at Sydney in 1843.[47]

Millstones were tailored locally but iron fittings were imported, though fashioned by local blacksmiths. There was an iron foundry in Lingan, Cape Breton County, as early as the 1860s, casting metal worth £1,200, used in the local mine.[48] In 1871 alone Cape Breton had 149 blacksmith shops employing 221 people.[49] Besides working for mills, blacksmiths produced carriages of which there were only 19 officially listed on the island in 1871, and 30 in 1881.[50] Blacksmiths played an important role in the life of each community. Colin Cash of Irish Cove not only forged horseshoes but made carriages, horse-drawn sleighs, cart wheels and hubs, and wagons. In July and August of 1882 alone he made 11 wagons. People came to him for service and wagons from as far away as North River.[51]

Mills for the carding and fulling of wool were less common, but as the number of sheep increased and the population became more affluent and could afford to have the work done outside their homes, the number of such mills increased, reaching 17 in 1881.[52] A well-known fulling, dyeing, and dressing mill was opened by Angus MacDonald at Middle River in 1852, just as the local economy there rebounded from the famine.[53] An even more famous fulling mill was erected by Donald MacLean MacDonald, who came to Mabou in 1848 at the age of 23. He soon added a dyeing mill, hence the name "Glendyer Mill." After his death in 1866, his sons took over the business and, in 1880, set up the integrated Glendyer Woolen Mills, the first of its kind in Cape Breton. Despite a fire that totally destroyed the works in 1885, the industry flourished and provided local employment for up to 50 people.[54]

Other features of the countryside in the 19th century were sawmills, again located near streams that could be dammed. Local timber was used, and barrel staves and lumber and shingles were produced for second-generation housing that replaced the log cabin.

Small industry was everywhere. The Canadian Census of 1891 lists 1420 industrial establishments in Cape Breton County, 529 in Inverness, 245 in Victoria, and 94 in Richmond.[55] Writing of 1871, the economist M. C. MacLean commented:

> It is a striking fact that of the 111 [manufactured] items or group of items listed in the [Canadian] census [of 1871] one or other of the Cape Breton counties led in 62. When we remember that the population of the island was only one-fiftieth of that of Canada, we realize the magnitude of the achievement.[56]

Emerging communities—like Baddeck, Port Hood, Mabou, Sydney, Ship Harbour (Port Hawkesbury), and Arichat—were the locations for tradesmen such as carpenters, saddle and harness makers, furniture makers, carriage makers, and shoemakers, as well as tailors, printers, and family businesses supplying exotic imports like tea and rum.

Despite these settlements, the island was mainly rural. In 1891, there were around 4,000 people living on Isle Madame with only 370 in Arichat town. The other largest settlements were North Sydney (2,513), Big Glace Bay (2,459), Sydney Mines (2,442) and Sydney (2,426). Though not incorporated, the Chéticamp district—extending for 30 kilometres along the shores of the Gulf of St. Lawrence—was home to 3,142 people.[57] This, with a total island population of 100,000.

THE LARGER SETTLEMENTS were generally found near water. There was no scheduled boat transport on the island before the 1840s, all travel arrangements being made on the spot. And any trip could be hazardous. Around 1823, Judge John Marshall described trying to reach Cape Breton in the spring:

> As the drift ice was constantly passing along the Strait [of Canso], I was apprehensive that if I did not get over, the ice might be brought down more closely and heavily, and so block up the passage.... The ferryman was [away] from home, and there was no boat at the place. [Likely at Port Mulgrave. Marshall heard of a boat available a kilometre or more up the coast; he found the boat and two men to row.] It was not until we got a short distance, that I perceived the boat was very leaky, and that both of the men were what is commonly described as "the worse for liquor"— in fact they were *intoxicated.*

Marshall carried on anyway. "There was a small tin measure in the boat, which I kept in constant use, in hopes to keep the water in the boat so low as to reach the opposite shore in safety." The boat was swept along past their hoped-for landing place to the base of a high cliff that plunged into the water. They decided not to risk a landing and to go back but just then "a cake of ice was driven against one side of the bow of the boat, which threw her round, so as greatly to endanger her being upset." They managed to turn the boat around, but "finding the water in the boat still increasing, and that it had gained nearly a third of her depth, I took off my hat and employed it in discharging water, during the rest of the passage back." They reached the shore more than a kilometre below where they had started. He did not reach Cape Breton for two more days.[58]

A trip from Sydney to St. Peter's meant a canoe paddled by Mi'kmaq via Sydney River with a portage near East Bay, hence the present name "Portage." Up until the 1840s, most long trips were undertaken with the aid of the Mi'kmaq, both male and female. Like Judge Dodd earlier, whenever Judge John Marshall performed his judicial circuit, which included all the county seats on the island, "large portions of my journeys were performed in Indian canoes, in which I have sometimes passed a great part or whole of the night, occasionally paddling to lessen chilliness, and to afford the poor tired Squaw a partial relief."[59] The trip to Port Hood from Sydney, over 150 kilometres, was particularly arduous, "nearly two-thirds of it were performed with Indians in bark canoe, and during the whole of the journey, of three days and nights, I never parted with an atom of my apparel, except hats and boots...."[60]

Reliable transportation to Halifax appears to have begun in 1828, when Sydney Captain John Lorway's schooner the *Nancy* began a summer passenger-and-freight run.[61] By 1839, Arichat had regular steam communication with Halifax.[62] Steamboats had reached Cape Breton shores 14 August 1830, when the *Richard Smith* entered Sydney Harbour, "to the consternation...of the finny tribes, and to the wonder of the terrestrial inhabitants of this harbor." The steamboat belonged to the General Mining Association and was built at Pictou. The local militia turned out and gave a salute of 13 rounds from two field pieces. The rejoicing can be compared to the 1955 opening of the Canso Causeway, representing—like that project—a major step toward overcoming Cape Breton's isolation. A public dinner was held, followed by a trip by "officers of the garrison and gentlemen of the town" up the Bras d'Or. The *Smith* then made a circuit of the harbour, "with an assemblage of the youth and beauty of Sydney" at the rate of 15 or 16 kilometres an hour, "as if unconscious of [the] opposition [of the water]."[63]

Another step came after 1844, when Cape Breton benefitted from reliable international mail service with Britain and Boston.[64]

The expansion of shipping, travel, and communications came up against the reality of the dangers involved: the rugged seacoast without lighthouses or rescue stations. St. Paul's—20 kilometres northeast of Cape Breton—and Scatarie Island—off the easternmost point of Cape Breton—were dangerous dark islands waiting for ships. In the early part of the 19th century an average of five ships a year were wrecked somewhere in Cape Breton. The English ship, *Sovereign*, carrying 800 troops on their way home after the War of 1812, sank off St. Paul's Island with only 12 survivors.[65] Petitions were sent asking for the erection of a lighthouse there. After bickering as to which government should undertake the project, the governments of all three Maritime colonies and Canada finally set up rescue stations on St. Paul's Island in 1832.

But the need for a light remained. On 8 May 1834, a 207-passenger emigrant ship *Astrea*, from Ireland heading for Québec, struck a rock eight kilometres east of Louisbourg near Little Lorraine. Only three people were saved. Bodies were strewn along the coast, "a prey of pigs, dogs, fish etc." This news helped provoke the establishment of lighthouses—first at St. Paul's Island in 1837, then at Scatarie two years later.[66]

Almost as important as the Atlantic routes was the internal steamboat travel on the Bras d'Or Lakes and the Mira River. These runs boosted local trade and improved the chance for timely arrival of goods at Arichat, North Sydney, and Port Hood for scheduled shipment abroad. In 1846 George Handley, a Halifax merchant, began a fortnightly steamer service through the Bras d'Or Lakes to Sydney. Between runs, the steamer supplied regular service between Sydney and North Sydney.[67]

By 1852, the side-wheeler *Banshee* became the first steamer built in Cape Breton and the first to perform scheduled lake service. Constructed at Bras d'Or, its machinery was brought from England; the hull was sheathed in galvanized iron. Runs from Sydney to Bras d'Or, Baddeck, Whycocomagh, and St. Peter's carried passengers, farm produce, cattle, tea, and rum between these ports. The formation of the Bras d'Or Steamship Company by Captains J. Howard Beatty and George Burchell of North Sydney brought in enough capital to buy ferries like *Lady of the Lake* and the *Magnolia*, a former hospital ship of the American Civil War. The *Magnolia* eventually served as a link for train traffic between Baddeck and Iona. The company also introduced the *Neptune* between East Bay and Port Mulgrave on the Nova Scotia mainland, as well as the *May Queen* which ran between Baddeck and Whycocomagh. When the railroad was completed across Cape Breton in 1891, the ferries continued to serve settlements at a distance from the tracks. The *May Queen* herself then served as one in a long line of scheduled ferries sailing between Sydney and North Sydney. It was replaced by the *Peerless*, then the *Electronic*, and finally the *Mary*, which ceased operations in 1947.

The sidewheeler *Marion* was put into operation by the Bras d'Or Steamship Company in 1883 and followed the weekly Sydney-Baddeck-Mulgrave run in conjunction with the *Neptune's* East Bay-Mulgrave route. Though more comfortable than road travel, it still had its complainers. Despite inconveniences, boats remained essential well into the 20th century. The *Neptune*, the last lake steamer, ran until 1922, ending its life as a coal barge before it was deliberately sunk in Muggah Creek, Sydney.

There were also numerous smaller ferries subsidized by the provincial government, at Mira Ferry (later Albert Bridge), Mira Gut, Lennox Passage, and the well-remembered *Minnehaha* at Lake Ainslie.

ANOTHER MAJOR LINK in the transportation chain was the long-debated St. Peter's Canal. As we have seen, the narrow isthmus between the Bras d'Or Lakes and the ocean at St. Peter's was used as a haulover for centuries by the Mi'kmaq, as well as by merchants like Nicolas Denys and Laurence Kavanagh. It had been fortified by the French as Port Toulouse. After Cape Breton was annexed to Nova Scotia in 1820, shippers and merchants on Isle Madame sought markets in the United States, around the Bras d'Or Lakes, and in the Sydney area. Since Sydney was 70 kilometres closer to Arichat via the Lakes than by the dangerous outside passage around Scatarie Island, they began to pressure for a canal to be cut through the isthmus at St. Peter's. There was also discussion of another canal at Portage which would allow goods to sail from Sydney through East Bay to St. Peter's, shortening the distance even more.[68]

148

The proposed Shubenacadie Canal on the Nova Scotia mainland had recently been surveyed, and the province decided to use the remaining funds to hire an engineer to survey the Cape Breton isthmus at St. Peter's.[69] In 1825 Francis Hall reported that a 2,700-foot canal, 21 feet wide and 13 feet deep, could be constructed for around $68,000. There was no immediate movement, but in 1840 an act was passed incorporating the St. Peter's Canal Company. Further surveys followed but, as the years went by, controversy brewed as to whether a railroad across the island might be a better investment than the canal, since a railroad—replacing most commercial sailing—would render the canal useless.[70]

By the 1850s the government gave in and tried to attract private investment to the canal project.[71] When this failed, the government undertook the project—but only in fits and starts. 1854 saw 200 men, "grubbing and clearing...trees and brushwood, removing manure heaps, taking down and replacing fences and cutting...trees near the Atlantic shore."[72] But the job proved a greater challenge than anticipated and began to drag. Mainland politicians reviled it as a "ditch" that should be abandoned—and work was suspended. Politicians from Cape Breton persisted, and the job started up again in 1864.

Given the primitive equipment, the St. Peter's Canal was a major engineering project. It entailed cutting through a solid granite hill for most of the canal's 800-metre (2,600-foot) length. The dredging suffered numerous setbacks with rock falls. Locks and gates had to be installed, strong enough to withstand the different tidal levels between the Bras d'Or Lakes and the Atlantic Ocean.

Patrick Purcell, a contractor and successful railroad and canal builder from Upper Canada, was finally hired and, with more money from the new federal government, the project was completed in 1869.[73]

Again and again, the size of ships out-paced the width of the canal and though it was twice enlarged—in 1875-1881 and in 1912-1917—it could not handle the traffic.[74]

More significant was the arrival of the railroad in Cape Breton, which drew traffic from the water routes and eventually destroyed not only the Bras d'Or Lakes ferry service but any hopes for the success of the St. Peter's Canal. Arichat, already in decline with the advent of steamships which simply passed through that port on their way to and from the Bras d'Or Lakes, was now further hurt by the railroad since goods were carried east and west through the centre of the island via the Sydney-Grand Narrows-Port Hastings tracks.

RELATIVE EASE OF WATER TRANSPORT on Cape Breton had always made the development of roads less urgent. Before the island's annexation to mainland Nova Scotia, roads were hardly more than paths between homes. The French had established land links between Louisbourg and the Mira River, across Boularderie Island, and to Gabarus. Under British rule, Lieutenant-Governor DesBarres planned roads spoking out from Sydney, some of which were cleared before 1820. These included the road to Mira in the 1790s, the Cow Bay Road, and the road from Sydney along the North West Arm to North Bar (today's North Sydney) and on to Sydney Mines, with a branch to Coxheath.

A start was made before 1820 on the road from Sydney to St. Peter's—today's Route 4—called the "King's (or Post) Road," though in the end it did not follow the route drawn by DesBarres. Instead, as today it hugged the shore of Sydney River to Portage where 19th century travellers would canoe up the Bras d'Or Lakes to St. Peter's. By land, the path westward to East Bay was treacherous and hard to follow.

In 1798 Reverend James McGregor lost his way in the 10-kilometre portage between East Bay and Sydney River and was terrified of attack by "water kelpies," strange highland beasts he expected to encounter. He finally gave up and returned to East

Bay, sailing across the lake and through the Great Bras d'Or channel to Sydney—a 60-kilometre trip.

At Portage, the Mi'kmaq guided travellers to East Bay. They would paddle and carry the canoes, but passengers were expected to transport their own provisions and spare clothing on a pole on their shoulders as they waded through brooks. From East Bay, passengers often helped paddle to St. Peter's where they might stay with the affable Laurence Kavanagh family. Next day, they would leave from there for D'Escousse, sailing up the Gut of Canso to the Strait area—today's Port Hastings—where the Balhashe (or Balhace) family provided overnight lodgings.[75] If a traveller continued by land west of East Bay, there was a provincially subsidized "house of entertainment"—the equivalent of a bed-and-breakfast—at Red Islands where one could spend the night.[76]

The only other roads of any significance were one that ran across Isle Madame from Grand Digue to Arichat; another from Baddeck Bridge and Big Baddeck to Margaree (called "the Old Road"); and possibly one from Judique over River Denys Mountain.

Nova Scotia's Lieutenant-Governor Sir James Kempt, visiting the St. Peter's area in 1826, found the roads terrible and felt road money had been injudiciously spent in Cape Breton—"almost indeed thrown away." The road along the Bras d'Or toward St. Peter's (Route 4), was "almost impassible."[77] A newer road between Grand Digue and Ship Harbour (Port Hawkesbury) was in better condition.[78] Kempt used some of his discretionary money to develop main roads, and the following year £300 was set aside to improve the main post road between Sydney and St. Peter's.[79]

Road commissioners, whose job it was to oversee construction, were political appointees who often had only slight knowledge of road-building techniques. Each able-bodied landowner was expected to perform roadwork, and the amount paid depended not on the amount of work done but on the time spent on the job.

This led to inefficiency and waste. Wealthier people could pay others to do their roadwork. Farmers, who rarely saw coin, worked on the roads to pay taxes or, begrudgingly, to avoid fines.[80] Roadwork became a form of political payment to labourers, and often alcohol was exchanged as part of the pay or to avoid working on the roads.

One of the prime challenges to road building, especially in Inverness and Victoria counties, was the narrow space that farmers, loath to give up any property, allowed along cliffs for right of way. People frequently fell over the edges when roads were swept away by storms. A ten-kilometre-long trail was blazed in the early 1820s between Margaree and Chéticamp, which Judge John Marshall described as "passable for foot passengers."[81]

By the 1830s the road between East Bay and St. Peter's was still only a saddle road, but was safe enough that judges could go from Sydney to St. Peter's on horseback instead of by canoe.[82] Farmers brought their produce to the Sydney market on drays— a pair of poles, one end hanging on each side of the horse, the other end dragging on the ground—thus negotiating the rutted roads. The poles were left behind in town for firewood and the rider returned home on horseback. A drawback to this efficient system seemed to be the cows that roamed the streets; they ate the horses' harnesses, which were made of straw.[83]

Within the next few decades after the 1830s, trails were being constructed around St. Ann's Harbour in Victoria County, through North River Bridge to near Indian Brook. This was the beginning of the North Shore Road as far as Ingonish. Still, the only safe way to travel north of Cape Smokey before the 1850s was by boat. The first route between Englishtown and Cape Smokey was little more than a footpath, developed along the shore in the 1850s. Beyond Ingonish to Cape North, it was "over crags and cliffs and trackless mountains." In many places the essential Mi'kmaw guide had to cut tracks with an axe to prevent travellers from "tumbling headlong into eternity."[84] By 1853 there was the semblance of a road from Ingonish to Aspy Bay, though it was described as merely a mud path.[85]

The road was finally more or less passable to Bay St. Lawrence in the 1860s. Cape Smokey remained a formidable barrier, especially with the winter snow and spring mud. A narrow footpath was blazed, but it was too treacherous for most travellers. By 1874 a rough road for wagon travel over Smokey Mountain was completed. This in effect opened Ingonish to the rest of Cape Breton.[86] In the late 1870s, the provincial government began opening "halfway houses" to put up travellers at Neil's Harbour, Cap Rouge near Chéticamp (1902), and at Fishing Cove near Pleasant Bay (1878).[87] These halfway houses provided food and shelter and were points where local mail could be dropped off.

The Gulf or Inverness side of Cape Breton remained neglected. A road between Chéticamp and Pleasant Bay was built in the 1850s, but it hardly deserved the name, since it could not accommodate carriages or even wagons.

Roads of varying width and reliability were forged by mid-century across Boularderie Island and from Louisbourg along the coast to Main-à-Dieu, Lennox Passage to River Inhabitants, Ship Harbour to West Bay—an extension of the original Post or King's Road—and Whycocomagh to Lake Ainslie, with branches to Port Hood, Mabou, and Broad Cove.

Between Sydney and Louisbourg, roads were in good enough condition by the 1840s that two-wheeled horse-drawn gigs could negotiate the distance, though Sydney's postmaster, Robert Martin, claimed he took from early morning till after dark to make the trip.[88] There were still no carriage routes across the island in the 1840s. Even near Sydney carriage travel was impossible in 1844,[89] and canoe remained the best way to make a journey.[90]

By the 1850s, however, the King's or Post Road to St. Peter's was in fair enough condition that a coach could go "in stages" of

24 kilometres and reach the Strait of Canso in two days. "Our Cape Breton stage is an easy, two-seated vehicle; a quiet little rockaway-wagon, with a top," wrote one traveller.[91] It was drawn by three or four horses depending on travel conditions. From Sydney, it stopped at Big Pond, then Red Islands, then changed horses, coach and driver at St. Peter's,[92] leaving the next day for Plaister Cove (Port Hastings). After an overnight stay, a ferry would take passengers across the Strait to the Nova Scotia mainland, where they boarded a coach to link up with the railroad at Truro.

However, all bets were off in winter and especially in spring. In March 1854 the member for Victoria County, on his way to the sitting of the provincial legislature, took 18 days getting from his home in Baddeck to the Gut of Canso and another eight days to reach Halifax.[93]

During the 1860s, the Post Road from Sydney to the Strait of Canso had so much improved that horse-drawn carriages could negotiate the route in one day—still in 15 stages, using 46 horses. This was truly a revolution in communications and coincided with progress in lake-ferry travel and the first telegraph line (1851) across the island, which followed that same road.[94]

"Down North" travel was not so smooth. The terrain was the most challenging on the island. Between 1873 and 1887 a carriage track was finally carved out between Smokey Mountain and Cape North. But the area remained isolated, especially in winter. As late as the 1920s, two teams of men, working toward one another, shovelled the length of Smokey Mountain to get the mail through.[95]

For this reason, the settlers were careful to complete all preparations for winter by that time; they made their last trip to North Sydney for supplies in December and, with few exceptions, did not leave their own community again till spring.[96]

Finally, in 1891 a better wagon road was completed over Smokey, "although it was only wide enough to accommodate one wagon at a time."[97] In the same year an "excellent road" was ready for use between Ingonish and Aspy Bay. On the more neglected Gulf side, a trail was blazed eastward from Pleasant Bay to the Victoria County line in 1893, but it was dangerously precipitous and narrow.

As we shall see, it was not the needs of the local inhabitants that led to the final improvement of the roads on the island, but the growing tourist industry.

THE MOST PROMISING transportation development by the 1860s was the railroad, since it could carry large, heavy loads of commodities like coal to nearby ports for shipment abroad and to the growing markets in the continental North American interior. Cape Bretoners had some familiarity with railroads since the 1830s when wooden tracks were first laid for the horse-drawn haulage of coal cars from Sydney Mines to nearby shipping piers at North Sydney. There was a burst of railroad fever during the 1860s when the combination of the American Civil War and free trade of the Reciprocity Act attracted American capital in its search for coal to sell in the United States. In 1864, the International Coal and Railway Company was incorporated by New York capitalists headed by John Jacob Astor. In the same year another American, Robert Belloni, formed a group incorporated as the Louisbourg Railway Company to build a railroad from the coal reserves at Cow Bay (Port Morien) to the ice-free port at Louisbourg. These initiatives were put on hold, however, when Reciprocity was cancelled by the Americans in 1866.

With Confederation in 1867, the promise of new Canadian markets for coal loomed. By 1870, the Glasgow and Cape Breton Railroad Company had built an 18-kilometre stretch of track from Reserve Mines to an International Wharf, which Sydney residents demanded be located far from town—the site of the present Cambridge Suites Hotel. In 1881 this company, the Lorway, and the Schooner Pond Coal Company joined to become the Sydney and

Louisbourg Coal and Railway Company, established to carry passengers as well as coal between Louisbourg and Sydney.[98]

Across the island, the coal reserves at Broad Cove in Inverness County also attracted attention. In 1874, the first incorporation took place of a hundred-kilometre rail line between Broad Cove and the Strait of Canso.[99] It was not until 1901 that the railroad magnates MacKenzie and Mann completed it as the Inverness and Richmond Railway.[100]

The Halifax and Cape Breton Railway and Coal Company developed plans to construct an extension from New Glasgow to Louisbourg—with a train ferry link across the Strait of Canso—but was unable to raise the capital. The federal government took over the company as part of the Intercolonial Railway, which it planned to extend from Windsor, Ontario, through to Sydney.

Surveys for the line were completed in 1886, but the question of the route the ICR would follow across Cape Breton raised controversy. One possibility was a southern route from the Strait of Canso to Louisbourg, while the other—known as the Central Route—would cross the Barra Strait at Grand Narrows, continuing to Sydney via East Bay. The Central Route was strongly lobbied for by H. F. MacDougall, MP and cabinet minister from Victoria County. He argued that 40,150 people living within 16 kilometres of both sides of this route would be served, while the southern route would serve only 23,932. The central region tapped more fertile areas for the shipment of grain, potatoes, and hay, not to mention the coal from the Sydney region.

The supporters of the southern route alleged that the cantilever bridge that would have to be built at Grand Narrows would block boat traffic. MacDougall replied that only 10 to 15 ships sailed through the Narrows daily and, besides, the southern route would miss the limestone mines in Victoria County and the coal mines at New Campbellton.[101]

Political favouritism and the argument that this line would

open up the most land with the fewest branch lines won the day for the Central Route. In the end, though, the train passed through Bras d'Or rather than East Bay.

In 1887 work was begun on the line from Point Tupper to Iona, and on the Sydney-to-Grand Narrows section. At the same time the 1,494-foot-long railroad bridge over the Barra Strait was constructed.

The prospective cost of the bridge was alarming to politicians. To ensure its completion MacDougall invited Prime Minister Sir John A. Macdonald to Cape Breton to convince him of its necessity.

The Grand Narrows bridge was a major engineering feat. The water there was 90 feet deep in places. Under the supervision of R. G. Reid—the man who was contracted to complete the Intercolonial Railway across Cape Breton Island, and the same man who oversaw the building of the railroad across Newfoundland—the bridge was finished in 1891. It cost an alarming $530,000—a sum about which Sir John A. Macdonald said, "I do not regret it for a moment."[102]

The completed bridge sat on 90-foot pillars sunk into the bedrock, rising 4 or 5 feet above the surface of the lake. The pillars had been constructed by first building and sinking wooden cofferdams, then pumping out the water and sending men down to dig into the bedrock and put in anchoring bars—big long bolts. Captain John Parker told the story years later:

> They couldn't pour. They didn't have cement like that in those days. Cut stone. And build up the pier from the bedrock [90 feet below] to a distance say of 4 or 5 feet above high tide.... The tide is 6 feet. Big stones, good size, mortared them together....[103]

Cement piers were placed on the pillars. The bridge was floated on barges in sections and lowered onto the piers.[104] The bridge was ready for use 15 July 1889 when an impromptu group, made up of H. F. MacDougall and a few guests, boarded a flatcar and made the first rail crossing of the Barra Strait.[105]

But there were more challenges than the Grand Narrows crossing. One narrative describes:

At Little Crossing, near Alba, it was found necessary to construct three trestles before a base was found. Immediately the bridge was finished it commenced to move upstream until, finally, it was so out of line trains could not negotiate it.... It was learned afterwards that the bridge was erected over a plaster deposit which failed to provide the footing required. Eventually solid rock was reached and an immovable base was provided.[106]

Another serious problem occurred west of Orangedale where the tracks mysteriously disappeared in a swamp under seven feet of water. A train passing through stuck to the rails, however, and got through. Huge loads of fill solved the problem.

The completed line was offically opened in the summer of 1891 when Governor General Lord Stanley and his party crossed the island, passing through "profusely decorated" towns and villages along the route, to end up in Sydney. There Mayor Colin MacKinnon met the party, which paraded under a triumphal arch erected on Charlotte Street.

In 1884, the Cape Breton Extension Railroad was incorporated. It was planned to run from Port Hawkesbury to Louisbourg via St. Peter's, for shipping winter mail and coal through Louisbourg's harbour. By September 1903, the line was opened as far as St. Peter's. The rest was never completed; it cost too much to build through the difficult terrain leading to Louisbourg. The completed section to St. Peter's was eventually purchased by the Canadian government and added to the Intercolonial Railway network in 1920.[107]

As well as giving faster passenger service, the railroads reduced the isolation of communities, especially those located at a distance from water; and they speeded up delivery of coal and other commodities to outlying island settlements—spelling the end of the Bras d'Or Lakes steamship service. As well, the St. Peter's Canal's importance declined, further dashing Arichat's hopes of becoming a major hub of commerce. The village of St. Peter's, on the Cape Breton Extension Railroad, soon outpaced declining Arichat as a service centre, leaving it as a small fishing village.[108]

The railroad heralded the end of the 19th century economy and, more important, prepared the way for Cape Breton's major economic developments of the next century.

ALL OF THAT DEVELOPMENT would rest on one commodity—coal. The coal industry had been slow to grow due to poor technology and restricted markets. Beginning in the 1720s, the French had taken coal from the cliffs at Lingan for heating and smelting purposes, but the availability of wood made it cheaper and easier to use than coal. After the fall of Louisbourg (1758), British troops stationed at Lingan undertook some mining and erected a blockhouse near the workings to protect it from Yankee smugglers and raids during the American Revolution. A later mine located there was called the "Blockhouse Pit." A mine worked by troops was also opened at present-day Sydney Mines to supply the needs of regional troops. Governor DesBarres assumed control of these works in 1785, and they were operated by local merchants like Thomas Moxley, Richard Stout, Ritchie and Leaver, and the Bown family on short-term leases. Moxley simply sank pits into the seams and hauled out the surface coal, leaving ruined and flooded holes in the ground.

It was not until James Miller arrived in the 1790s that real technological progress was made. Miller was an Irish-born geologist who understood the nature of coal and, working with local merchant Richard Stout, ran levels into the seams through the cliffs at Sydney Mines. He emphasized drainage, the hiring of trained colliers, and shipment of the product.

Miller and the operators faced a number of challenges. Though coal was dug at Sydney Mines, the coast there is exposed and wharves were continually swept away by storm and ice. The quality of the output was poor, since it was not graded and sizes varied from dust to boulders. It could not compete with the British product which, due to more advanced technology—including steam engines to haul coal and drain the mines and advanced coal screening methods—was cheaper and of better quality. As well, colonial authorities restricted use of Cape Breton's coal to heating and to the needs of the naval yards and troops in Nova Scotia and Newfoundland. There was no question of permitting the use of coal for any local industrial development that would lead to competition with the mother country.

The work force was a motley crew, many of them Irish from the Newfoundland fishery who mined, some for twelve months, others for four at a time, the latter supplementing their living by farming or fishing. Their lives were rough, sheltered

in two barracks or cook-rooms (as they were called), where they took their meals and slept in the same apartments...it may easily be imagined what sort of a place the cook-room was, where forty men ate, slept and washed—when they did wash, which was only once a week—in a single apartment...in summer it became so very *lively* that most of the men preferred sleeping...under the spruce trees in the vicinity.... Brawling and fighting seemed to be the order, or rather the disorder of the day, from Monday until Saturday, Sunday being truly a day of rest, which, strange to say, was devoutly observed.[109]

In 1823 Judge Marshall described the miners as "lawless and violent characters." When one of their number was convicted in Sydney for violating a woman and was on his way to prison in Halifax aboard a coal boat which stopped to load at Sydney Mines,

[a] lawless band [of miners] with their faces disguised, rushed down the Shute, as it is called, by which the coal was being conveyed into the vessel, seized and secured the guards, carried away the prisoner to a blacksmith's shop near the mines, had his irons taken off, and set him at liberty.[110]

The man was never recovered by authorities, but Marshall was ready for the next incident.

This time it involved a shipwreck near Sydney. A boat which was on its return from salvaging some of the cargo, "was proceeding to Sydney, and in passing up the mouth of the harbour, near to the grounds where the coal mines were situated, a band of the lawless labourers there, went off to the boat, and after threatening the persons in charge of the goods, to throw them overboard, if they resisted, they carried off the goods...." When the sheriff from Sydney went over, he found "a large band, with various arms, prepared to oppose him, a part of their defenses being a small mounted swivel, ready for action." When Marshall got news of this, he ordered 20 riflemen from the Sydney garrison to take charge. They landed about six kilometres from the mines and went the rest of the way by land. "None dared to offer any opposition, or hindrance." They captured a miner and proceeded to search the miners' quarters. One man escaped, but no one dared go after him since he was "a very powerful man" and fully armed. However, the quick action worked, and Marshall declared "that visit...to the miners, had such good effects, that ever after, the laws could be as readily and peaceably enforced in that locality, as in any other quarter."[111]

The mine operators supplied the miners with goods on credit, a precursor of company stores and company control of all aspects of workers' lives. Miners escaped by leaving for the fishery, their debts unpaid. This unstable work force was rarely above 100 men. Though there was some specialization, jobs were interchangeable: cutting coal, loading it into tubs, propping the roofs of the levels. Some served aboveground as cooks, boatmen, stable keepers, and hoist operators.[112]

Large-scale mining did not develop until external forces intervened. The mines by royal prerogative belonged to the Crown, which in the 18ᵗʰ century was literally the King. In 1788 George III gave his son, the Duke of York, a 60-year lease to the unworked mineral resources of Nova Scotia. In the years following, the duke contracted a number of gambling debts and in 1825, in order to pay them, turned to his jewellers, the firm of Rundell, Bridges and Rundell. He proposed that he sublet the lease to them. In the spring of 1826, the jewellers sent out their agent, a young mining engineer named Richard Brown, to investigate the resource. Brown reported back that the coal reserves, both in Cape Breton and in Pictou County, were extremely promising. In 1827 the jewellers set up a joint stock company, the General Mining Association (G.M.A.), to develop the resource. The G.M.A. negotiated with the government of Nova Scotia for a fixed rent of £3,000 a year while the duke would receive one-fourth of the net profits. Richard Brown would stay on as general manager.

The long-term lease of the G.M.A. allowed it to undertake reasonable planning and commit large expenditures to the development of the Sydney coal field.[113] By 1846 the G.M.A. had spent some £300,000 developing the mines at Cape Breton and Pictou.[114] Steam-powered engines were installed to drain the mine levels and to power winding winches to raise the coal. New mine shafts were dug, coal was now sorted, and in 1834 a permanent rail line was constructed to a sandbar up the harbour, known simply as "The Bar"—today's North Sydney, the root of its nickname "Bartown." The sandbar protected the wharves from storm and ice; this permitted secure shipping conditions and led to the growth of settlement there.

Another new mine was opened further down the coast at Bridgeport, named for Robert Bridge, treasurer of the G.M.A. The G.M.A. made improvements hoping to capture the American market. They had succeeded in pressuring the provincial government to declare Sydney a "free port" in 1828. Yet, the American market failed to fulfil its promise. U.S. tariffs protected Pennsylvania coal; and the hard anthracite coal of that region was more in demand for industry than the soft bituminous Cape Breton product. The demand was so slow that, in 1842, the Bridgeport Mine was closed.

In 1854, however, negotiation of the Reciprocity Treaty with the United States successfully opened that market to natural products such as fish, lumber, and coal. After the War of 1812, the Americans had lost the right to fish within five kilometres of Maritime shores. By the new 1854 treaty that right was reinstated, to the benefit of places like the Strait of Canso, to which American fishermen returned to fish and buy supplies from local dealers.

The coal industry was the chief beneficiary of the Reciprocity Treaty. There was not an immediate rapid rise in sales, though they reached 126,000 tons in 1857.[115] Rather, the promise of a growing American market stimulated an increase in coal exploration. Within five years of the treaty, more than 40 exploration leases were issued in the Sydney coalfield. The growing interest in the resource resulted in increased pressure on the provincial government to break the restrictive coal monopoly of the General Mining Association. Local politicians, in particular William Young, crusaded for the admission of new players into the field. In 1858 the G.M.A. gave up most of its mineral rights to the government of Nova Scotia, though it retained areas on the north side of Sydney Harbour and tracts around Lingan and Bridgeport, including their three mines there.[116]

Outside these areas, new mines were quickly opened to take advantage of the Reciprocity Treaty. Local merchants like Charles Campbell of Baddeck, Marshall Bourinot of Jersey ancestry from Arichat—who ran the Blockhouse Mine—the Lorway family of Sydney, and the Archibalds of North Sydney who invested in the Gowrie Mine—all faced with the decline of the wooden shipbuilding industry—switched their investments to mining. They did not, however, have the capital required to go it on their own. So by the 1860s American capitalists like the Belloni brothers of New York controlled most of the newly-opening mines.

With the outbreak of the American Civil War (1861-1865), great amounts of coal were needed to supply *both* sides in that struggle. By 1865, most of the Cape Breton coal output of 320,610 tons was being shipped to the United States.[117] In 1866, however, the Americans abrogated the Reciprocity Treaty and returned to a protectionist policy. The result was the immediate loss of the coal market and economic depression in Cape Breton's mining areas through the late 1860s and most of the 1870s. Smaller coal companies failed or amalgamated to stave off bankruptcy.

The hope of prosperity that the island's vast coal reserves might bring remained only a dream until late in the century.

Richard Brown, in his 1869 *History of the Island of Cape Breton*, could only hope that young Cape Bretoners "may live to see your country attain the high rank to which it is justly entitled by its geographical position and vast natural resources."[118]

# 9

# The Cape Bretonian Emerges

## The 19ᵗʰ Century Roots of Cape Breton Culture

"If Louisbourg had not been demolished, it is very probable
that Cape Breton would at this time [1828] have been a
populous and flourishing colony. To the levelling of that
town and fortress may justly be attributed the oblivion
which has so long enveloped Cape Breton."[1]
—J. McGregor

NOVA SCOTIAN STATESMAN Joseph Howe took a tour of Nova Scotia in the late 1820s and managed to reach the Sydney area over "roads...rascally, beyond any conception,"[2] but he did not even bother to mention the island in his published description of the province. The rugged geography which separated communities preserved local traditions, but it was the evolving and predominant Gaelic culture and language among a large part of the population that really kept outside influences at bay. The same may be said for the Acadian settlers—tightly concentrated in two areas, Isle Madame and Chéticamp—with their own language, family ties, and cultural norms that easily overcame outside impacts. Likewise the Mi'kmaq lived with their own language in remote reserves, and travelled the back country.

Only the principal county seats—all important ports, like

Arichat, Sydney, Port Hood, and Baddeck, and to a lesser extent the Mabou and Port Hawkesbury areas—experienced any strong outside influences and of these, only the former capital at Sydney could boast a colonial society worthy of the name.

Internal communications gradually grew as lake shipping and roads improved and factors like cattle drives and the coal trade brought about community interaction. Religion brought people together at services, church picnics, and concerts and, as in the case of the Catholics, linked them to the mainland, while four-day mass communion services with large numbers travelling long distances were important social occasions for Presbyterians, beginning in the 1830s. The arrival of newspapers out of Sydney also allowed those literate in English, and later Gaelic, to experience contact with both island and off-island cultures.

The most threatened group was the Mi'kmaq, faced with the provincial government's policy of assimilation. The 1859 "Act Concerning Indian Reserves" allowed squatters to buy native land, and the Legislative Assembly in Halifax informed a Mi'kmaq delegation from Cape Breton that the money so acquired would be used to "educate" and to "settle" them. These were code words for assimilation into the official English-speaking culture. Accordingly, lands were surveyed and boundaries of reserves clearly marked. But neither the natives, whose culture involved communal as opposed to individual land ownership, nor the Scottish settlers who refused to give up or pay for the land on which they squatted, conformed to the act.[3]

With Confederation in 1867, the native population came under the jurisdiction of the new federal government. According to the Indian Act of 1876, Nova Scotia was divided into districts, each with an Indian Agent who reported directly to Ottawa on native matters. A Department of Indian Affairs was created to "raise the level of Indians"[4] so they could become "regular" citizens. Christianity was emphasized and church-run boarding schools were organized, where the use of the Mi'kmaw language and of any traditional Mi'kmaq practices—from hunting to self-governance—were forbidden.

The new system was even more paternalistic than that of the provincial regime, the federal government having the sole right to decide who were Mi'kmaq and what was a reserve. By this policy, the government hoped to turn native settlements into communities parallel to white municipalities. Hence the election of chiefs was introduced and the traditional system of lifetime tenure chiefs was abolished. Grand Chiefs were ignored, though the Catholic Church, to keep a close relationship with the natives, recognized them as spiritual leaders.[5] The Church also used the Grand Councils to keep the Mi'kmaq loyal to the religion. According to Grand Captain Alex Denny the missionaries "started changing the role of the Grand Council from it being a political thing into it being religious...."[6] The Grand Council "were responsible to pass down the Catholic doctrine to their children."[7]

With the decline of the influence of the Grand Chiefs, Indian Agents who controlled reserve finances became more powerful. They decided on the legality of the elections of chiefs and their removal from office.[8]

Education was perhaps the most powerful tool in the destructive assimilation policies. Native or "indigenous culture" was considered "unworthy of perpetuation."[9] Primary schools were set up on reserves to teach natives to live "socially responsible and useful lives."[10] Most early instructors were non-Indian Roman Catholics, though by the end of the century more Mi'kmaq teachers were appearing.

The power of the Indian Agents led many Mi'kmaq to keep them at a distance.[11] They tried to live their traditional lives, but growing settlement limited the range of their hunting and fishing territory, while the absence of fish and game in many regions forced them to turn to non-traditional activities.[12] Ancient cultural practices were retained but modified to the new economic and political realities. For example, native handcrafts like basketry and quill work found expression in "made for trade" items like sewing boxes, chair seats, moccasins, snowshoes, canoes, woven baskets of all kinds, and even "luxury items" such as calling-card cases and whisk broom holders.[13] Old Mi'kmaq motifs were used, but beads often replaced traditional materials like shells and porcupine quills.

Instead of travelling seasonally between the sea and the Bras d'Or Lakes, and between the coast and the highlands, natives camped near white settlements like Sydney and Baddeck and, of course, in the St. Peter's-Arichat corridor. Some Mi'kmaq men entered the labour market, working at sawmills and in logging camps. Government was only too happy to encourage their possible absorption into white culture with training in barrel, tub, bucket, and churn making.

Robert Elmsley, a Baddeck merchant, described the industry of the Mi'kmaq who camped on Mutton Island off Baddeck in the mid 19th century. Besides trout and eel fishing they

made mast hooks, and oil tanks, baskets, keeled tubs, ox yokes, axe handles, quill boxes, pretty moccasins, bows and arrows, kites, toy canoes, staves, fish barrels, washtubs. Any wares not sold in Baddeck were conveyed to Little Bras d'Or or North Sydney by canoe. Dozens of canoes skipped off to Boularderie Head and soon returned with proceeds.[14]

On the whole, however, the Mi'kmaq kept apart from the European settlers who in turn saw them as mysterious creatures, or like children, often objects of ridicule.

The Cape Breton Mi'kmaq were more isolated and conservative than mainland natives and retained longer the old lifestyle of hunting, fishing, and food gathering, and attendant customs in dress. Women, less likely to experience outside contact, changed more slowly.

Birch-bark wigwams were popular in some areas until the 1880s, though by then they were not used year round, natives preferring frame houses of logs or board, "furnished like a backwoodsman's shanty."[15] These were often built away from reserves to avoid the restrictions of reserve life.[16]

Along with traditional ways, the Mi'kmaq in Cape Breton retained stories peculiar to their experiences. Tales based on the lives of magic heroes or powerful chiefs who triumph over cowardly opponents were popular. Some tales related the exploits of Mosi Mayal—Monsieur Abbé Maillard, the missionary who served them after the fall of Louisbourg and developed their ideographic writing—attributing to him the powers of a traditional medicine man.[17]

Max Basque remembered:

Father really could tell some great stories. My grandfather, anyway, on my mother's side.... Everything would be quiet, be ready to go to bed. Over at Grandfather's place. And somebody'd say—well, it's a signal for somebody to tell a story—"Ke'skw a." Everything just went quiet. Ke'skw a. That means that somebody would tell a story. And Grandfather would tell—I wish to goodness I'd marked some of them down, or remembered. All the weird stories about the Badger and about the Rabbit. And even about the Frog and the Wild Geese. About the Wild Geese and the Turtle.... And then, all the strange tales about the Cold... Tkey. Just another word for cold. Tkey ne'apa'sit Ka'qniktuk. The Cold was peeking in the door.... Ketu' mnaqnewa'lit. He was peeking to see if I was getting any weaker. I was getting colder.... Oh, a long tale. All evening's tale about how he got the best of that Cold, kept the Cold from coming in.

...No wonder they could tell stories, because there was no radio, no grammophone, or no nothing in the evenings, when it got dark. Might keep the home fires, keep the bonfire going, inside a camp. If it was outside, good enough—outside. Sitting all around it. And there would be nobody say anything. And then somebody would say, "Ke'skw a. Ke'skw a."[18]

Numerous chants were also retained from the past, examples being feast or hunting chants which today are impossible to translate. A musicologist has found traces of Gregorian Chant in some Mi'kmaq chants, perhaps recalling the hymns of the early Jesuits at St. Ann's.[19] Traditional dance persisted as well. The Mi'kmaq commonly used sticks to beat birch bark or pieces of wood before drums became popular later, though there is debate as to whether the natives had used them before contact with Europeans.[20]

Although many customs and the lifestyle of their ancestors were preserved—the game of "Waltes" has come down, possibly unchanged—contact with Europeans continued to take their toll on the Mi'kmaq. Richard John Uniacke, though displaying typical 19th century attitudes toward the natives, summed up their problems in 1860:

His contact with the white man has infected his nature with vicious habits, that he was in a great measure free from when he reigned in his native woods. Indolence and intemperance are his besetting evil habits; and these together with the small pox and consumption make great ravages upon him. He is however generally honest, or rather disdains to steal. Although he dislikes regular labour he is very patient and persevering in work that suits his taste and is not heavy: and he still retains a large share of the fortitude and endurance that have always characterized the North American savage.[21]

Like most white people, Uniacke displayed prejudice and pessimism as to their future:

The probability of their ever constituting a civilized and industrious race is too little to inspire expectation even in the most sanguine. Some slight approach, however, is made in some cases to more improved habits, which may have the effect perhaps, of rescuing a small remnant from further extinction.[22]

But they did not disappear. By the end of the 19th century the number of Mi'kmaq on the island had increased to nearly 1,000, but with few signs that the policy of assimilation was working.

THE GAELIC-SPEAKING Scottish settlers, although far more numerous than the Mi'kmaq, also faced assimilating forces from the official English-based culture of Nova Scotia. Like the Acadians, they brought with them a culture which they were adapting to their new island home.[23] So we see spinning, weaving, dying, rug hooking, and quilting based on Old Country practices. These work sessions were often accompanied by songs which preserved both history and romance. Charles Dunn refers to this as their "folk culture transplanted." New songs and poems articulated the new experiences, such as the voyage to America, the seemingly impenetrable forests, even encounters with bears. They kept alive Old World stories and created new ones in home entertainment we call ceilidhs today—from the Gaelic word for "a visit."

Gaelic culture had been disadvantaged in Scotland so no more than one-fifth of family heads in the 1830s were literate.[24] Much of the culture that Scots brought to Cape Breton was thus oral; for nearly 150 years, stories, music, and social practices were handed down in Gaelic, the everyday language of most island Highland Scots.

And Highlanders they were! As late as 1873, Charles Dudley Warner, on a visit to Cape Breton, came across a man who could speak a little English. Warner asked him if he had heard of the poems of Robbie Burns. The man said he did not know Burns, but he had heard of Robert the Bruce. Warner was amazed and compared it to an American not knowing George Washington.[25] Warner was wrong of course; Burns was a Lowlander from another culture and knew little Gaelic, while Robert the Bruce was a Highlander like the Cape Bretoner.

In such a society bards, or poets, held an honoured place and their works played a great part in people's lives. "In a sense they were the true Highland dominies (schoolmasters), robbing illiteracy of its worst consequences."[26]

Before long Cape Bretoners were producing their own bards. Many of these men are still revered. Malcolm Gillis composed Gaelic songs such as "Hills and Dales of Upper Margaree" which is sung today throughout the Gaelic-speaking world. Another outstanding bard of this period is Allan "The Ridge" MacDonald (1794-1868) from Southwest Mabou Ridge. He arrived in Mabou around 1816. The historian of Inverness County, John L. MacDougall, a Gaelic scholar in his own right, proclaimed himself "fully convinced that [MacDonald's] Gaelic songs are evidence that Allan the Ridge was, not only an entertaining songster but, also, a natural poet of singular genius."[27]

And there were the tales. Twentieth-century storyteller Joe Neil MacNeil told folklorist John Shaw:

It was mostly during the long winter months that people engaged in this kind of activity. The nights were so long. Nightfall would come early on and the day's work would be done.... People didn't come just from one house or two houses for a house-visit; people would come from perhaps three or four houses, and some people would come over a distance as great as three miles.... There were special houses for story-telling.... The wake-house was an especially good setting for story-telling.... I feel after all that they used to get pleasure from sitting and listening to tales. People were so united; they were like one person—one being— inside. And that was the kind of entertainment they derived from tales and rhymes and songs and poems of every sort.[28]

In 1847, instruction in Gaelic in Nova Scotia was finally officially allowed where warranted, but a scarcity of teachers limited its use. Social pressure was strong "to get ahead" by speaking English like the successful merchants in Port Hood, Mabou, and Baddeck.[29] On the other hand, all through the 19th century the more remote areas of Victoria and Inverness Counties remained major centres of the Gaelic language. They lived their daily lives in Gaelic. Historian Ray MacLean claims that Gaelic survived longer in Roman Catholic areas since their culture was more oral than that of the Presbyterians, whose culture was based on the written word of the Bible, available mainly in English.[30] But certainly Gaelic remained a household language in many Protestant homes along Cape Breton's North Shore through the first half of the 20th century. "Ministers in that region continued the nineteenth-century practice of giving equal time to both Gaelic and English."[31]

Along with the Gaelic language, music played an important

role in the retention and development of the Scottish culture in Cape Breton. Settlers brought their bagpipes and fiddles with them. "Marches, strathspeys, reels and jigs were common in a traditional style.... The bagpipe, though, had several functions which went beyond entertainment. No wedding or funeral was complete without a Piper."[32] And for many, the pipes were the music for dance. Bagpipes were not readily available, however, and the fiddle—easier to make and maintain—took over, with a repertoire of Old Country tunes and hundreds of locally composed tunes.[33] It was used for social events, and popular fiddlers became almost semi-professional, accepting money as well as alcohol. It was the attendant drunkenness that caused some of the clergy to rail against the fiddle and to foster temperance societies. Despite this, fiddlers were cherished and fiddling flourished as an accompaniment to square and stepdancing with their regional variations, particularly in Catholic sections.[34]

Religion played a key role in the lives of all Cape Breton Scots. When the Presbyterian Church arrived in Cape Breton it was in the midst of change, emerging from a period of tolerance and "moderation" and entering one of evangelical zeal with no room for alcohol or tobacco. This austere form of Presbyterianism spread to the Highlands of Scotland in the 1820s just as large numbers of Scots were leaving for Cape Breton. In 1825 the Glasgow Colonial Society was formed, and began exporting evangelical clergy and reading material to the colonies. The mainland Presbyterians, who had been settling in Nova Scotia since the 1770s, favoured the earlier, moderate form of the faith and resisted the Society's teachings. Cape Bretoners on the other hand felt at home with these more rigorous beliefs and eagerly sought their missionaries.[35]

In 1833 the Edinburgh Ladies' Association was formed as an auxiliary of the Glasgow Colonial Society, and chose Cape Breton as a mission. Isabelle Gordon MacKay, prime mover of the Association, sent Rev. Alexander Farquharson and Rev. John Stewart to the island. They opened 16 Presbyterian churches and brought in other clergymen. Education was central to their belief system. "Without knowledge," said Rev. James McGregor in 1786, "people can be neither good Christians nor good citizens."[36] In 1836 the Presbyterian Church of Cape Breton was formed. The following year, Hugh Munroe established an academy at Boularderie where Alexander Munro and his wife taught. By 1840 they had 110 pupils, including some Catholics, from all over Cape Breton. Teachers educated at the Boularderie Academy were soon evangelizing off the island in Canada and the United States.[37]

The close connection between Presbyterianism, education, discipline, thrift, and industry is perhaps most striking in the person of Rev. Norman McLeod, who settled in St. Ann's in 1820. McLeod, a native of Sutherlandshire, Scotland, had experienced a sudden religious conversion and could not abide the "Moderate" brand of Presbyterianism. Accordingly, he began preaching a puritanical type of faith, and with his followers was blacklisted by the Established Church. They headed for Pictou, Nova Scotia, where McLeod made a number of converts before the Moderates there opposed him. Leaving for Ohio, a storm drove their ship to St. Ann's Bay. The land was beautiful, and available. They stayed. Isolation allowed them to practice their brand of faith without interference. McLeod taught school, emphasizing thrift, austerity, and industry. He attacked "unchristian giddiness and gaudry, vanity and folly, pride and passions" and fulminated against the "deep-rooted worldliness and dreadful malignity...hiddenly lurking in the breast of every carnal and unregenerated man."[38]

McLeod's settlement flourished and attracted new arrivals imbued with the zeal of the Reformed Church. His success also attracted the admiration of government authorities who made him a local magistrate. This, together with his formal ordination from a rather dubious school in New York State, gave him both spir-

174

itual and political dominance in what now became a strict theocracy.

By the 1830s, as the surrounding population continued to grow, McLeod came into conflict with neighbouring clergymen, which led to slanderous quarrels over his credentials. As a result, he lost some of his "Normanites." And when the potato blight destroyed his crop in 1851, he took it as a sign for him and his flock to leave Cape Breton and join his son in Australia. They eventually settled in Waipu, North Island, New Zealand. Over a period of years, Cape Breton people built or bought six ships for the 33,600-kilometre journey. Though McLeod was gone and a more moderate regime followed, his influence on Cape Breton Presbyterianism remained, particularly in attitudes toward temperance, education, and strict observance of the Bible.

All the while, that church continued to expand on the island. By the late 1850s three presbyteries had been established—at Richmond, Victoria, and Cape Breton Counties—each with a number of charges. In 1860, what we might call the "Free Church in Cape Breton" merged with the Presbyterian Church of Nova Scotia, over the objections of some clerics who saw this as tampering with the norms of their Cape Breton congregations.[39] However, the cultural influence of this brand of Presbyterianism remained as a strict moral code, a Bible-oriented faith, a passion for formal education, and a continual devotion to the Communion gatherings.[40]

The Communion events were a vital part of the social life of Presbyterian Cape Bretoners. These were huge gatherings; people came from all over the island, by water, horse power, and on foot. They filled the local homes and barns. It was a tremendous drain on local food resources. Services were held in the summer months in open fields and often lasted several formal days. The days featured hymn singing and sermons, mostly in Gaelic, and intense religious discussion.

One minister reported that at the Mira Communion of 1853:

The arrows of conviction flew thick amongst them, and not only were serious looks, grave comportment, and weeping eyes seen in all directions, but also more unmistakable indications of deep distress. Thousands were melted. Some of both sexes trembled under the word, and in a variety of ways manifested deep feeling.[41]

Since there were few avenues for social intercourse among the mainly rural population, people used this opportunity to meet and gossip with friends. "Church attendance thus provided an emotional outlet in some directions, particularly for women [and] ...the younger people usually found means of getting to know each other."[42]

The milling frolic was another example of getting work done, combined with entertainment. Since it involved the useful job of fulling home-woven blankets, clerics did not forbid the practice. Men and women could join together in laughing and singing while the otherwise onerous task—rhythmically pounding and passing along fistfuls of wet wool, sizing the cloth—was completed.[43] The frolic was also a good opportunity for passing culture along. John Alex John X. MacDonald of the North Shore told a story of his father, too young to attend, listening to a new song at a milling frolic from outside, through the window. "When he woke up in the morning, [my father] was lying in bed, and he had the whole fourteen verses!"[44]

Their religion gave the Presbyterian settlers solace, and as historian Laurie Stanley-Blackwell writes:

Presbyterianism gave a sense of direction to a society in a state of transition, a society, once static, agrarian and Scottish, and now faced with the realities of spatial mobility, economic diversification and a Cape Breton identity.[45]

This same transition took place among the Roman Catholics. Starting with Isle Royale in 1713, there were close links to the Church in Québec, and until 1827 the Catholic Church in Cape Breton was still part of the Diocese of Québec. By the 1820s native-born priests were already at work, in contrast to the Presbyterians whose charges were not manned by native Cape Bretoners until 1851.[46] By 1823 Acadian chapels had been built at Chéticamp, Margaree, and Arichat. Scottish Catholic churches were located at Grand Narrows, East Bay, and L'Ardoise, each with a resident priest.[47] The influence of the Catholic Church was profound since, unlike among the Presbyterians, there were no internal theological conflicts.

Catholic men wishing to study for the priesthood were trained in Québec or even Europe, where they became well-educated and cultured, far above the level of their parishioners. It was therefore natural that they should become the unquestioned leaders of their communities. From their "glebe houses" or rectories, they gave political, legal, and social advice that extended well beyond the confines of religious practice.[48] Moreover, the priests' ability to speak and conduct religious services in Gaelic, which was not as common among the Presbyterian ministers,[49] helped keep the language alive in Catholic communities. Cape Breton Catholics' greater tolerance of folk music and ceilidhs also tended to foster preservation of the old culture. By 1824 Rev. Bernard MacLeod had established a school at Grand Narrows and, shortly afterwards, a school/seminary at East Bay which was moved to the more populous diocesan seat at Arichat in 1853.

As the Catholic population of Nova Scotia grew, particularly in Cape Breton, the island was separated from the Diocese of Québec and attached to the Vicariate of Nova Scotia. In 1844 Nova Scotia was divided into two dioceses, the largely Irish mainland diocese of Halifax, and the other centred in Cape Breton with Arichat as the diocesan capital. Arichat was the logical choice because of its large population, economic importance, ranking status that dated from the French regime, central location, and access by water. Two-thirds of the Catholics in the Diocese of Arichat lived on Cape Breton (31,892) with another 17,000 or so in the three adjoining mainland counties (Antigonish, Guysborough, and Pictou).[50]

In 1851,when the first Bishop William Fraser died, the Rector of Arichat, Etienne Chartier, would normally have been expected to succeed him. Instead, the position went to a Scot, Reverend Colin MacKinnon from the mainland village of Antigonish. The appointment of a Scot was reasonable, since this represented the national origin of most Catholics in the Diocese. In 1851 MacKinnon carried matters further and moved the Arichat college to his hometown of Antigonish, where priests could be trained in a Scottish milieu.[51] This was a serious blow to the already declining fortunes of Arichat, but worse came in 1880 when the diocesan centre was also moved to Antigonish. The Diocese of Antigonish, as it was now called, was henceforth firmly rooted in a Scottish environment, albeit far from the majority of its communicants. For Arichat, it meant a further decline in importance and the isolation of its French population on Isle Madame. For Cape Breton it meant the loss of an institution of higher learning—for the next 80 years!

Though the latter years of the 19th century saw both the Presbyterian and Roman Catholic churches amalgamated with mainland centres, indigenous developments within the two faiths ensured the retention among Scottish and French Cape Bretoners of their sense of religious and cultural identity. Their faithful, though differing in tenets, rarely quarrelled or fought, at least not openly. Protestant and Roman Catholic lived in separate areas according to their island or region of origin in Scotland. Intermarriage was considered scandalous, and both agreed that alcohol was a pernicious scourge of the age. The Temperance Movement which began in the 1830s was led by clergy of both persuasions.[52]

This religious peace was briefly disturbed in 1857, particularly in Sydney and Whycocomagh, when a Protestant Alliance led largely by a group of "political parsons" became involved in local politics, warning against the "chimerical perils of Catholic despotism."[53] Cooler heads prevailed, however, and the movement died out. Both bodies were more likely to quarrel among themselves over religious jurisdiction and faith tenets than with each other. Scots of all stripes were serious about their religion, which bound them together and provided a framework for the growing cultural identity of Cape Breton in the 19th century.

THE IRISH BEGAN ARRIVING in Cape Breton as fishermen and merchants after the fall of Louisbourg. Then, after the War of 1812, some of the Irish veterans settled at Irish Cove on the Bras d'Or Lake; others made their way up the River Inhabitants or over to the Port Hawkesbury region on the west coast where they could live free of British interference. Low Point near present-day New Waterford was popular with the Irish at the end of the 18th century due at first to its arable land. Known as the "Irish Grant," settlers were attracted there from Isle Madame.

When Governor DesBarres undertook coal mining in 1786 at present-day Sydney Mines, more Irish sailed in from Newfoundland to work in the pits. Place names like Kilkenny Lake, River Ryan, and New Waterford bear witness to the Irish presence. Though they generally had to be content with Scottish priests, there were enough Irish in the Low Point-Sydney Mines area to warrant their own priest, the sometimes irascible Rev. Henry McKeagney. McKeagney oversaw construction of St. Patrick's Church in Sydney in 1828. The church was built by its parishioners, and the Irish sailed in from as far away as Bras d'Or and Main-à-Dieu. Though the Bishop had decreed the new church being erected was to be called St. William's, McKeagney refused to do so and called it St. Patrick's and referred to the graveyard as St. Henry's, perhaps after himself.

More seriously, McKeagney was at the head of a band of voters supporting Richard Smith's candidacy in the Great Election of 1832. "Father MacKechnie (*sic*) was struck down and a general melee ensued."[54] For this, and for disobedience to the Bishop, McKeagney was suspended from the pastorate of Sydney in 1840.[55]

On the whole, however, the Irish population was never large or concentrated enough to sustain old customs. Though no native Irish language survived in Cape Breton, the Irish had a strong influence on stepdancing and certain square dances, particularly where Irish were more concentrated, such as North East Margaree.[56] The Irish clergy were also more tolerant of dance than the Scottish and Acadian clergy, and Irish parishes were centres of music, song, and dance.[57] Particularly in Margaree and Judique, certain jigs and waltzes of Irish origin were introduced.[58] Being mainly Roman Catholic, Irish intermarried with Catholic Scots or Acadians. Within a generation, though they kept alive their consciousness of being Irish, they had cast aside many of their old beliefs. Irish folklore and supernatural notions—such as stories of fairies—survived longest in areas of heaviest concentration, as at Low Point, and in rural areas like Margaree.[59]

A challenge in discovering the threads of Irish music that made their way into the Cape Breton musical style is the closeness of the Irish and Scottish musical traditions. Paul MacDonald writes in *The Irish in Cape Breton*:

> The round dance portions of most dances are danced to Irish songs.... With the exception of dances like those at West Mabou and Glencoe Mills, [today] it is a rare dance that is not interspersed with Irish songs. Although the instrumental dance music is considered to be Scottish, there are numerous Irish reels and hornpipes and hundreds of Irish jigs which have been adapted for the dance repertoire. An example is "The West Mabou Reel," one of the most popular reels in Inverness County.... And then there are the jigs. The Scottish collections contain only a handful. But in Cape Breton the dance tradition often includes two jig figures followed by a reel figure. This would require more than a handful of jigs, and the Irish repertoire provided the great body of jigs still used in dances today.[60]

There was doubtless a good deal of cross-fertilization in some areas, resulting in an increase in tempo that is noticeable when comparing Cape Breton music with that found in Scotland. One scholar has remarked that Irish music was "absorbed and reshaped, thus contributing to the evolution of a new and distinct Cape Breton musical sound."[61]

The Irish confirmed their identity in the celebration of religious holidays. At Sydney Mines, Irish miners refused to work on St. Patrick's Day and other feast days. There were Irish Societies such as the Ancient Order of Hibernians and Orange Lodges with links to Ireland. Both Catholic and Protestant belonged to an Irish philanthropic society in Sydney, and in 1845 the Irish in Isle Madame raised money in support of the temperance movement in Ireland.[62]

THE ACADIANS, as the French in Cape Breton have been known since the fall of Louisbourg, were heavily concentrated in the St. Peter's-Isle Madame corridor. As we have seen, they lived under the economic control of the bilingual and Anglican Jersey merchants who occupied all important posts, judicial and military, until the 1850s. The Jerseymen's superior education, religious affiliation, and British connections gave them dominance over the Acadians who were dependent on them to buy their fish. In turn, the Jerseymen provided vital supplies, from nets and hooks and salt to their molasses and tea. Though Isle Madame's prosperous trade and fishery attracted Irish, Scottish, and English, the Acadians with 66 percent of the population in 1838 had a solid majority.[63]

Like the Mi'kmaq and the Scots, the Acadians had to fight the government's policies of assimilation. Their first teachers were anglophones, though their everyday discourse was in the rich French of their ancestors.[64] With the 1840 election of their first Acadian MLA, Henry Martell, they began the fight for the right to teach French in their schools.[65] The establishment of the Arichat Academy brought hopes of higher education to the Acadians, but the naming of a Scottish bishop foretold its loss to the mainland in 1855. In that same year, however, Rev. Hubert Girroir opened a secondary school with French instruction at Arichat. Girls were educated at the convent established by the Congregation of Notre Dame in 1856.[66] All this guaranteed the survival of the written French language.

The Acadians' language, religion, and family connections gave them a social cohesiveness. Since most people were illiterate, their culture was oral with a rich musical tradition dating back to old Louisbourg and beyond. Chéticantins in particular observed singular religious festivals and devotions which added to their sense of identity. Striking examples are seen in the feast of Candlemas, or Chandeleur, when the blessing of religious candles in February provided an occasion for a mid-winter break. At Chandeleur a dance, L'Escaouette, is performed, along with little songs about the sea or other facets of nature, rooted in old France.[67] At mid-Lent or Mi-Carême, people dressed in costumes and went from house to house performing dances, particularly at Chéticamp. Their songs were a repertoire of 18th century folk songs, sung a cappella.[68]

At the end of the 20th century, Father Daniel Boudreau, nearly 90 years old, was brought home by the local radio station to record a wide variety of over 500 old Acadian songs. As far as dance, the earliest consisted of French *rondes* or song dances. As in the case of the other Cape Breton settlers, as time went on much of their music became a mixture of Scottish, Irish, and French styles.[69]

The storytellers were also important figures in Chéticamp, "as necessary as the services of a violinist were for a wedding...."

The storyteller, sometimes completely illiterate, was an artist. He knew how to describe his characters and make them come alive for his audience. He knew how to thrill his listeners by demonstrating the feelings of his heroes. "P'tit" Paddé is still remembered for beginning his stories while sitting on a chair, but soon, caught up in the excitement of his story, rising to his feet and completing the tale with all appropriate gestures.[70]

Though Chéticamp had been used as a summer fishery during the French Regime, there was no permanent settlement before 1782. In that year, the Jersey firm of Robin set up shop and gained control of the best coastal areas. Their presence in Chéticamp attracted Acadians who had fled from attacks on Arichat and New Brunswick's Baie de Chaleur during the American Revolution. Others came from eastern Prince Edward Island.[71] Their economic life was dominated by the Jerseymen even more so than that of the Acadians of Isle Madame, since the Jerseymen owned their boats and they were not paid for their catch in money, but in food supplies and credit.

In any case, the Jersey business practices suffocated local enterprise and investment and kept the settlement poor. Alex John Boudreau recalled:

They [the Jerseymen] provided—when they first settled—they provided ships, they provided equipment, they provided, well, all of the necessities of life, you know, to the people.... Nails...paint...flour...shoes, they could get it there at Robin. And it was the only place. So they had a lot of money invested. And their only fear at that time was to lose control.... Any fisherman who was fishing for Robin Jones and was kept in debt by them, could not get married without permission from the manager.... The wedding rings were made out of 50¢ pieces, silver pieces, by Robin Jones.... You couldn't even get your wedding ring if you didn't have permission.[72]

On the other hand, the Catholic Church played a strong economic as well as cultural role in the lives of the Chéticantins. Unlike other francophone areas like East Margaree or even Isle Madame, where priests were often Scottish or Irish, most priests in Chéticamp spoke French.

The first priest permanently stationed there, Rev. Gabriel Champion, arrived in 1801, in flight from the French Revolution.[73] The most influential priest however was Pierre Fiset, a great organizer, who not only had the magnificent landmark church, Église Saint-Pierre, erected in 1892, but fought to break the fishing monopoly of the Robin Company. He managed to obtain regular steamboat service for the settlement in 1886, laying the foundation for the area's fish and gypsum shipping industry.

The isolation of the Chéticamp region ensured a stronger preservation of the Acadian traditions than happened in the older but more culturally-mixed Isle Madame. As we will see, it was not until the 20th century that the Chéticantins would wrest a substantial share of their economy from the Robin Company.

An interesting feature of Acadian folklore in Cape Breton was the belief in sorcery, particularly relating to the Jerseymen. Perhaps due to Jersey influence over them, many Chéticamp Acadians saw some Jerseymen as sorcerers who, for example, could adversely affect their fishery. The Acadians dealt with these Jerseymen on a daily basis. They were fellows the Robin firm brought out just for the season as middle-level workers to handle the stores, warehouses, accounts, and so forth—young Jersey Islanders, also Protestant, whom Herbert LeBoutillier of Jersey descent described as "full of devilment...full of hellery, they'd do anything for a joke."[74] They were kept at a social distance by both the Jersey leadership and the local priests—but their pranks, and even rumours of sorcery, have come down in the Acadian folklore to this day. The brand of "sorcery" was not confined to Jerseymen; anyone—even other Acadians—who displayed atypical behaviour or outstanding skills like mathematics could be considered a *sorcier*. Sometimes whole families were suspect. Sick horses or cows who failed to give milk were thought to have been bewitched.[75]

DURING MOST OF THE 19TH CENTURY the Scottish, Acadian, Mi'kmaq, and Irish peoples retained a strong sense of their ethnic identity. As the years passed, however, there was some intermarriage, especially between Catholic Scots, Irish, and Acadians. The old Loyalist families tended to marry Loyalists. Since many were Anglican, or at least Protestant, some married into

Presbyterian families. In this way old loyalties to the previous homelands, though continuing, were softened, particularly after a few generations of life in Cape Breton Island.

It is indeed difficult to pinpoint the period when settlers developed a sense of being "Cape Bretonians" rather than simply members of an ethnic group. The feeling of "them" and "us" seems to have evolved first in the Sydney area, since it had been the seat of colonial government and later of Cape Breton County, which included the whole island before 1835.

Whereas most of the island was growing rapidly with a simple hierarchy centred around the local clergyman and wealthy merchant, Sydney's social structure was more complicated. There was stratification even among the earliest settlers, between the Loyalists and those who arrived from England aboard the *Blenheim,* "with intense rivalry and fistic encounters between the two groups."[76] Even after annexation to mainland Nova Scotia in 1820, society bore the signs of a colonial capital with the Loyalist families, former government officials, and retired military officers at the top. In 1846, one observer reflecting on Sydney's "ruling class" found people "very flashily dressed, with airs of considerable pride and conceit."[77] As late as 1875, Sydney's society was said to be of "a high order of culture and exclusive dignity. It possesses many of the social attributes of an old capital...."[78]

The military played a significant role in the social structure. The first troops had arrived to defend Sydney and the colony in 1785, and the garrison remained at the town's North End until 1854. During that time, whether stationed or choosing to retire there, military personnel intensified Sydney's air of being a colonial garrison town. In her diary Anna Kearny, wife of Lieutenant-Colonel Francis Kearny, stationed in Sydney in 1803-1804 during the administration of John Despard, describes the fêtes, dances, card parties, "elegant suppers," social visits and other pastimes of Sydney's society during the period.[79] Frequent social events were common where "all of the Inhabitants of Sydney both civil and military" took part, with "Ices, Cakes, negus and a variety of refreshments ...cold meat for the Gentlemen...with cold beef pye etc etc handed about to the Ladies in the [Lieutenant-Governor's] Ball Room."[80]

Even after Cape Breton's annexation to Nova Scotia, many military commanders who chose to retire in Sydney were at the pinnacle of local society. Samuel Rigby, former Town Major, took Dorothy Cox, daughter of Loyalist landowner Captain William Cox of Coxheath, as his second wife; retired Captain William Ousley lived in his estate at Brooklands; Major Edward Sutherland was a fine artist who left two beautifully composed paintings of Sydney in the 1840s and 50s. His daughter married the customs collector, Henry Davenport, whose estate "Ashby" was one of those that surrounded the town. Besides "Ashby" and "Brooklands," there was "Sherwood" owned by the prestigious Dodd family, and "Colby" where the Rigbys resided.

These families closely guarded their social positions. Arguments dating from before annexation lingered on, and duelling was not uncommon. Richard Gibbons, Junior, fought a duel with William Pooley, a schoolteacher who had married into the rival Dodd family. In his anger, Gibbons declared Sydney's tightly-knit aristocracy to be "rum puncheons and sugar hogsheads, liars, slanderers and oath breakers, broken auctioneers and wreckers."[81] In the duel, Gibbons was shot in the hip; he never rode again.

The military also fought duels, and even the high sheriff came close to fighting one.[82] Archibald Dodd, son of MLA Edmund Murray Dodd, raped the daughter of Nicholas Martin, one of Sydney's early postmasters, but refused to marry the girl. Martin shot Dodd, killing him—but a local jury, siding with Martin over the aristocratic Dodds, acquitted him.[83] To add insult to injury, the Martins married into the Gibbons family, cementing an anti-Dodd social alliance that lasted into the 1890s.

Below the highest social echelons was a group of professionals and officeholders, often powerful men in their own right. Henry Crawley, the Commissioner of Crown Lands, surveyed much of Cape Breton and laid out and defended the Mi'kmaq reserves. Charles E. Leonard, Collector of Customs and High Sheriff; Charles R. Ward, also High Sheriff and editor of the *Cape Bretonian*, Peter Hall Clarke, merchant and agent for Lloyds of London; the McKeagneys, who produced one of Cape Breton's first Members of Parliament in 1867—who was appointed to the Court of Queen's Bench in the newly-established Province of Manitoba in 1872[84]—and Sydney's first resident priest Henry McKeagney; as well as Anglican priests stationed in Cape Breton, like Charles Inglis and R. J. Uniacke—all these wielded considerable influence.

Considered socially inferior to these were the merchants, tradesmen, and hotel keepers whose businesses were located along the Esplanade and Charlotte Street, north of Dorchester.

Social organizations flourished in this milieu. Before annexation, societies like the Friends had played a role in giving people a voice in the political affairs of the Colony. There were Masons who arrived among the Loyalists, like Ranna Cossit, David Mathews, and David Tait. They met at Loyalist John O'Brien's tavern and lodge, still standing on the Esplanade at the corner of Amelia Street. Anna Kearny mentions their meeting "to see old Mr [David] Tate made a mason an *exhibition* from which all the *Brethren* promis'd themselves an infinity of amusement...."[85] The Masonic Lodge not only attracted Loyalists, but gave help and social influence to its members throughout the 19th century.

Temperance societies were also popular and necessary in a world with few official controls on the alcohol trade. The Cape Breton Island Branch of the Temperance Society was inaugurated in Sydney in October 1831. All religious leaders came together in support of that society, including Rev. Henry McKeagney and the powerful Baptist families like the Crawleys, the Weekses, and later

C. H. Harrington, mayor of the town. By 1850, the Star of the East, Division Number 61, Sons of Temperance, had built a hall on Charlotte Street, in the building where ironically the Capri Club pub is now located, where they sponsored musical evenings and addresses at which tea was served.[86]

In the 1870s, records show that a Sydney area population of 2,000 supported at least two temperance societies, the Masonic Lodge, a snowshoe club, a cricket club, six clergymen of the Roman Catholic, Anglican, Methodist, Presbyterian, and Baptist faiths, and four doctors.[87]

As the island's county seat and chief port of entry, by the 1830s Sydney had become a centre of education, newspapers, and intellectual development. Private schools existed there since Ranna Cossit's day, and by the 1820s the settlement had a "regular" or public school. In 1836 Otto Weeks, son of a Loyalist and an Anglican priest, was appointed principal of Sydney's grammar and common schools. In 1840, the two were combined to form the first Sydney Academy, a one-room school near DesBarres Street.[88]

Private schools remained common: by the 1860s there were at least three of them in Sydney, one run by John L. Hill, the sheriff, another for girls located opposite St. George's Church, and a third on Charlotte Street, which met six days a week. The Congregation of Notre Dame arrived in Sydney in 1885 to establish a school for girls on George Street—today's Holy Angels High School—which meant quality education for girls of all religious persuasions. This affected the artistic as well as the educational level of the population.

Besides schools, the town supported a Mechanics Institute dedicated to the enlightenment of working people beyond school age. Otto Weeks organized a group in the late 1830s, and by 1844 it could claim 50 members and a library. Regular lectures were given. In 1845 Weeks and the newspaper publisher Richard Huntington founded a Scientific and Literary Society which sponsored debates on current issues like evolution and human rights.

The importance of Weeks and Huntington in the cultural life of mid 19th century Sydney cannot be overstated. While Weeks focussed on education and cultural improvement, Huntington was mainly a newspaper man. A native of Yarmouth, he came to Sydney in 1840 to establish the *Cape Breton Advocate*, the Island's first regularly published newspaper. It had only a brief run, but Huntington soon founded *The Spirit of the Times*. He realized that Sydney in the 1840s, with only around 500 people, could hardly support such a publication, so he wrote for an island-wide audience. Though its circulation was limited, since most rural inhabitants could not read English, he hired regional agents to make the paper available in the county capitals where the literate English-speaking population was clustered.

Besides news, the *Times* featured locally-composed poetry and political diatribes, often calling for Cape Breton's separation from Nova Scotia. With the poor communications prior to the steamboat era, and a cash-poor society, the *Times* publication was uncertain; but it lasted till 1846, when it was replaced by the *Cape Breton Spectator*.[89]

The fact that a newspaper as well as an academy and cultural societies could even exist in a small place like Sydney points to the presence of an intellectual elite. Teachers, clergymen, military leaders, and well-educated families like the Wards, Martins, Sutherlands, the operators of the mines like the Bown family and the Bourinots—to name but a few—were quite aware of current intellectual developments. As a growing port, Sydney came into contact with outside ideas, and off-island publications were readily available. John Bourinot, the French Consul, who became a prominent Sydney merchant representing French coaling interests, sold the publications of current British authors and, from his home on the waterfront, entertained visitors from all over Europe and the United States.[90]

With current literature available and intellectual stimulation provided by the cultural societies, Cape Breton's first novelist—William C. McKinnon of Loyalist descent—was inspired to publish poetry in *The Spirit of the Times*. In the 1850s, he began publishing serialized novels influenced by island events, as in *Castine, A Tale of Louisbourg* and *The Midnight Murder*. The latter was based on the 1833 Flahaven murder in North Sydney, the story of an innkeeper's wife who had a love affair with a passing sailor. He murdered her husband only to be reported by their daughter. The sailor, his accomplice, and Mrs. Flahaven were all three hanged in Victoria Park.[91]

Other writers like Otto Weeks published poems in the *Cape Breton Advocate* and *The Spirit of the Times*. The publisher, Richard Huntington, wrote poetry of the tenor of the following:

> Hail, Sydney, to thy Noble port
> May ships from many a clime resort!
> May Commerce hither waft her stores,
> With circling wealth to glad thy shores!
> May Learning flourish—Science here
> The gloom of mental darkness cheer."[92]

The influence of artistically trained retired soldiers is seen in military bands that were established in the 1840s, Sutherland's elegant paintings of Sydney from Hardwood Hill, and the water colours of Colonel Alexander Cavalie Mercer (1783-1868) depicting the barracks and landscape at Battery Point. The presence of these artists in turn stimulated Arthur Hill in his drawings of Sydney from Hardwood Hill in the 1870s and his illustration of the International Coal Company's newly completed wharf (1870).

While Sydney's longer settled population was showing signs of intellectual awakening, most communities outside the former capital were also enjoying an invigorated cultural life. In English-speaking areas we see mechanics institutes, local subscription libraries, and agricultural societies. Arichat had its own Academy, and Ship Harbour (Port Hawkesbury) and Mabou were the homes of literary societies.[93] The Mabou Literary and Scientific Society met at the schoolhouse in nearby Hillsborough, a heavily Loyalist region. The Ship Harbour Young Men's Debating Society, founded in 1843, mirrored developments in Sydney.[94] Huntington's newspaper was an important tool in keeping islanders informed about news and literary subjects, which helped the island population cohere toward a common sense of place and of self.

Arichat, dominated by the Jersey, held special prominence. It boasted a decent courthouse as early as 1814, a Post House (1824), and industries attendant on fishing and shipbuilding like the LeNoir forge, operational since 1811. For newspapers it had to depend on Sydney or Halifax until 1891 when the *Warden* was first published. By the 1870s Arichat's fortunes were on the wane, though it remained an important population centre for another 20 years.

Though not as populous, Baddeck gained importance when it became the shire town of Victoria County, carved from Cape Breton County in 1851. Founded by Loyalists, it was first located on the Baddeck River in 1785—what we now call Big Baddeck. Little Baddeck, which is now simply Baddeck, was settled by merchant James Duffus in 1825. This location on the Bras d'Or Lakes made it a shipping and commercial centre before it became capital of Victoria County. Other merchants arrived in the 1840s and began ship construction for the export of timber to Europe and the United States. Behind a cluster of wharves along the waterfront, merchants, shoemakers, a post office, county offices, and churches were located.[95]

An agricultural society (1848) followed. By the 1880s Baddeck was the communications centre for the Lakes area with its own newspaper, the *Island Reporter*, established in 1884. Charles Dudley Warner, visiting in 1873, described Baddeck as a "straggling village" but

clean-looking...of white wooden houses, of perhaps seven or eight hundred inhabitants.... There were a few country-looking stores and shops, and on the shore three or four rather decayed and shaky wharves...and a few...decaying warehouses leaned about the docks. A peaceful and perhaps a thriving place, but not a bustling place.[96]

Port Hood, with a protected harbour—rare on the west coast—was a regional shipping and communications centre. Because of its early start as a Loyalist, then a Scottish, settlement, in 1835 it was named capital of Juste-au-Corps—later Inverness County. Education came early to the shiretown. In 1835 there were three teachers at the newly established school, who received their salaries by public fundraising and tuition. Port Hood's claim to being a regional centre was strengthened in the 1880s with the publication of its newspaper, *The Referee*.

The remains of the Fortress of Louisbourg were already becoming a "must see," attracting visitors to the small fishing village that had grown up east of the ruins. There, 19th century visitors could marvel at the past glory of the place. In the early 1830s, John McGregor observed that "the remains of all the batteries and the foundations of many of the public buildings, the stockades and, in calm weather, the sunken ships of war, are still to be seen."[97] Even 17 years later, symbols of greatness were evident to Abraham Gesner:

> The arched places of arms and bomb proofs of the citadel are still entire. Three of them are sheepfolds—another is occupied by a fisherman for a cabbage cellar. The foundations of the barracks, chapels, the nunnery, hospital and other public buildings are still perfect.[98]

By 1885, much had disappeared. Hezekiah Butterworth described the site as "a sheep pasture.... A broken sea-wall of hewn stones, the outlines of a vast amphitheatre, a glacis, avenues amid buried ruins, still remain. The green grass grows over all...."[99]

ALREADY IMBUED with a deep sense of their history and cultures, by the end of the 19th century Cape Bretoners represented an evolving regional character. The rural Gaelic-speaking Scots had accommodated their society to their island home; the Acadians, though largely under the economic domination of the Jersey merchants, were developing their own culture supported by their Church; the Irish, loosely concentrated in the Margarees and near the growing eastern mining towns, were already showing signs of cultural assimilation into the life of their fellow Scottish Celts. The Mi'kmaq, walking the fine line between adjusting to European economic and social demands while keeping their traditions, were far from the doomed race that government policies had envisioned. In the towns, particularly in the Sydney region, a local culture based more and more on a sense of Cape Breton identity was developing, though not yet fully expressive of all facets of the island's cultural mosaic.

Meanwhile, international trade in fish, coal, and lumber nurtured the growth of places like North Sydney, Port Hood, Port Hawkesbury, and the Gabarus-Framboise region, while technological advances in shipping and communications stimulated the economies not only of North Sydney but of Port Hastings and Baddeck. The old political centres of Sydney and Arichat failed to benefit from many of these changes, though their primacy in government matters assured their importance. All in all, the end of the 19th century witnessed a Cape Breton with a balanced economy and a growing population, despite out-migration. After the fall of Louisbourg and the Great Famine, the island had indeed risen again.

## END BOOK ONE

# Notes

### INTRODUCTION
### The Geology of Opportunity

1. Barrett, *Cape Breton Highlands National Park: A Park Lover's Companion*, 39-40.
2. Ibid., 40.
3. Ibid., 44.
4. Ibid.
5. Ibid., 45.
6. Ibid., 47-48.

### CHAPTER 1
### In the Land of the Mi'kmaq

1. Hoffman, *The Historical Ethnography of the Micmac of the Sixteenth and Seventeenth Centuries*, 7.
2. Strouthes, *Change in the Real Property Law of a Cape Breton Island Micmac Band*, Vol. I, 2.
3. Wicken, *Encounters with Tall Sails and Tall Tales: Mi'kmaq Society, 1500-1760*, 70, 71, 76.
4. Ibid.; also Prins, *The Mi' kmaq: Resistance, Accommodation, and Cultural Survival*, 276 *et seq.*
5. "The Micmac Birch-bark Canoe," *Cape Breton's Magazine*, No. 10, back cover, based on *The Bark Canoes and Skin Boats of North America*, Adney and Chapelle.
6. Ganong, *Crucial Maps in the Early Cartography and Place-Nomenclature of the Atlantic Coast of Canada*, 80.
7. Wallis and Wallis, *The Micmac Indians of Eastern Canada*, 54.
8. Prins, 32 *et seq.*
9. Ibid., 33-34.
10. Ibid., 34.
11. Ibid., 32.
12. Ibid., 25.
13. Ibid., 75.
14. D. B. Quinn, "The Voyage of Etienne Bellenger to the Maritimes in 1583: A New Document," in Whitehead, *The Old Man Told Us: Excerpts from Mi'kmaw History 1500-1950*, 16.
15. *Cape Breton's Magazine*, No. 28, back cover; quoted from Father J. Perrault, *Jesuit Relations*, Vol. VIII, 159; reprinted 2000 in Lamb, *Hidden Heritage*, 145-146.
16. Wallis and Wallis, 142.
17. Martin, "The European Impact on the Culture of a Northeastern Algonquian Tribe: An Ecological Interpretation," in Coates and Fisher, *Out of the Background: Readings on Canadian Native History*, 66-87.
18. Ibid., 25.
19. Prins, 36-37.
20. Ibid., 56-57.
21. Ibid., 44.
22. Rand, *Legends of the Micmacs*, 152-153.
23. Wilson, "The Icelandic Trade," in Power and Postan, eds., *Studies in English Trade in the Fifteenth Century*, 180.
24. Ganong, 8-23.
25. Quoted in Bourinot, *Cape Breton and Its Memorials*, 10.
26. For a full discussion of the various claims for Cabot's landing see Ganong, 135-175, and Hoffman, *Cabot to Cartier*, 94.
27. Wicken, 69.
28. Prins, 48.
29. Brown, *A History of the Island of Cape Breton*, 41.
30. Marc Lescarbot, *History of New France*, 1968, 1:32-33, in Whitehead, *The Old Man Told Us*, 24.
31. Hoffman refutes this settlement, favouring a Newfoundland location.

32. Prins, 48-49.

33. Ibid., 48.

34. Martin, "The Four Lives of the Micmac Copper Pot," *Cape Breton's Magazine*, No. 24, 26.

35. Martin, 20.

36. Denys, *The Description and Natural History of the Coasts of North America (Acadia)*, 440.

37. Campbell, "The Micmacs of Cape Breton from Acadia to Confederation," *Cape Breton Post*, 19 January 1985.

38. Hoffman, 214.

39. Pastore, "The Sixteenth Century: Aboriginal Peoples and European Contact," in *The Atlantic Region to Confederation*, 29.

40. Denys, 445.

41. Prins, 53-54.

42. Wicken, 204.

43. *Jesuit Relations*, Vol. I, 177.

44. MacLean, "Baleine," unpublished Staff Report, Parks Canada, n.d., pp. 7-8, in Biggar, ed., *The Works of Samuel de Champlain*, 157-158.

45. Ochiltree to King James I, quoted in Brown, 80.

46. Ibid., 85.

47. Prins, 71.

48. Wallis and Wallis, 182.

49. Prins, 76.

50. A. J. B. Johnston, *Storied Shores: St. Peter's, Isle Madame, and Chapel Island in the 17th and 18th Centuries*, 33.

51. Ibid., 34.

52. Ibid., 37.

53. Denys, 378.

54. Ibid., 380.

55. Ibid., 380-381.

56. MacBeath, "Nicolas Denys," *Dictionary of National Biography*, Vol. I, 257.

57. Ibid., 256-261.

58. Denys, 106.

59. Ibid., 443.

## CHAPTER 2
## Isle Royale, The First Boom

1. Memoir [of a 1692 visit, written by Anonymous in 1706], "Les Avantages de cet Etablissement," in McLennan, *Louisbourg*, 27

2. Brown, 143.

3. MacNutt, *The Atlantic Provinces: The Emergence of Colonial Society 1712-1857*, 11.

4. Pothier, "Les Acadiens à L'Isle Royale, 1713-1734," *La Société Historique Acadienne*, Vol. 3, No. 3, 105.

5. Fortier, "The Development of the Fortifications of Louisbourg," *Canada, An Historical Magazine*, Vol. I, No. 1, 16-34.

6. Ibid., 19.

7. Moore, "The Maritime Economy of Isle Royale," *Canada, An Historical Magazine*, Vol. I, No. 1, 33-46.

8. Moore, "Street Life and Public Activities in Louisbourg: Four Studies for Animators," *Parks Canada Ms. Report 317*, 20-29.

9. Morgan and MacLean, "Social Structure and Life in Louisbourg," *Canada, An Historical Magazine*, Vol. I, No. 1, 61-75.

10. Ibid., 69.

11. Moore, "Street Life...," 34.

12. Ibid., 35.

13. Denys De La Ronde, "An account of the Island of Cape Breton, English Harbour, 13 October 1713," in Donovan, "The History of Ingonish and Northern Cape Breton: From the Beginning to 1758."

14. "Receipts and expenditures of His Majesty's Collieries, Spanish River," nos. 50 and 51, in Donovan, "History of Ingonish...."

15. McDougall Maude, *Settlements of Isle Royale and Isle St. Jean, 1713-1758*, n.p.

16. Ibid.

17. Ibid., 134.

18. Dickason, *Louisbourg and the Indians...1713-1760.*

19. Ibid., 39-70.

20. "Voyage Made to Isle Royale or Cape Breton Island in Canada in 1716 Aboard the Frigate *Atalante* commanded by M. de Courbon St. Leger," in Whitehead, *The Old Man Told Us,* 92-93.

21. Dickason, 70-71.

22. Ibid., 86-87.

23. *Journals, House of Representatives of Massachusetts, 1744-1745,* XXI, 8-11.

24. Baker, *A Campaign of Amateurs: The Siege of Louisbourg, 1745,* 16.

25. "Lettre d'un Habitant de Louisbourg (Cape Breton)" in Wrong, *Louisbourg in 1745,* 53.

26. Baker, 37.

27. Bower, "Louisbourg: A Focus of Conflict, 1745-1748," 190-191.

28. Anonymous [possibly Thomas Pichon], in *An Account of the Customs and Manners of the Mikmakis and Maricheets, Savage Nations, Now Dependent on the Government at Cape Breton,* in Whitehead, *The Old Man Told Us,* 105.

29. Rawlyk, *Yankees at Louisbourg,* 157; reprint 1999, 157.

30. McLennan, 173.

31. Pepperrell to Shirley, 6 August 1745, in *Collections of the Massachusetts Historical Society,* 6, X, 348-349.

32. McLennan, 174-175.

33. Fortier, 27.

34. MacNutt, 35, 36, n. 16.

35. McLennan, 187.

36. Downey, *Louisbourg,* 148.

37. A. J. B. Johnston, 81.

38. Ibid.

39. Fortier, 25.

40. MacNutt, 48.

## CHAPTER 3
### "A Little Republick of Our Own"

1. Harvey, ed., *Holland's Description of Cape Breton Island and Other Documents,* 85.

2. Pitt to Amherst, 9 February 1760, in McLennan, 290.

3. Downey, 185-186.

4. Ibid., 186.

5. Harvey, 85.

6. Knox to the Clerk of the [Privy] Council, William Faulkener, July 1764, C.O. 323/176 ff 234-239.

7. Ray, "Settlement and Population Growth in Acadia" in Daigle, ed., *The Acadians of the Maritimes,* 151.

8. Dickason, 101.

9. Ibid., 105.

10. Upton, "Indian Policy in Colonial Nova Scotia 1783-1871," *Acadiensis,* Vol. 5, No. 1, 4.

11. Ibid., 4.

12. Harvey, 11.

13. Ibid., 10.

14. Brown, 361, 373; McDougall Maude, n.p.

15. Harvey, 93.

16. K. MacDonald, *Port Morien: Pages from the Past,* 6-7.

17. PANS Vol. 338, Doc. 128, 10 No. 24.

18. Brown, 370.

19. Harvey, 11.

20. De La Corne, "The Wreck of the *Auguste* 1761," *Cape Breton's Magazine,* No. 18, 10-15; reprinted in Caplan, *Cape Breton Shipwreck Stories,* 1-12.

21. Campbell, *Ensign Prenties's Narrative: A Castaway on Cape Breton,* 51; reprinted 2001 as *Castaway on Cape Breton,* 57-58.

22. Harvey, 93.

23. Webster, "Joseph Frederick Wallet DesBarres and *The Atlantic Neptune,*"

*Transactions of the Royal Society of Canada,* Section 2, 24.

24. Ibid., 26.

25. Ibid., 24.

26. Ibid., 34.

27. Ibid., 38.

28. Ibid., 31.

29. Brown, 379.

30. Murdock, *A History of Nova Scotia,* Vol. 2, 470, 475.

31. Haldimand to Sydney, 25 October 1782, MG 21, Q20, 310-316.

32. Investigating into the Conduct of Abraham Cuyler, 31 July 1789, Cape Breton, B6 (henceforth C.B. B), 119-124; Audit Office 13/13 ff 496-507.

33. Parr to Lord North, 6 July 1783, N.S. A 103, 126-127.

34. Morgan, "The Loyalists of Cape Breton," in *Early Cape Breton,* 33.

35. Parr to Cuyler, 13 September 1784, Cape Breton A 7 (Henceforth C.B. A) 25-26.

36. Memorandum of Thomas Ashfield, DesBarres Papers, MG23, F1, Series 4, 23; ibid., Series 1, Vol. 1, 169.

37. DesBarres to Yonge, 27 July 1785, War Office 1, Vol. 3, 310-312.

38. H. W. Perry, Memorandum, 1785, C.B. A1, 252.

39. DesBarres to Roberts, 3 August 1785, ibid., 90-91.

40. Statement of Lieutenant-Governor DesBarres, MG23, F1(3), file VIII photostat of Audit Office 3/142, 128.

41. Fergusson, ed., *Uniacke's Sketches of Cape Breton and Other Papers Relating to Cape Breton Island,* 145.

42. Jackson, *Cape Breton and the Jackson Kith and Kin,* 60. Other examples include Joseph Hart and Ingram Ball, who did not arrive in Cape Breton until 1808.

43. Harvey, *Holland's Description,* 87-93.

44. Proclamation of Lieutenant-Gover-nor DesBarres, 1 September 1785, C.B. A, 87-89.

45. Lease of DesBarres, 27 July 1787, C.B. A4, 87-89; 18 July 1786, C.B. B3, 53-59.

46. Additional Instructions to Parr, 11 September 1784, MG11, Supplementary 11, No. 13(4), Section 16.

47. Fergusson, 145.

48. Smith, *A Caveat Against Emigration to America,* passim.

49. Remonstrance and Petition of the Principal Inhabitants of the Island of Cape Breton, DesBarres Papers, Vol. 2, 370-371.

50. Richard Gibbons (d. 1794) had served as Attorney General of Nova Scotia before coming to Sydney.

51. Macarmick to Nepean, 18 May 1790, C.B. A17, 125. Friendly Societies were popular in Britain at the time and offered mutual support, often financial, to their members.

52. Mathews to Nepean, 10 June 1786, ibid., A12, 105-110.

53. Macarmick retained his position of lieutenant-governor until his death in 1815 even though he left the island in 1795. In the interim, the colony was run by administrators who had the same powers as a lieutenant-governor. The third lieutenant-governor, George Robert Ainslie, was appointed in 1815.

54. Burke, "Irish Convicts Abandoned on Cape Breton's Shore, 1788," *Cape Breton's Magazine,* No. 72, 13-19.

55. Ibid., 18.

56. Council, 1 August 1798, C.O. 217, Vol. 115, 216-218; Miller and Ball to Mathews, 18 May 1797, ibid., Vol. 113, 389-390.

57. Wentworth to King, 8 November 1797, N.S. A126, 174.

58. Wentworth to King, 23 January

1795, ibid.,121, 21.

59. Bishop Charles Inglis, Transcript of a Journey to Cape Breton, 13 July 1805, MG 13,103, 5.

60. Inglis, 17 July 1805, M.G. 23, C6, Vol. 6.

61. Jones to Solomon Jones, 26 March 1797, BI, MG 17, 42. Original at Queen's University Archives.

62. Gillies, at Port Hood website: *http://www.porthood.ca/history.*

63. Council, 3 December 1801, C.O.217, Vol. 120, 27.

64. Despard to Portland, 18 December 1800, ibid., Vol. 118, 340-341.

65. Cottrell to King, 28 July 1801, ibid., Vol. 121, 8.

## CHAPTER 4
### The Hebridean Connection
### and the Roots of Discontent

1. *Seasonable Advice to the Landholders and Farmers in Scotland,* 1770, 14, quoted in Bumstead, *The People's Clearance 1770-1815,* 15.

2. Council, 1 August 1802, C.O.217, Vol. 121, 8.

3. Ibid.

4. Captain Thomas Henry Crawley (1757-1851) was the father of Henry W. Crawley. Thomas H. was appointed Surveyor General of Lands around 1805 or '06, and later Mines Superintendent. He kept the Lands job after annexation. Henry W. was appointed Commissioner of Crown Lands for Cape Breton 1832-1848. He conducted the County Grammar School in Sydney before 1834.

5. Land Petitions (1811), C.B. 2405, Public Archives of Nova Scotia (henceforth PANS).

6. Ibid. (1825), C.B. 1825.

7. Ibid. (1820), C.B. 2505.

8. Council, 20 July 1803, C.O. 217,

Vol. 122, 23.

9. Cambden to Despard, 7 June 1804, ibid., 73-75.

10. Despard to Hobart, 4 March 1803, ibid., Vol. 121, 49-50.

11. Council, 21 August 1806, ibid., Vol. 125, 11-12.

12. A. C. Dodd, "Observations," 1805 (written in 1816), ibid., Vol. 134, 148; Parker, *Cape Breton Ships and Men,* 26; reprinted 2003 in *Ships and Men,* 53-54.

13. Swayne to Bathurst, 7 January 1813, C.B. A34, 12-13.

14. Draft, A. C. Dodd to Swayne, 8 April 1813, Dodd Papers, PANS, doc. 84.

15. C.O.217, Vol. 136, 291; ibid., Vol. 134, 30-31.

16. Ibid., 32.

17. Dodd to Bathurst, 25 May 1818, ibid., Vol. 136, 66.

## CHAPTER 5
### The Forced Marriage
### with Nova Scotia

1. Brown, 442.

2. *The Spirit of the Times,* 19 July 1842.

3. The vote was 594 to 433, indicating that a large number of unqualified voters had cast ballots.

4 Beck, *The Government of Canada,* 51.

5. Petition to Ainslie, 10 November 1819; Rev. Hibbert Binney to S.P.G. 4 September 1817, S.P.C., Papers, Vol. 31, 299-301.

6. Petition of the Inhabitants of the North Eastern District of Cape Breton, 7 August 1819, C.O. 217, Vol. 138, 13.

7. For an in-depth discussion of annexation see R. J. Morgan, "Separatism in Cape Breton," in *Early Cape Breton,* 104-118.

8. The mines were now operated by

the General Mining Association. See Chapter 8.

9.   *Cape Breton Spectator*, 14 August 1847.

10.   *The Times and Cape Breton Spectator*, 21 April 1849.

11.   Hugh MacDonald of Mabou, 1868-1871.

12.   Charles Boudrot.

13.   Murray Dodd's mother was Susannah Gibbons and his second wife was Caroline Maria Ritchie, of an influential Halifax family. John Ritchie was operating the coal mines at the time of annexation.

14.   *Cape Breton Spectator*, 22 May, 21 August 1847.

### CHAPTER 6
### "The Epidimical Fury
### of Emmigration"

1.   Boswell, *Journal of a Tour of the Hebrides*, entry for Saturday, October 2, 1773.

2.   A. A. Johnston, *A History of the Catholic Church in Eastern Nova Scotia*, Vol. I, 66.

3.   C.B. B7, 183-185, 28 November 1792.

4.   Prins, 270.

5.   The following is from Mi'kmaq Spirit website: *http://www.muiniskw.org/pgCulture4a.htm*:

"The existence of the Mi'kmaw ideograms and their development as a teaching tool was documented by the missionaries of the day. The timeline goes something like this:

"In 1652, Father Gabriel Druillettes, a Jesuit missionary to the Abenaki, reports seeing the Mi'kmaq use ideograms to record lessons in the 'Jesuit Relations' of that year:

"'...They made use of a small piece of charcoal instead of a pen, and a piece of bark instead of paper. Their characters are novel, and so individual that one could not know or understand the writing of the other; that is to say, that they made use of certain marks according to their own ideas as of a local memory to preserve the points and the articles and the maxims which they had remembered. They carried away this paper with them to study in the repose of the night.'

"In 1677 Father Chrétien Le Clercq, a Franciscan Récollet, made note in his journals of observing Mi'kmaq children taking notes using charcoal and birch bark as he was teaching them prayers:

"'They preserve these instructive papers with so much care, and they have for them so particular an esteem, that they keep them very neatly in little cases of birch-bark bedecked with wampum, with beadwork, and with porcupine quills.'

"In 1738, l'Abbé Pierre-Antoine-Simon Maillard (French Seminary of Foreign Missions) also worked out the Mi'kmaw symbols, and published a grammar of the language. It appears that his work was independent of Le Clercq's, and Maillard devoted 8 years to the task."

6.   Prins, 171.

7.   Conversation, Ronald Caplan with Sakej Henderson of the University of Saskatchewan, 2008.

8.   Prins, 165.

9.   Upton, 4.

10.   *Journals*, Legislative Assembly, 1860, 327-328, in McGee, *The Native Peoples of Atlantic Canada*, 86-87.

11.   Indian Commissioner of Nova Scotia Report, 1867, in McGee, 90.

12.   McGee, 14.

13.   Prins, 165.

14.   Ibid.

15.   Blanchard, *Histoire des Acadiens de*

*l'Île du Prince Édouard,* in Chiasson, *Chéticamp: History and Acadian Traditions,* 23; 1998 edition, 13.

16. Chiasson, 23-25; 1998 edition, 12-17.

17. Ibid., 39; 1998 edition, 25.

18. MacKenzie, *The Irish in Cape Breton,* 21; 1999 edition, 19.

19. Mitcham, *Island Keepers,* 165.

20. Harvey, *The Wreck of the* Astraea.

21. *Freeman's Journal,* 29 May 1788, in *Cape Breton's Magazine,* No. 72, 14.

22. "With John J. and Sadie Theriault," *Cape Breton's Magazine,* No. 50, 103-108; reprinted in Caplan, *The Cabot Trail in Black and White,* 116-118.

23. "With Winston 'Scotty' Fitzgerald," *Cape Breton's Magazine,* No. 46, 2; reprinted in Caplan, *Talking Cape Breton Music,* 48.

24. Conversations, Ronald Caplan with Jack MacLeod of Baddeck and with Jack Ingraham of Neil's Harbour, 1972.

25. MacKenzie, 21 *et seq;* 1999 edition, 50 *et seq.*

26. J. Hunter, *West Highland Free Press,* 18 January 1985.

27. Dunn, *Highland Settler,* 25.

28. Ibid., 25.

29. "Johnny Allan MacDonald of Enon," *Cape Breton's Magazine,* No. 48, 1-7; reprinted in Caplan, *Cape Breton Works,* 68-72.

30. "Mary MacMillan at Ben Eoin," *Cape Breton's Magazine,* No. 39, inside front cover; reprinted in Caplan, *Cape Breton Lives,* 97-98.

31. *Patterson's History of Victoria County,* 58.

32. T. C. Haliburton, *An Historical Sketch and Statistical Account of Nova Scotia,* Vol. 2, 234.

33. Dunn, 66. A few lines of Donald MacDonald's song, translated from the

Gaelic by Effie Rankin in *Cape Breton's Magazine,* No. 59, convey his passion for the beauties of "the rear": "It is the Rear to which I gave my affection and there I'd always like to be: where the forest grows dense with bending branches and limbs: iris dark-green, soft-shooted, full of sap when fresh foliage clothes it: a sweet fragrance rises from every flower which grows among its winding hummocks."

34. *Cape Breton's Magazine,* No. 59, 64. Opposing images like: "Far better to be beside the sea, watching the ebb and flow, than to be observing dense foliage among the winding meadows."

35. Nova Scotia, *Journals of the House of Assembly,* 1839, Appendix 32.

36. Hornsby, *Nineteenth-Century Cape Breton,* 52-53.

37. Stanley, "The 'well-watered garden': A Study of Presbyterianism in Cape Breton in the Early Nineteenth Century," 54.

38. Ibid., 51; Gentilcore, *The Agricultural Background of Settlement in Eastern Nova Scotia,* 40 *et seq.*

39. [A. DesBarres,] *A Description of the Island of Cape Breton in North America,* 43.

40. C.O. 221, Vol. 36 (1827), 76.

41. Gentilcore, 49.

42. Campbell and MacLean, *Beyond the Atlantic Roar,* 64-65.

43. Bittermann, "Agricultural History in Nova Scotia: Middle River—A Case Study," 2 (BIR).

44. *Patterson's History...,* 82-84.

45. Ibid., 84-85.

**CHAPTER 7**
**"Poverty, wretchedness, and misery"**

1. McPherson, *Watchman Against the World,* 130.

2. *Journals,* House of Assembly, 1847, Appendix 39, 197.

3. Ibid., 1857, Appendix 71, 413; W.

J. Ousley to William Young, 12 February 1848.

4.   McLeod to Gordon, 1 June 1848, in Harvey, *Letters of the Reverend Norman McLeod, 1835-1851*, 22.

5.   *The Times and Cape Breton Spectator*, 17 March 1849; *The Nova Scotian*, 9 April 1849.

6.   *The Nova Scotian*, 1 May 1848.

7.   *The Times and Cape Breton Spectator*, 17 March 1849.

8.   *Presbyterian Witness*, 14 September 1850; 15 August 1851.

9.   PANS, RG 5, Series P, Vol. 84, Petition 68, 1848; see also Gesner, *The Industrial Resources of Nova Scotia*, 200.

10.   Ibid., Series P, Vol. 83, Petition 109, 30 December 1846; Vol. 84, Petition 24, 5 February 1848.

11.   *Journals*, 1848, Appendix 67.

12.   *The Nova Scotian*, 1 May 1848.

13.   Ibid., 26 January 1846.

14.   MacDougall, *A History of Inverness County*, 91.

15.   *Cape Breton News*, 24 November 1852.

16.   Harvey to Grey, 1 April 1847 in *Journals*, 1848, 42-43.

17.   Grey to Harvey, 29 April 1847, ibid., 42, 44.

18.   Bennett, *The Last Stronghold: Scottish Gaelic Traditions in Newfoundland*, 76, 84.

19.   McPherson, 167.

20.   Hornsby, 186.

21.   "Neil A. MacKinnon of Rear Beaver Cove," *Cape Breton's Magazine*, No. 44, back cover; reprinted in Caplan, *Cape Breton Lives*, 131.

22.   Hornsby, 194.

## CHAPTER 8
### The 19ᵗʰ Century Economy

1.   "John Bourinot" in Tennyson, *Impressions of Cape Breton*, 161.

2.   *Nova Scotia Legislature*, Acts 1850, Ch. 41, 28 March 1850.

3.   Hornsby, 128-131.

4.   M. C. MacLean, "Cape Breton a Half Century Ago" in *Public Affairs*, 187.

5.   "Hattie Carmichael of the Meadow Road," *Cape Breton's Magazine*, No. 35, 1-11; reprinted in Caplan, *Cape Breton Works*, 85-99; R. Caplan, "Questioning the 1871 Census."

6.   N. MacNeil, *The Highland Heart in Nova Scotia*, 54; reprinted 1998, 54.

7.   Ibid., 70; reprinted 1998, 68.

8.   Ibid., 51; reprinted 1998, 50.

9.   MacLean, 187.

10.   Howell, "Agricultural Exports From Cape Breton, 1797-1865" (BIR).

11.   Ibid., 6.

12.   M. C. MacLean, 70.

13.   H. MacDonald, "Evolution of Sheep Farming on Cape Breton," 12 (BIR).

14.   Hornsby, 152; Canada, *Report of the Royal Commission Investigating the Fisheries of the Maritime Provinces and the Magdalen Islands*, 96.

15.   Chiasson, 49.

16.   Canada, *Sessional Papers* 1885, Vol. VI, 132-133.

17.   A. DesBarres, *A Description...*, 37.

18.   Chiasson, 36-38.

19.   Hornsby, 159.

20.   Ibid.

21.   Ibid., 160; Mann, *Gull Cove Remembered*, n.p.

22.   Hornsby, 146.

23.   Lavery, *Tides and Times*, 65, 71.

24.   Ibid., 71.

25.   Ibid., 83.

26.   Hornsby, 155.

27.   A. DesBarres, *A Description...*, 11; Lomas, *Industrial Development of Nova Scotia, 1830-1854*; T. C. Haliburton,

206, 253.

28. *The Commercial Herald,* 23 March 1850.

29. Gesner, 311.

30. Parker, *Cape Breton Ships and Men.*

31. Ibid., 34.

32. Parker, *Sails of the Maritimes,* 48.

33. Parker, Appendix, 178-192.

34. Hornsby, 183-184.

35. R. Brown, *The Coal Fields and Coal Trade of the Island of Cape Breton,* 69-70.

36. Hornsby, 107-108.

37. Jackson, *Windows on the Past: North Sydney, Nova Scotia,* 27.

38. Ibid., 25.

39. Ibid., 27.

40. Ibid., 29.

41. Ibid., 28.

42. Gillies.

43. Ibid.

44. MacDougall, 179-181.

45. Lomas, 95.

46. Howell, 9.

47. Lomas, 357-359.

48. *Lovell's Canadian Dominion Directory for 1871,* Vol. 2; Lomas, 433; Hornsby, 81.

49. Canada, Census 1871, Vol. 3, Table XXVII.

50. Census, 1871, Table XXX; 1881, Vol. 3, Table XXXI.

51. Colin Cash, Diary, MG12, 2 (BI).

52. Census, 1881, Vol. 3, Table XXXI.

53. Lomas, 382; Nova Scotia, Journals House of Assembly, 1853, "Agricultural and Industrial Petitions."

54. *Sydney Post,* 26 July 1922.

55. Census, 1891, Vol. IV, Table VII; M. K. MacLeod, "Manufacturing industries very small in 19th century Cape Breton," *Cape Breton Post* (henceforth *Post*), 25 July 1986.

56. M. C. MacLean, 187.

57. Census, 1891, Bulletin No. 1, 9, and No. 3, 16.

58. Marshall Papers, AK B4, M35 (PANS); Pamphlet 1400, BI.

59. Ibid., 71.

60. Ibid.

61. *The Nova Scotian,* 20 November 1828.

62. Ibid., 4, 11 December 1839.

63. Ibid., 1 September 1830.

64. *Belcher's Farmer's Almanac for the Province of Nova Scotia,* 37.

65. *Post,* 19 November 1959; Zinck, *Shipwrecks of Nova Scotia,* Vol. 1, 90.

66. Nancy MacNeil, "The Wreck of the Barque *Astrea* and the Development of Lighthouses in Cape Breton," 10-12 (BIR).

67. R. D. Evans, *Transportation and Communication in Nova Scotia, 1815-1850,* 94.

68. *Cape Breton News,* 29 December 1852.

69. *The Nova Scotian,* 25 May 1825.

70. *Cape Breton News,* 22 December 1852.

71. Ibid., 19 January 1853.

72. Stone, *Journey Through a Cape Breton County,* 67.

73. Ibid., 68.

74. *Journals,* House of Assembly, 19 March 1840, 790; ibid., 1851, 178; ibid., 6 April 1851, n.p.; *Sydney Post,* 11 August 1832.

75. Dennis, *Cape Breton Over,* 257; C. B. Fergusson, "Charles Rogers Ward, Editor of *The Cape Bretonian,*" *The Nova Scotia Historical Quarterly,* Vol. 8, No. 4, 273-288.

76. A. DesBarres, *A Description...,* 36.

77. Kempt to Marshall, 8 September 1832, Marshall Papers, MG 1, Vol 1283/449.

78. Ibid.

79. *Journals,* House of Assembly, 24

February 1827, 44.

80. Black, "Cape Breton's Early Roads," *Nova Scotia Historical Quarterly*, Vol. 5:3, 294.

81. R. H. McDonald, *Transportation in Northern Cape Breton*, 4.

82. Reminiscences of Robert Martin, *Island Reporter*, New Year's Edition, 1885.

83. Ibid.

84. Williams, "Shank's mare and other things...," *Nova Scotia Historical Quarterly*, Vol.10, 215.

85. R. H. McDonald, 6.

86. Ibid., p. 7.

87. Ibid., 6; C. H. Farnham, "Cape Breton Folk," *Harper's New Monthly Magazine*, BI, Pamphlet 2102; *Post*, 14 April 1979; *Chronicle Herald*, 20 April 1979.

88. Reminiscences, *Island Reporter*, *op.cit.*

89. R. H. McDonald, 5.

90. Black, 295.

91. Cozzens, *Acadia; or, A Month with the Blue Noses*, 197-198; W. M. MacLeod, *Memoirs*, 30.

92. Cozzens, 205.

93. *Cape Breton News*, 18 March 1854.

94. *Nova Scotian*, 6 October 1851.

95. Danny MacAskill, "Mail and Snow and Roads and Mud," *Cape Breton's Magazine*, No. 16, 43-44; reprinted in Caplan, *The Cabot Trail in Black and White*, 9.

96. *North Sydney Herald*, 14 December 1881, as quoted in R. H. McDonald, 11.

97. Ibid., 14.

98. G. M. Haliburton, *A History of Railways in Nova Scotia*, 452.

99. *Journals*, House of Assembly, 1876, Appendix 10.

100. G. M. Haliburton, 453.

101. Text of speech, H. F. MacDougall, 11 April 1889, *The Post-Record*, 5 January 1947.

102. "How the Railway Came to Cape Breton," *Post*, n.d., BI.

103. J. P. Parker, "Building the Grand Narrows Bridge," *Cape Breton's Magazine*, No. 23, 16.

104. Ibid., 16-17.

105. *The Cape Breton Highlander*, 19 January 1972.

106. *Post*, "Weekly Cape Bretoner," 25 August 1956.

107. G. M. Haliburton, 453.

108. Fergusson, *Places and Place Names of Nova Scotia*, 19, 599.

109. R. Brown, *The Coal Fields...*, 71.

110. Marshall, *Personal Narratives*, 50.

111. Ibid., 55.

112. Hornsby, 15-18.

113. Millward, "Mine Operations and Mining Leases on Nova Scotia's Sydney Coalfield, 1720 to the Present," *Nova Scotia Historical Review*, Vol. 13, No. 2.

114. Hornsby, 96.

115. Ibid., 97.

116. Millward, "Mine Locations and the Sequence of Coal Exploitation on the Sydney Coalfield, 1720-1980," in K. Donovan, ed., *Cape Breton at 200*, 184.

117. Hornsby, 171.

118. Brown, viii.

## CHAPTER 9
### The Cape Bretonian Emerges

1. McGregor, *Historical and Descriptive Sketches of the Maritime Colonies of British America (1828)*, 118.

2. Quoted in Donovan, "May Learning Flourish" in *The Island*, 110.

3. Upton, "Indian Policy in Colonial Nova Scotia, 1783-1871," *Acadiensis*, 1975, Vol. V, No. 1, 28-29.

4. Prins, 184.

5. Ibid., 185.

6. "A Talk with Grand Captain Alex

Denny," *Cape Breton's Magazine*, No. 40, 45.

7. Ibid., 47.

8. Prins, 185.

9. Ibid.

10. Ibid.

11. Ibid.

12. B. Campbell, "The Micmacs of Cape Breton, Confederation and Its Aftermath," *Post*, 26 January 1985.

13. Ibid.

14. "Robt. Elmsley's Early History of Baddeck," *Cape Breton's Magazine*, No. 42, 25-26.

15. Prins, 180.

16. Ibid., 187.

17. Ibid.

18. "Max Basque, Whycocomagh—Part Two," *Cape Breton's Magazine*, No. 52, 63-65; reprinted in Caplan, *Another Night*, 136-140.

19. Skupin, "Micmac Music," *Epigraphic Society Occasional Papers*, Vol. 20, 235.

20. Diamond *et al.*, *Visions of Sound: Musical Instruments of First Nation Communities in Northeastern America*, 176-177.

21. Fergusson, *Uniacke's Sketches*, 112.

22. Ibid., 166.

23. Donovan, "Reflections on Cape Breton Culture" in *The Island*, 3.

24. Dunn, 36; Campbell and MacLean, *Atlantic Roar*, 179.

25. Tennyson, 167-168.

26. Ferguson, *Scotland 1689 to the Present*, Vol. 4, 222.

27. MacDougall, *A History of Inverness County*, 569.

28. MacNeil, *Tales Until Dawn: The World of a Cape Breton Gaelic Story-Teller*, 27-35.

29. *Atlantic Roar*, 179; Dunn, 36.

30. *Atlantic Roar*, 179.

31. Elizabeth Mertz, "'No burden to Carry': Cape Breton Pragmatics and Metapragmatics," in footnote 182 of Stanley-Blackwell, "'Tabernacles in the Wilderness': The Open-Air Communion Tradition in Nineteenth- and Twentieth-Century Cape Breton," in Scobie and Rawlyk, eds., *The Contribution of Presbyterianism to the Maritime Provinces of Canada*.

32. N. MacDonald, "Celtic Society in Cape Breton," 11.

33. Gibson, *Old and New World Highland Bagpiping*, 197.

34. *Atlantic Roar*, 189-190.

35. Stanley, *The Well-Watered Garden*, Chapter 1.

36. Robinson, *To the Ends of the Earth*, 55.

37. Stanley, 107-115.

38. McLeod to "My Dear Friends," 10 March 1840, 10; 29 March 1845, 16, in Stanley, 161-162.

39. Ibid., 173.

40. Ibid., 174.

41. *Presbyterian Witness*, 27 August 1852, in ibid., 146.

42. *Atlantic Roar*, 200-201.

43. Dunn, 38-40.

44. John Alex John X. MacDonald, "A Milling Frolic on the North Shore," *Cape Breton's Magazine*, No. 21; reprinted in Caplan, *The Cabot Trail in Black and White*, 91.

45. Stanley, 149.

46. *Atlantic Roar*, 215.

47. Stanley, 32.

48. *Atlantic Roar*, 218-219.

49. Stanley-Blackwell, "'Tabernacles in the Wilderness': The Open-Air Communion Tradition in Nineteenth- and Twentieth-Century Cape Breton," in Scobie and Rawlyk.

50. A. A. Johnston, *A History of the*

# Notes

Catholic Church in Eastern Nova Scotia, Vol. II, 213, 231.

51. Ibid., 231, 278.

52. *Atlantic Roar*, 222.

53. Stanley, 171-172.

54. Gillis, *The Great Election*, 11.

55. A. A. Johnston, Vol. II, 115.

56. Sheldon MacInnis, "Stepdancing," in Corbin and Rolls, *The Centre of the World at the Edge of a Continent*, 114.

57. LeBlanc and Sadowsky, "Report Inverness County Dance Project Cape Breton, Nova Scotia," 12, 14.

58. Doherty, *The Paradox of the Periphery: Evolution of the Cape Breton Fiddle Tradition c. 1928-1995*, 75.

59. MacKenzie, 104; reprinted 1999, 62-65.

60. Paul M. MacDonald, "Irish Music in Cape Breton," in MacKenzie, *The Irish in Cape Breton*, 1999, 120-121.

61. Doherty, 75.

62. Doyle, "Treatise on Early Irish Settlers in Cape Breton," 97-98.

63. Ross and Deveau, *Les Acadiens de la Nouvelle-Écosse*, 178-180.

64. Ibid., 180.

65. Ibid., 183.

66. Ibid.

67. Chiasson, 159-160.

68. LeBlanc and Sadowsky, 6.

69. Ibid., 206-208.

70. Chiasson, 212.

71. Ross and Deveau, 154. See also Chapter 6 in this book.

72. "With Alex John Boudreau, Chéticamp Island," *Cape Breton's Magazine*, No. 32, 2-3; reprinted in Caplan, *Acadian Lives in Cape Breton Island*, 90-91.

73. Ross and Deveau, 160.

74. "A Talk About George LeBrun," *Cape Breton's Magazine*, No. 30, 15; reprinted in Caplan, *Cape Breton Lives*, 223.

75. Boudreau, *Chéticamp Memoirs*, 210-212.

76. MacLeod, *Memoirs*, 8.

77. Fergusson, *Uniacke's Sketches*, 155.

78. Osgood, *The Maritime Provinces: A Handbook for Travellers (1881)*, 150-151.

79. Kearny ms., MG1, Vol. 526A, PANS; copy in MG 3, 34, BI.

80. Ibid.

81. *Island Reporter*, January 1885.

82. Ibid.

83. Patterson, "The Queen and Nicholas Martin" in *Studies in Nova Scotia History*, 78-82.

84. R. MacDonald, *In and Out of Order*, 97-99.

85. Kearny ms. *op. cit.*

86. *Cape Breton News*, 23 February 1853.

87. Osgood (1883), 150-151; *Lovell's Canadian Dominion Directory for 1871*, 1762-1763.

88. Donovan, *The Island*, 104.

89. Ibid., 90-95.

90. Ibid., 100.

91. MacKinnon, *Old Sydney*, 58-67; chapter reprinted in W. C. McKinnon, *The Midnight Murder*, 133-137.

92. Donovan, 104.

93. Ibid., 105-106.

94. Ibid., 105.

95. "Robt. Elmsley's Early History of Baddeck," *Cape Breton's Magazine*, No. 42, 25-31.

96. Warner, in Tennyson, *Impressions of Cape Breton*, 171-172.

97. McGregor, *British America*, 389-391.

98. Gesner, 93.

99. Butterworth, *Zigzag Journey in Acadia and New France*, 205-206.

# Bibliography

NOTE: The following abbreviated forms are used throughout this book:

BI refers to the Beaton Institute, Cape Breton University.

BIR refers to reports or studies found in the Beaton Institute.

PAC refers to the Library and Archives Canada (formerly the Public Archives of Canada).

PANS refers to the Nova Scotia Archives and Records Management (formerly the Public Archives of Nova Scotia).

## PRIMARY SOURCES

### Government Documents and Records

**Great Britain** (unless otherwise noted, found at PAC)

Audit Office 13/ff. 496-507.

Colonial Office 217. Copied as Cape Breton A and Nova Scotia A (composite series of reports and correspondence).

Colonial Office 220. Copied as Cape Breton B (minutes of the Executive Council, 1785-1807).

Colonial Office 323/176 ff. 334-239.

Colonial Office Papers, Colonial Office 42. Included in MG11, in particular, MG11, Supplementary No. 13.

Haldimand Papers, MG21, including Q Series, number 20.

Privy Council Records, 1843. File ; Island of Cape Breton. In the matter of the Petition of certain Inhabitants of the Island of Cape Breton, against the Annexation of that Island to the Province of Nova Scotia. Harvard University, Houghton Library: Can/1750/15/F.

War Office 1, Volume 3.

**Canada**

General Censuses, 1871-1891.

House of Commons. *Sessional Papers, 1885.*

*Report of the Royal Commission Investigating the Fisheries of the Maritime Provinces and the Magdalen Islands, 1928.*

**Massachusetts**

*Journals of the House of Representatives of Massachusetts, 1744-1745.*

**Nova Scotia** (unless otherwise noted, found at PANS)

House of Assembly. *Journals,* 1758-1867.

_____. *Acts,* 1850, Chapter 41, 28 March.

_____. *Report of the Committee of the House of Assembly of Nova Scotia on fisheries*, 1852.

_____. *Report on the fisheries of Nova Scotia*, 1867.

_____. *Report of Committee On Strait of Canso*, c. 1862.

Petitions, including land petitions, are found in two series: Land petitions and other material, and Cape Breton land petitions and other material (1787-1843). Record Group 5 was particularly useful. An index to the Cape Breton petitions is available at BI.

Volume 338, Document 128, p. 10, Number 24 (militia).

## Manuscript Collections

Cash, Colin (1849-1934). Diary. MG 12, 2. BI.

DesBarres, Joseph Frederick Wallet. MG 23, F1. PAC.

Dodd Family, MG13, 4. BI;. MG 13, 103. PAC. MG 23, C 6, Vol.6.

Inglis, Charles (Bishop), MG 13, 103. PAC. MG 23, C 6, Vol.6.

Jones, Jonathan. MG 17, 42. BI. Originals at Queen's University Archives.

Kearny, Anna, Diary, 1802. MG 1, Vol. 526A. PANS. MG 3, 34. BI.

Macarmick, William. MG 23, F2 (PAC).

## Published Manuscripts

Biggar, H. P., ed. *The Works of Samuel de Champlain*. Toronto: 1936.

*Collections of the Massachusetts Historical Society*. 6, X.

Denys, Nicolas. *The Description and Natural History of the Coasts of North America (Acadia)*. Original publication in French: 1672. Translated and edited—with a memoir of the author, collateral documents, and a reprint of the original—by William F. Ganong, Toronto: The Champlain Society, 1908. Facsimile edition, New York: Greenwood Press, 1968.

Harvey, D. C., ed. *Holland's Description of Cape Breton Island and Other Documents*. PANS, 1935.

_____. *Letters of the Reverend Norman McLeod, 1835-1851*. PANS Bulletin 11 (2), 1939.

Jesuits. *The Jesuit Relations and Allied Documents: Travels and Explorations of the Jesuit Missionaries in North America*. New York: 1925.

Marshall, John George. *Personal Narratives; with Reflections and Remarks*. Pam. 1400. BI. MG 1, Vol. 1283/449. PANS.

Wrong, G. W. "Lettre d'un Habitant de Louisbourg (Cape Breton)." *Louisbourg in 1745*. Toronto: 1897.

# SECONDARY SOURCES

## Unpublished Articles and Studies

Bittermann, R. "Agricultural History in Nova Scotia: Middle River—A Case Study."

BIR, 1983.

Bower, P. "Louisbourg: A Focus of Conflict, 1745-1748." Unedited ms., Fortress of Louisbourg, 1970.

Caplan, R. "Questioning the 1871 Census." n.d.

Coleman, E. "Ship Building in Cape Breton: a major industry in 19th century." BIR, 1980.

Donovan, K. "The History of Ingonish and Northern Cape Breton: From the Beginning to 1758."

Doyle, W. "Treatise on Early Irish Settlers in Cape Breton." 2007.

Evans, R. D. "Transportation and Communication in Nova Scotia, 1815-1850." M.A., Dalhousie, 1936.

Haliburton, G. M. "A History of Railways in Nova Scotia." M.A., Dalhousie, 1955.

Howell, F. "Agricultural Exports from Cape Breton 1797-1865." BIR, 1980.

Lomas, A. A. "Industrial Development of Nova Scotia, 1830-1854." M.A., Dalhousie, 1950.

MacDonald, H. "Evolution of Sheep Farming on Cape Breton." BIR, 1978.

MacDonald, N. "Celtic Society in Cape Breton." CTV University of the Air script, BIR, 1981.

MacLean, T. D. "Baleine." Staff Report, Parks Canada, n.d. BI.

McDougall Maude, M. C. "Settlements of Isle Royale and Isle St. Jean 1713-1758." Research paper, Fortress of Louisbourg, 1965.

McGee, H. F. "Ethnic Boundaries and Strategies of Ethnic Interaction: A History of Micmac-White Relations in Nova Scotia." Ph.D., Southern Illinois, 1974.

McKinnon, K. L. "A Short Study of the History and Traditions of the Highland Scot in Nova Scotia." M.A., St. Francis Xavier, 1964.

Morgan, R. J. "Orphan Outpost: Cape Breton Colony, 1784-1820." Ph.D., Ottawa, 1972.

Stanley, L. "The 'well-watered garden': A Study of Presbyterianism in Cape Breton in the Early Nineteenth Century." M.A., Dalhousie, 1980.

Strouthes, D. P. "Change in the Real Property Law of a Cape Breton Island Micmac Band." Vol. I, Ph.D., Yale, 1994.

Wicken, W. C. "Encounters with Tall Sails and Tall Tales: Mi'kmaq Society, 1500-1760." Ph.D., McGill, 1994.

## Published Articles, Reports, Studies

"A Theory of the Vikings on Cape Breton." *Cape Breton's Magazine* 18: 22-25.

Bittermann, R. "Economic Stratification and Agrarian Settlement: Middle River in the Early Nineteenth Century," in Donovan, ed., *The Island*: 71-87.

Black, M. "Cape Breton's Early Roads." *Nova Scotia Historical Quarterly* 5:3 (1975).

Brown, R. R. "Railroads of the General Mining Association (Part 1)." *Canadian Railroad Historical Association Bulletin* 6 (August 1938).

Burke, C. A. "Irish Convicts Abandoned on Cape Breton's Shore, 1788." *Cape Breton's Magazine* 72: 13-19.

# Bibliography

Campbell, B. "The Micmacs of Cape Breton Long Before the White Man." *Cape Breton Post*, 5 January 1985.

_____. "The Micmacs of Cape Breton, from Acadia to Confederation." *Cape Breton Post*, 19 January 1985.

_____. "The Micmacs of Cape Breton, Confederation and Its Aftermath." *Cape Breton Post*, 26 January 1985.

De La Corne, St. Luc. "The Wreck of the Auguste, 1761." *Cape Breton's Magazine* 18: 10-15; reprinted in Caplan, ed. *Cape Breton Shipwreck Stories*. Wreck Cove: Breton Books, 1999.

Donovan, K. "'May Learning Flourish': The Beginnings of a Cultural Awakening in Cape Breton During the 1840's," in Donovan, ed., *The Island*: 89-112.

Evans, R. D. "Stage Coaches in Nova Scotia, 1815-1867." *Collections of the Nova Scotia Historical Society* 34.

Farnham, C. H. "Cape Breton Folk." *Harper's New Monthly Magazine*, n.d., pamphlet 2102, BI.

Fereday, J. "Career of Richard Smith." Article taken from M.A., Keele. BI.

Fergusson, C. B., "Charles R. Ward, Editor of *The Cape Bretonian*." *The Nova Scotia Historical Quarterly* 8 (1978): 4.

_____. "John Cabot's Landfall, 1497—'It was Cape Breton!'" *Cape Breton's Magazine* 70: 53-62. Taken from *The Dalhousie Review*, "Cabot's Landfall," 1953.

Fortier, M. "The Development of the Fortifications of Louisbourg." *Canada, An Historical Magazine* 1:1 (1974).

Gillies, C. Port Hood website: *http://www.porthood.ca/history*.

Graham, W. "The Fisheries of British North America and the United States Fishermen." *Collections of the Nova Scotia Historical Society* 14 (1910).

Harvey, D. C. "Educational Experiments, 1825-1832." *Journal of Education*, 1935.

_____. "A Documentary Study of Early Educational Policy." PANS *Bulletin* 1:1 (1937).

_____. "The Wreck of the *Astraea*." *Dalhousie Review*, 21:1 (1941). Pamphlet 2904, BI.

Harvey, M. "The Voyages and Discoveries of the Cabots." *Collections of the Nova Scotia Historical Society* 9 (1893-1895).

Innis, H. "Cape Breton and the French Regime." *Transactions of the Royal Society of Canada*, Section 2 (1935).

LeBlanc, B. "'It Is Wrong, Wrong to Dance...' An Introduction to Cheticamp Dance Prohibition." *Cape Breton's Magazine* 51: 37-84.

LeBlanc, B., and Laura Sadowsky. "Report Inverness County Dance Project Cape Breton, Nova Scotia." Centre for Canadian Folk Culture Studies, Museum of Man, 1986. BIR.

MacBeath, G. "Nicolas Denys." *Dictionary of National Biography* Vol. 1. University of Toronto, 1967.

MacDonald, P. "How the Railway Came to Cape Breton." n.d. Clippings File, BI.

MacLean, M. C. "Cape Breton a Half Century Ago." *Public Affairs* (June 1939).

MacLeod, M. K. "Manufacturing industries very small in 19th century Cape Breton." *Cape Breton Post*, 25 July 1986.

MacNeil, N. "The Wreck of the Barque *Astrea* and the Development of Lighthouses in Cape Breton." *Dalhousie Review* 21:1.

Martin, C. "The European Impact on the Culture of a Northeastern Algonquian Tribe: An Ecological Interpretation," in Coates, K., and R. Fisher, eds., *Out of the Background: Readings on Canadian Native History*. Toronto: Copp Clarke Pitman, 1988.

_____. "The Four Lives of the Micmac Copper Pot." *Cape Breton's Magazine* 24: 17-29. Reprint from *Ethnohistory* 22 (1975).

Mi'kmaq Spirit website: *http://www.muiniskw.org/pgCulture4a.htm*.

Millward, H. "Mine Locations and the Sequence of Coal Exploitation on the Sydney Coalfield, 1720-1980," in Donovan, ed., *Cape Breton at 200*: 183-202.

_____. "Mine Operators and Mining Leases on Nova Scotia's Sydney Coalfield, 1720 to the Present." *Nova Scotia Historical Review* 13:2, 67-87.

Moore, C. "The Maritime Economy of Isle Royale." *Canada, An Historical Magazine* 1:1, 33-46.

_____. "Street Life and Public Activities in Louisbourg: Four Studies for Animators." Parks Canada, Mss. Report 317 (1978).

Morgan, R. J. "The Loyalists of Cape Breton," in Morgan, *Early Cape Breton*. Wreck Cove: Breton Books, 2000.

_____ and T. MacLean, "Social Structure and Life in Louisbourg." *Canada, An Historical Magazine* 1:1, 61-75.

Parker, J. P. "Building the Grand Narrows Bridge." *Cape Breton's Magazine* 23: 15-17.

Pastore, R. "The Sixteenth Century: Aboriginal Peoples and European Contact," in *The Atlantic Region to Confederation: A History*.

Perrault, J. Excerpts from his narrative in *Jesuit Relations*, Vol. 8; reprinted in *Cape Breton's Magazine* 28.

Pothier, B. "Les Acadiens à L'Isle Royale 1713-1734." *La Société Historique Acadienne* 23:3 (1969), 3.

Ray, M. K. "Settlement and Population Growth in Acadia," in Daigle, J., ed., *The Acadians of the Maritimes: Thematic Studies*.

Skupin, M. "Micmac Music." *Epigraphic Society Occasional Papers*, 20.

"The Micmac Birch-bark Canoe." *Cape Breton's Magazine* 10, back cover. Based on Adney and Chapelle, *The Bark Canoes and Skin Boats of North America*.

Toward, L. "Influence of Scottish Clergy on Early Education in Cape Breton." *Collections of the Nova Scotia Historical Society* 29 (1951): 153-177.

Upton, L. F. S. "Indian Policy in Colonial Nova Scotia 1783-1871." *Acadiensis* 5:1, 3-31.

Webster, J. C. "Joseph Frederick Wallet DesBarres and *The Atlantic Neptune*." *Transactions of the Royal Society of Canada*, Section 2, (1937): 21-39.

Williams, F. "Shank's mare and other things…" *Nova Scotia Historical Quarterly* 10:3, 213-220.

# Bibliography

Wilson, E. C. "The Icelandic Trade," in Power, E., and M. Postan, eds., *Studies in English Trade in the Fifteenth Century.*

"With John J. and Sadie Theriault." *Cape Breton's Magazine* 50: 99-116.

## Books and Published Theses

Atlantic Geoscience Society. *The Last Billion Years: A Geological History of the Maritime Provinces of Canada.* Halifax: Nimbus, 2001.

Baker, R. F. *A Campaign of Amateurs: The Siege of Louisbourg, 1745.* Canadian Historic Sites, 45, 1978.

Barrett, C. *Cape Breton Highlands National Park: A Park Lover's Companion.* Wreck Cove: Breton Books, 2002.

Beck, J. M. *The Government of Canada.* Toronto: 1957.

*Belcher's Farmer's Almanac for the Province of Nova Scotia.* Halifax: 1862.

Benjamin, S. G. W. *The Atlantic Islands As Resorts of Health and Pleasure.* New York: Harper, 1878. Excerpts in *Cape Breton's Magazine* 51: 49-57.

Bennett, M. *The Last Stronghold: Scottish Gaelic Traditions in Newfoundland.* St. John's: Breakwater, 1989.

Boudreau, A. *Chéticamp Memoirs.* Private Printing, c. 1997.

Bourinot, J. *Cape Breton and Its Memorials.* Montreal: W. Foster Brown, 1892.

Brown, R. *A History of the Island of Cape Breton.* London: 1869.

_____. *The Coal Fields and Coal Trade of the Island of Cape Breton.* London: 1871.

Bumstead, J. M. *The People's Clearance 1770-1815.* University of Manitoba Press, 1982.

Butterworth, H. *Zigzag Journey in Acadia and New France.* Boston: 1885.

Cameron, A. *A Guide to Eastern Canadian Mammals.* Ottawa: National Museum of Canada, 1956.

Campbell, D., and R. A. MacLean. *Beyond the Atlantic Roar: A Study of the Nova Scotia Scots.* Toronto: McClelland and Stewart, 1974.

Campbell, G. G. *Ensign Prenties's Narrative: A Castaway on Cape Breton.* Toronto: The Ryerson Press, 1968; reprinted in *Castaway on Cape Breton: Two Great Shipwreck Narratives.* Wreck Cove: Breton Books, 2001.

Caplan, R. *The Cabot Trail in Black and White: Voices and Photographs from Northern Cape Breton.* Wreck Cove: Breton Books, 2007.

_____. *Cape Breton Lives: A Book from Cape Breton's Magazine.* St. John's: Breakwater Books, 1988.

_____. *Cape Breton Shipwreck Stories.* Wreck Cove: Breton Books, 1999.

_____. *Cape Breton Works: More Lives from Cape Breton's Magazine.* Wreck Cove: Breton Books, 1996.

_____. *Talking Cape Breton Music: Conversations with People Who Love and Make the Music.* Wreck Cove: Breton Books, 2006.

Chiasson, A. *Chéticamp: History and Acadian Traditions.* St. John's, Breakwater, 1986; reprinted Wreck Cove: Breton Books, 1998.

Corbin, C., and J. A. Rolls. *The Centre of the World at the Edge of a Continent: Cultural Studies of Cape Breton Island.* Sydney: UCCB Press, 1996.

Cozzens, F. S. *Acadia; or, A Month with the Blue Noses.* New York: Derby and Jackson, 1859.

Daigle, J., ed. *The Acadians of the Maritimes: Thematic Studies.* Moncton: Centre d'etudes acadiennes, 1982.

Dennis, C. *Cape Breton Over.* Toronto: Ryerson, 1942.

[DesBarres, A.] *A Description of the Island of Cape Breton in North America.* London: 1820.

Diamond, B., *et al. Visions of Sound: Musical Instruments of First Nation Communities in Northeastern America.* Chicago: University Press, 1994.

Dickason, O. *Louisbourg and the Indians: A Study in Imperial Race Relations 1713-1760.* National Historic Parks and Sites, Parks Canada, 1971.

Doherty, E. *The Paradox of the Periphery: Evolution of the Cape Breton Fiddle Tradition c. 1928-1995.* Ph.D., Limerick, 1996.

Donovan, K., ed. *Cape Breton at 200: Historical Essays in Honour of the Island's Bicentennial 1785-1985.* Sydney: UCCB Press, 1985.

_____, ed. *The Island: New Perspectives on Cape Breton History 1713-1990.* Sydney/Fredericton: UCCB/Acadiensis, 1990.

Downey, F. *Louisbourg: Key to a Continent.* Englewood Cliffs: Prentice-Hall, 1965.

Dunn, C. *Highland Settler: A Portrait of the Scottish Gael in Cape Breton and Eastern Nova Scotia.* University of Toronto, 1953; reprinted Wreck Cove: Breton Books, 1991.

Evans, G. *Uncommon Obdurate: The Several Public Careers of J. F. W. DesBarres.* Toronto: University Press, 1969.

Ferguson, W. *Scotland 1689 to the Present.* The Edinburgh History of Scotland, Vol. 4. Edinburgh: Oliver and Boyd, 1978.

Fergusson, C., ed. *Places and Place Names of Nova Scotia.* PANS, 1967.

_____, ed. *Uniacke's Sketches of Cape Breton and Other Papers Relating to Cape Breton Island.* PANS, 1958.

Forbes, E., and D. Muise. *The Atlantic Provinces in Confederation.* University of Toronto, 1993.

Fry, B. *"An Appearance of Strength": The Fortifications of Louisbourg.* Vol. 1, National Historic Sites, Parks Canada, 1984.

Ganong, W. *Crucial Maps in the Early Cartography and Place-Nomenclature of the Atlantic Coast of Canada.* Toronto: University Press, 1964.

Gentilcore, R. *The Agricultural Background of Settlement in Eastern Nova Scotia.* Association of American Geographers, 1956.

Gesner, A. *The Industrial Resources of Nova Scotia.* 1849.

Gibson, J. *Old And New World Highland Bagpiping.* McGill-Queen's, 2002.

Gillis, J. *The Great Election.* North Sydney, n.d.

Gillis, R. *Historic Sydney.* Halifax: Nimbus, 2003.

Gould, G., and A. Semple. *Our Land: The Maritimes.* Fredericton: St. Anne's Point Press, 1980.

# Bibliography

[Grove, E.] *Little Grace OR Scenes In Nova Scotia By Miss Grove.* Halifax: 1846.

Haliburton, T. *An Historical Sketch and Statistical Account of Nova Scotia.* Vol. 2, 1829.

Hamilton, P. *Nova Scotia Considered As a Field for Emigration.* 1858.

Hoffman, B. *Cabot to Cartier: Sources for a Historical Ethnography of Northeastern North America, 1497-1550.* Toronto: University Press, 1961.

_____. *The Historical Ethnography of the Micmac of the Sixteenth and Seventeenth Centuries.* Ph.D., University of California, 1955.

Hornsby, S. *Nineteenth-Century Cape Breton: A Historical Geography.* McGill-Queen's, 1992.

Jackson, E. *Cape Breton and the Jackson Kith and Kin.* Windsor: Lancelot Press, 1971.

Jackson, E. *Windows on the Past: North Sydney, Nova Scotia.* Windsor: Lancelot Press, 1974.

Johnston, A. A. *A History of the Catholic Church in Eastern Nova Scotia.* 2 Vols., St. Francis Xavier University Press, 1960.

Johnston, A. J. B. *Storied Shores: St. Peter's, Isle Madame, and Chapel Island in the 17th and 18th Centuries.* Sydney: UCCB Press, 2004.

Lamb, J. *Hidden Heritage: Buried Romance at St. Ann's, Cape Breton Island.* Windsor: Lancelot Press, 1975; reprinted Wreck Cove: Breton Books, 2000.

Lavery, M. and G. *Tides and Times: Life on the Cape Breton Coast at Gabarus and Vicinity, 1713-1990.* Scarborough: private printing, 1991.

Lotz, P., and J. Lotz. *Cape Breton Island.* Vancouver: Douglas, David and Charles, 1974.

*Lovell's Canadian Dominion Directory for 1871*, Vol. 2. Montreal: 1871.

MacDonald, K. *Port Morien: Pages from the Past.* Sydney: UCCB Press, 1995.

MacDonald, R. *In and Out of Order.* North Sydney Historical Society, 2005.

MacDonald, W. J., ed. *Patterson's History of Victoria County.* Sydney: College of Cape Breton Press, 1978.

MacDougall, J. *A History of Inverness County.* [1922] Mika Reprint, Belleville: 1972.

MacGillivray, D., and B. Tennyson, eds. *Cape Breton Historical Essays.* Sydney: College of Cape Breton Press, 1980.

MacKenzie, A. *The Irish in Cape Breton.* Antigonish: Formac, 1979; reprinted as *The Irish in Cape Breton with an Essay on Cape Breton's Irish Music by Paul M. MacDonald.* Wreck Cove: Breton Books, 1999.

MacKinnon, J. *Old Sydney.* Sydney: MacKinnon, 1918.

MacLeod, W. *Memoirs.* Private printing, 1930.

MacNeil, J. (J. Shaw, ed.) *Tales until Dawn / Sgeul gu Latha: The World of a Cape Breton Gaelic Story-Teller.* McGill-Queen's, 1987.

MacNeil, N. *The Highland Heart in Nova Scotia.* New York: Scribners, 1948; reprinted Wreck Cove: Breton Books, 1998.

MacNutt, W. *The Atlantic Provinces: The Emergence of Colonial Society 1712-1857.* Toronto: McClelland and Stewart, 1965.

Mann, S. *Gull Cove Remembered, 1900-1920.* Private printing, n.d.

McDonald, R. H. *Transportation in Northern Cape Breton*. Parks Canada, Mss, Report 363, 1979.

McGee, H. *The Native Peoples of Atlantic Canada: A History of Ethnic Interaction*. McClelland and Stewart, Carleton Library 72, 1974.

McGregor, J. *British America*. London: 1832.

_____. *Historical and Descriptive Sketches of the Maritime Colonies of British America (1828)*. Johnson Reprint Corporation, 1968.

McKinnon, W. *The Midnight Murder: A Novel from Early Cape Breton*. Wreck Cove: Breton Books, 2002.

McLennan, J. *Louisbourg: From Its Foundation to Its Fall 1713-1758*. Original publication, London: MacMillan, 1918. Reprint, Sydney: Fortress Press, 1969.

McPherson, F. *Watchman Against the World: The Remarkable Journey of Norman McLeod & his People from Scotland to Cape Breton Island to New Zealand*. Wreck Cove: Breton Books, 1993.

Mitcham, A. *Island Keepers*. Windsor: Lancelot Press, 1989.

Mitchison, R. *A History of Scotland*. 2nd edition. London: Methuen, 1982.

Morgan, R. *Early Cape Breton: From Founding to Famine 1784-1851*. Wreck Cove: Breton Books, 2000.

_____, ed. *More Essays in Cape Breton History*. Windsor: Lancelot Press, 1977.

Murdock, B. *A History of Nova Scotia*. Vol. 2, Halifax: 1865.

Newton, P. *The Cape Breton Book of Days*. Revised edition, Sydney: CBU Press, 2005.

Nova Scotia. *Natural History of Nova Scotia*. Vol. 1, Maritime Resource Management Service Inc., Parks and Recreation Division, Department of Lands and Forests, 1984.

Osgood, J. *The Maritime Provinces: A Handbook for Travellers*. 1881, 1883.

Parker, J. *Cape Breton Ships and Men*. Toronto: George, 1967; reprinted as *Ships and Men: The Golden Age of Wooden Ships in Cape Breton Island*. Wreck Cove: Breton Books, 2003.

_____. *Sails of the Maritimes*. Aylesbury: Hazell Watson, 1960.

Patterson, G. *Studies in Nova Scotia History*. Halifax: Imperial, 1940.

Power, P., and M. Postan, eds. *Studies in English Trade in the Fifteenth Century*. London: Routledge, 1933.

Prins, H. *The Mi'kmaq: Resistance, Accommodation, and Cultural Survival*. Orlando: Harcourt Brace, 1996.

Rand, S. *Legends of the Micmacs*. New York: Longmans Green, 1894.

Rawlyk, G. *Yankees at Louisbourg: The Story of the First Siege 1745*. Maine: University Press, 1967; reprinted Wreck Cove: Breton Books, 1999.

Reid, J., and P. Buckner. *The Atlantic Region to Confederation: A History*. Toronto: University Press, 1994.

Robinson, N. *To the Ends of the Earth*. New Zealand: Harper Collins, 1997.

Ross, S., and J. Deveau. *Les Acadiens de la Nouvelle-Écosse*. Moncton: Editions d'Acadie, 1995.

Scobie, C., and G. Rawlyk, eds., *The Contribution of Presbyterianism to the Maritime*

# Bibliography

*Provinces of Canada.* McGill-Queen's, 1997.

Smith, W. *A Caveat Against Emigration to America.* London: 1803.

Stanley, L. *The Well-Watered Garden: The Presbyterian Church in Cape Breton, 1798-1860.* Sydney: UCCB Press, 1983.

Stone, A. *Journey Through a Cape Breton County: Pioneer Roads in Richmond County.* Sydney: UCCB Press, 1991.

Sweetser, M., ed. *The Maritime Provinces: A Handbook for Travellers.* Boston: Osgood, 1875, 1884. Also Houghton Mifflin, 1890.

Tennyson, B., ed. *Impressions of Cape Breton.* Sydney: UCCB Press, 1986.

Wallis, W., and R. Wallis. *The Micmac Indians of Eastern Canada.* Minneapolis: University of Minneapolis Press, 1955.

Whitehead, R., ed. *The Old Man Told Us: Excerpts from Mi'kmaw History 1500-1950.* Halifax: Nimbus, 1991.

Wrong, G. *Louisbourg in 1745.* Toronto, 1897.

Zinck, J. *Shipwrecks of Nova Scotia.* Vol. 1. Windsor: Lancelot, 1975.

## Newspapers and Magazines

(*indicates scattered issues)

*Cape Breton Advocate,* 1840-1841

*Cape Breton Highlander,* 1963-1976, 1980

*Cape Breton News,* 1850-1855

*Cape Breton Post* and its antecedents, 1899-

*Cape Breton's Magazine,* 1972-1999

*Commercial Herald,* 1849-1850

*Morning Chronicle,* Halifax, 1862-1867

*The Cape Bretonian*

*The Cape Breton Spectator,* 1846-1849

*The Guardian,* 1839-1851

*The Island Reporter,* 1885-1896

*The Nova Scotian,* 1824-1926

*The Presbyterian Witness,* 1848-1945*

*The Spirit of the Times,* 1842-1845*

*Times and Cape Breton Spectator,* 1849

*West Highland Free Press,* 1985

# Index

# Index

219

# Index

# Index

# Index

ALSO AVAILABLE FROM
# Breton Books
www.capebretonbooks.com

## The Cabot Trail in Black & White
### collected & edited by RONALD CAPLAN
HEARTBREAKING AND TRIUMPHANT, a collection of stories and photographs in stark black and white, as we rarely see the Trail or its people and, in many cases, as we will likely never see them again. From over 25 years of *Cape Breton's Magazine*, these are pieces of life along a trace of road that became the highway—the Cabot Trail.
**8.5 X 11 • 150 PHOTOS • 144 PAGES • $23.50**
**ISBN 1-895415-99-3**

## Cape Breton Highlands National Park
### A PARK LOVER'S COMPANION
### by CLARENCE BARRETT
FOR BOTH HIKER AND ARMCHAIR TRAVELLER, this excellent guide brings us northern Cape Breton in all seasons, both on and off trail. This noted naturalist, photographer, and "near-legendary" outdoorsman shares his lifelong love, respect, and enthusiasm for the rich landscape and lore of the Highlands.
**35 COLOUR PHOTOS • DRAWINGS • MAPS • 176 PAGES**
**$21.50 • ISBN 1-895415-62-4**

## Cape Breton Works
### MORE LIVES FROM CAPE BRETON'S MAGAZINE
### collected & edited by RONALD CAPLAN
THIS IS CAPE BRETON TALKING! This extraordinary mix of men's and women's lives delivers a solid dose of the courage, humour, and good storytelling that make a place like Cape Breton work. From Canada's longest-running oral history journal, these voices affirm, entertain, and inspire.
**151 PHOTOS • 300 PAGES • $23.50 • ISBN 1-895415-24-1**

## Rita Joe: For the Children
### by RITA JOE • woodcuts by BURLAND MURPHY
STRONG, ENCOURAGING POEMS by the Order of Canada recipient from Eskasoni First Nation. With the young person in mind—down-to-earth and often humorous—these poems tell stories of Mi'kmaw life, and of the concrete and spiritual world of this courageous elder. Illustrated with powerful, tender wildlife woodcuts.
**39 POEMS • 52 PAGES • $21.50**
**ISBN 1-895415-98-5**

# Breton Books
## Wreck Cove, Cape Breton, Nova Scotia B0C 1H0
bretonbooks@ns.sympatico.ca • 1-800-565-5140
### Over 200 Cape Breton books & videos at website:
### www.capebretonbooks.com